1 Sales and Percent Change

2 Percent to Total

3 Sell-Thru

4 Stock-to-Sales Analysis

5 Markup & Markdowns

Fundamentals of Retail Buying with Merchandising Math

Angella L. Hoffman
The Art Institute of California, San Francisco

PEARSON

Boston Columbus Indianapolis New York San Francisco Upper Saddle River
Amsterdam Cape Town Dubai London Madrid Milan Munich Paris Montréal Toronto
Delhi Mexico City São Paulo Sydney Hong Kong Seoul Singapore Taipei Tokyo

Editorial Director: Vernon R. Anthony
Acquisitions Editor: Sara Eilert
Assistant Editor: Laura Weaver
Editorial Assistant: Doug Greive
Director of Marketing: David Gesell
Executive Marketing Manager: Harper Coles
Senior Marketing Coordinator: Alicia Wozniak
Marketing Assistant: Les Roberts
Project Manager: Alicia Ritchey
Associate Managing Editor: Alexandrina Benedicto Wolf

Operations Specialist: Deidra Skahill
Senior Art Director: Diane Y. Ernsberger
Cover Designer: Suzanne Duda
Cover Image: kRie/Shutterstock
AV Project Manager: Janet Portisch
Full-Service Project Management: Element LLC
Composition: Element LLC
Printer/Binder: LSC Communications
Cover Printer: LSC Communications
Text Font: 9/15 Helvetica Neue

Credits and acknowledgments borrowed from other sources and reproduced, with permission, in this textbook appear on the appropriate page within the text. Unless otherwise stated, all artwork has been provided by the author.

Many of the designations by manufacturers and sellers to distinguish their products are claimed as trademarks. Where those designations appear in this book, and the publisher was aware of a trademark claim, the designations have been printed in initial caps or all caps.

Library of Congress Cataloging-in-Publication Data
Hoffman, Angella L.
 Fundamentals of retail buying with merchandising math / Angella L. Hoffman.
  p. cm.
 Includes bibliographical references and index.
 ISBN-13: 978-0-13-272414-2 (alk. paper)
 ISBN-10: 0-13-272414-6 (alk. paper)
 1. Fashion merchandising. 2. Retail trade—Mathematics. 3. Retail trade. I. Title.
  HD9940.A2H62 2013
  658.8'71—dc23
                          2011036792

Printed in the United States of America

21 2022

ISBN 10: 0-13-272414-6
ISBN 13: 978-0-13-272414-2

brief contents

contents

Fundamentals of Retail Buying with Merchandising Math bridges the gap between current merchandising math textbooks and retail buying textbooks. It incorporates both buying philosophies and merchandising math. Buying is a mindset, and the author acknowledges this reality through the incorporation of questions and problems that train the reader to *think* like a buyer. The problem-based method of learning is used to encourage group collaboration and critical thinking. Simulated exercises mimic real-life buying responsibilities. Additionally, the order of the chapters and content within each chapter mimic the training of an assistant buyer in a corporate buying office.

The Introduction defines retail buying and the key characteristics of successful buyers. Buyers will never be exceptional at all of these tasks; therefore, they should maximize their strengths and work on their weaknesses.

Chapter 1 starts with retail sales. In a corporate buying office, the first responsibility of the buyer is to check daily sales and then compare those sales to the plan, the division, and the company results. Chapter 2 asks the buyer to compare each classification of business to the total business. The results of this analysis indicate where buyers should focus their time. Buyers inherently know that they should spend 90% of their time on 90% of the business. This will ensure a successful season and year end.

In Chapter 3 the buyer evaluates sell thru by style. This breaks down the classification analysis into smaller, more manageable parts and incorporates stock. The buyer can now see how buying too much, or too little, can affect sales. Both adequate and exceptional sell thrus are defined. In Chapter 4, stock-to-sales analysis demonstrates how buyers can change focus and ultimately affect purchases based on current seasonal trends. This assumes that the buyer has a total stock plan that is directly tied to the original business plan. At the end of Chapter 4, a Merchandising Math Packet has been provided to review all formulas covered.

Unit 1 concludes with a focus on markdowns and markup. This chapter pinpoints merchandise opportunities by category to gain higher initial markup through assortment planning. It also includes different formulas for calculating markup when either retail or cost is known. It concludes with a section on markdown planning by week, month, and season.

In Unit 2 all aspects of managing the business are explored from purchase order dating and entry, to development of the Six-Month Merchandise Plan. Several examples are included with a step-by-step process for creating the initial six-month plan. Buyers continue to update the original merchandise plan mid-season; this process is commonly referred to as the rolling open-to-buy forecast. Several examples of profit and loss statements are included in this unit and the major components of the profit and loss statement are explored.

Unit 2 concludes with a chapter on cooperative advertising. The retail landscape has changed dramatically over the last 10 years. Most buyers today will negotiate with vendors for some type of advertising contribution. This chapter enables students to participate in a simulation that mimics the buyer's role in negotiating and managing cooperative advertising dollars.

Chapter 10 includes two different buying simulations. One simulation requires students to summarize a department's previous year's what is profit and loss statement performance. Another simulation allows students to create a buying plan from a floor plan and then negotiate with vendors. These vendor and buyer negotiations give students the opportunity to apply basic merchandising math principles in real time and negotiate the best deals for their individual businesses.

Chapter 11 summarizes the buyer's market week trip and the importance of planning. In addition, examples of vendor market sheets are analyzed and summarized. The vendor market sheets demonstrate how gross margin is calculated. Students have the opportunity to pinpoint how they would approach an end-of-season negotiation with each vendor.

This textbook concludes with a special feature, Monday Morning Reports. Monday is very important in the life of a buyer: buyers receive the reports that summarize the previous week's business results. Chapters 12 and 13 include examples of reports frequently used by buyers. Questions that help the reader to understand how these reports are used by the buyer are includes. The buyer gains a broader picture of the business through the summary of these reports and then makes educated buying decisions based on this comprehensive analysis.

This book provides a full and broad view of the retail buyer's role, while also including the key merchandising math formulas that are the basis of all retail buying analysis. It is impossible to separate retail buying theory from merchandising math. Well-trained buyers have learned to think through questions and problems in the buying office. The simulations and problems in this text mimic the buying office and should prepare the reader for the exciting and challenging career of retail buying.

acknowledgments

I'd like to express my sincere gratitude to reviewer Andrea Williams from the Art Institute, San Diego, who supported the progress of this text and believed in the value of Monday Morning Reports. Her perspective was extremely helpful and encouraging.

A special thank you to V. Ann Paulins for offering additional advice above and beyond the reviews. I am honored to have received feedback from someone I admire so much.

To the amazingly talented and hard-working students who have blessed my life, I give many thanks. My students have surprised me in numerous ways. May they all find careers that bring them joy and satisfaction that is comparable to what I have experienced working with all of them.

Thank you to the exceptional women who have guided and supported my development as a leader and professional. I am very grateful to have worked with both Lorrie Ivas and Brenda Vemich.

I extend much gratitude to my family and friends who inspire me to always do my best and, more importantly, to be of service in the world.

Thank you to the fabulous Pearson team! Pearson is truly an evolved and forward-thinking publisher and it is a privilege to work with this team.

Download Instructor Resources from the Instructor Resource Center

To access supplementary materials online, instructors need to request an instructor access code. Go to *www.pearsonhighered.com/irc* to register for an instructor access code. Within 48 hours of registering, you will receive a confirming e-mail including an instructor access code. Once you have received your code, locate your text in the online catalog and click on the Instructor Resources button on the left side of the catalog product page. Select a supplement, and a login page will appear. Once you have logged in, you can access instructor material for all Pearson textbooks. If you have any difficulties accessing the site or downloading a supplement, please contact Customer Service at *http://247pearsoned.custhelp.com/*

FORMULAS
and Basic
Principles

UNIT 1

Introduction: Getting Started

Retail buying is an exciting career filled with opportunity for advancement and personal growth. Whether you have personal experience in retail positions or are seeking further education in retail merchandising, this textbook will provide you with the merchandising math principles and retail buying philosophies applied in successful retail ventures. If you are already familiar with the world of retailing, the following chapters will give you the opportunity to apply previous knowledge of retail formats to merchandising math simulations and problem-solving sets.

Retail Buying Defined

Retail buying is the purchase of a large quantity of wholesale goods for resale to the ultimate consumer. The **ultimate consumer** is the individual or group that will use or consume the product.

The **retail buyer** is the individual responsible for negotiating the purchase of wholesale goods for resale to the ultimate consumer.

Retail buying requires a wide range of skills and applied practices that result in a firm understanding of how a business operates and identifies strategies a retail buyer can employ to create a successful business environment.

Retail Buying by Store Type

Common retail buying positions may be found within:

- Department stores
- Specialty stores

Retail Associate and Ultimate Consumer
Source: © Fotolia VI/Fotolia

- Discount stores
- Off-price retailers
- Warehouse clubs
- Category killers
- Boutiques
- Non-store retailers (i.e., catalog, Internet)

Familiarity with different store formats is the key to understanding what the retail buyer provides. Based on the different goals of each format, a variety of distinguishing strategies are used. In addition to the store formats listed above, retail buyers may be small business owners or work in procurement for a variety of large businesses. Buyers that work for the typical store formats listed above essentially operate a business within the larger retail corporation. These buyers may be in charge of the day-to-day operations of one or more departments within the retail corporation. This is an excellent way to learn the business of retail buying by a large business entity with years of experience. As a small business owner, the job of retail buying may be combined with the responsibilities of store management, visual display, and customer service. An example of buying as it applies to procurement is the responsibility of buying paper goods for a large hotel chain. These positions usually require years of experience buying in very large quantities, where one has established strong negotiation skills.

For the purpose of this textbook, the retail buying position is primarily described in the context of department stores. This is because department stores are all-encompassing and offer a wide variety of hard and soft goods. Buying for other retail formats is typically a specialization of one aspect described in context of the department store buyer. Many trained department store buyers continue on to a variety of other store formats.

What buying skills do you already possess?
Source: Andres Rodriguez/Fotolia

Retail Buying Responsibilities

What does a retail buyer's job entail?

- Analyzing past business results
- Creating and presenting seasonal business plans
- Sourcing of new designer and private label resources
- Negotiating and forming strategic alliances with vendors and other resources
- Attending market week and trade shows
- Managing the open-to-buy and merchandise plan, which include financial planning for sales, inventory, markdowns, shortage, and gross margin
- Planning assortments and forecasting trends
- Pricing and promotion
- Planning and developing advertising
- Analyzing markets
- Planning "by location"
- Developing visual signage and floor plans
- Developing people

Retail Buying Skills

What skills or characteristics describe successful retail buyers?

- Detail oriented
- Creative
- Analytical
- Intuitive
- Flexible
- Assertive
- Decisive
- Energetic
- Punctual
- Goal oriented
- Personable
- Meticulous

Do You Have These Skills?

Although this is a list of characteristics that are essential to retail buying, they can also be acquired and refined.

Which of the skills listed above do you already possess?

_____

_____

What skills do you need to develop further?

_____

How might you develop those skills?

_____

If you are not considering a career in retail buying, the strategies for analysis and development of business opportunities are also highly beneficial to small business owners, designers, and account executives.

The following chapters will walk you through the thought processes of retail buyers and a buyer's priorities as they relate to specific tasks. Analysis of past retail performance is the foundation of retail buying. This is a quantitative analysis. The first chapter focuses on retail sales and, specifically, how they are used in comparison to last year sales results. Imagine that last year sales are a benchmark for future sales performance. Retailers strive to achieve a better-than-last-year sales result. In addition to last year, retailers create planned sales that are developed from that last year benchmark. Sales results when compared to the previous year and plan either reduce or increase the amount of money available for future purchases.

Discount
Source: V. Yakobchuk/Fotolia

SALES
and PERCENT CHANGE

CHAPTER OBJECTIVES

- Define retail buying and the scope of the retail buyer's job.
- Describe common retail buying positions per store format.
- Relate personality attributes found in successful retail buyers.
- Analyze retail sales using TY and LY figures.
- Explain comparative sales and full-store sales analysis.
- Rank retailers based on MTD and STD sales statistics.
- Compare departmental sales to division and total company.

1

The Importance of Sales

Sales are the most important factor in determining the success and performance of a retailer. Sales affects all other aspects of merchandise planning and the open-to-buy. For now, think of **open-to-buy (OTB)** as the buyer's monthly checkbook.

Buyers start their day reading the daily sales report, sometimes called the daily flash. Then they make the rest of their business decisions based on these sales figures, or how well they are performing. In addition, they read industry media for updates on retailer sales performance and compare their business to that of similar stores.

Important Terms

In the realm of buying:

- **Net sales** are the sales achieved after all customer returns and adjustments are deducted.
- **Gross sales** are the total sales achieved before any customer returns or adjustments are accounted for.
- The **daily flash** is a report or online database of sales, often comparing sales this year to sales last year. The daily flash may also include a comparison of sales to a buyer's planned sales.
- **TY** means this year.
- **LY** means last year.
- The **plan** is a document outlining what the buyer or company intends to do to achieve seasonal and yearly business goals. The plan is usually derived from an analysis of last year results, and is followed by an action plan for achieving better results this year.

Retail Sales Analysis

In the following exercises, you will review a variety of sales results for different retail formats. Sales are given for the month of January, as well as year-to-date **(YTD)**. The end of the fiscal year for most retail companies is January.

YTD statistics are more important than monthly statistics, even though January is an important month for most retailers. If buyers have not made their planned sales in the month of December, they rely heavily on January to reach their year-end goals.

Table 1-1 presents TY and LY sales for December, for a number of stores. A comparison of TY and LY results provides the **percent change**.

Calculating Percent Change

Percent change is calculated by subtracting LY sales from TY sales, and then dividing by LY sales. This may also be referred to as the percent of increase or decrease in sales.

- The calculation for percent change is $\dfrac{TY - LY}{LY}$

- In an Excel spreadsheet the formula is = (TY − LY)/LY
  (In Excel, TY and LY would be replaced by the corresponding cell location.)
- Percent change may also be called % increase/decrease.

Buyers must review their sales daily, as well as the sales of the competition, if the information is accessible. This helps to determine how well a store is doing in comparison to industry trends. Some retailers report sales monthly, whereas others report on a quarterly basis.

Buyers compare their monthly and quarterly sales to other similar retailers. For example, a high-end department store buyer will compare sales to other limited-line or high-end department stores.

The third column of Table 1-1 is the **% Change** for January. In this case, 2011 (TY) sales are compared to 2010 (LY) same-month sales.

Comparative Sales Analysis

In the fourth column, **Comp %** refers to **comparative sales**. This means that only those stores open for a full year in both 2010 and 2011 are compared.

Stores without a full year of history, such as a recently opened store, are taken out of the calculation.

> ### Comp % = comparative sales
>
> **Comparative sales** only include sales for stores that have been open an entire year, both this year and last year.

The Impact of New Stores

A store that was not open last year would increase total sales for TY because it was not in existence last year. This is sometimes referred to as incremental (or additional) business. Even if the new store only earned $100.00, it would be $100.00 more than was possible last year, without that new store. Thus, it would appear that the retailer was performing better than last year.

New store openings are often heavily anticipated by buying offices and include celebrity appearances and big opening-day sales events. Store managers are often recruited from older high-performing stores, which can hurt the sales performance of the older stores. Occasionally, new stores are overemphasized at the expense of older stores.

New stores may also be placed in locations that are close to old stores, which can dilute sales for the old store, the new store, or both. Competition may also enter the marketplace and hurt old and new store performance. Therefore, to accurately pinpoint the performance of a retailer, comparative sales must be considered.

"same stores" may be used interchangeably with "comparative stores."

BUYING CYCLES

Buying generally occurs in three-month cycles—(1) February, March, April; (2) May, June, July; (3) August, September, October; and (4) November, December, January.

The **4th quarter** of the buying cycle is the most important, because of the holiday season.

Table 1-1 Data

Please review the following January 2011 sales results, and answer the questions regarding 4th quarter business. The dates of these particular statistics are not important; the examples that they provide are important.

Note: Sales are shown in millions of dollars unless otherwise indicated with a "B," indicating billions of dollars. For example, The Limited's January 2011 sales are seven hundred and seventy-two million, six hundred thousand dollars, expressed as $772.6.

Specialty Retail Sales

TABLE 1-1

Specialty Retailers	January 2011 $ Sales	January 2010 $ Sales	January Month % Change	January 2011 Comp %	YTD 2011 % Change	YTD 2011 Comp %
The Limited	772.6	622.6	24.0%	24.0%	11.0%	9.0%
Gap	843.0	797.0	6.0%	1.0%	3.0%	1.0%
Aéropostale	120.4	112.5	7.0%	1.0%	8.0%	1.0%
The Buckle	54.4	50.2	8.4%	4.3%	5.7%	1.2%
American Eagle Outfitters	145.0	160.0	−9.0%	−6.0%	1.0%	−1.0%

Specialty Retail Questions

1. Which retailer had the highest sales for January 2011?

_____

2. Which retailer had the highest % Change for the month of January, and what was the % Change?

_____

3. Which retailer had the lowest % Change for the month of January, and what was the % Change?

_____

4. Which retailer had the highest Comp % for the month of January, and what was the Comp %?

_____

5. Where is there a huge disparity between January % Change and January Comp %? Why might this be?

_____

6. Using YTD 2011 information, which specialty retailer had the highest % increase? Did they also have the highest % Change for the month of January? (YTD means Year-to-Date. YTD Comp % includes all stores open for a full year both TY and LY.)

_____

7. Using YTD 2011 information, which specialty retailer had the worst performance or smallest % increase? Was this performance consistent with their January % Change?

_____

8. Compare all statistics for the specialty retailers, and then determine the top three performers. The most important statistic for this exercise is YTD % Change. It takes priority over all other statistics. However, give an explanation for each retailer that explains % Change and Comp % for the month and the year.

#1

_____

#2

_____

#3

_____

Table 1-2 Data

Please review the following January 2011 sales results, and answer the questions regarding 4th quarter business. The dates of these particular statistics are not important; the examples that they provide are important.

Note: *Sales are shown in millions of dollars unless otherwise indicated with a "B," indicating billions of dollars.*

Department Store and General Merchandise Sales

Department store and general merchandisers are often grouped together due to the similarity of their merchandising strategies. Use Table 1-2 to answer the questions that follow.

TABLE 1-2

Department Store and General Merchandise Sales						
Department Store and General Merchandisers	**January 2011** $ Sales	**January 2010** $ Sales	**January Month** % Change	**January 2011** Comp %	**YTD 2011** % Change	**YTD 2011** Comp %
Saks Inc.	163.6	158.9	3.0%	4.4%	5.7%	6.4%
Dillard's	376.0	354.0	6.0%	6.0%	2.0%	3.0%
Macy's Inc.	1.31B	1.253B	4.6%	2.6%	6.5%	4.6%
J.C. Penney, Inc.	903.0	940.0	–3.9%	–1.2%	1.2%	2.5%
Bon-Ton	180.1	180.1	FLAT	0.3%	0.7%	0.9%
Stage Stores, Inc.	72.0	67.0	7.6%	5.1%	2.7%	0.2%
Kohl's	825.0	798.0	3.4%	1.4%	7.1%	4.4%

Department Store and General Merchandise Questions

9. Which retailer had the highest volume sales for the month of January, and what were the sales?

_____

10. Which retailer had the worst performance for the month of January?

_____

11. Which retailer had the same sales as last year, and in which category were the sales the same?

_____

12. Which retailer(s) had full-store sales that were higher than comparative store sales?

_____

13. Based on these statistics, which of these retailers is most in jeopardy?

_____

14. Compare all statistics for the general merchandisers provided, and then determine the top three performers. The most important statistic for this exercise is YTD % Change. Give an explanation for each retailer that explains % Change and Comp % for the month and the year.

    #1
    _____

    #2
    _____

    #3
    _____

Retail Sales in Other Fashion Occupations

Other fashion occupations that benefit from the analysis of retail sales include designers and vendor representatives. Designers and vendor representatives target successful stores for new product launches and additional lines of goods. If adequately informed, they may increase their sales by determining which stores are further expanding and negotiate a second sale of goods in these stores. In addition, if retailer sales are trending down for the quarter, or year, they can predict order cancellations and markdown allowance requests from the buyers of these stores.

Markdown Allowance

A **markdown allowance** occurs when the vendor agrees to pay for a reduction in the retail amount of a product or style. This often happens when a retailer decides to promote the product at a percentage off or reduce it to a lower retail price point in order to drive sales.

Expanding Product Lines

Designers may use retail sales performance to determine which classification of goods to expand. If the junior department is a strong seller in most specialty retailers, designers may target more of the junior market in their assortment of goods.

Forecasting

Small business owners can use industry retail sales as a guide to their own business forecasting. A small business owner who caters to the junior market may aspire to monthly sales increases like that of successful large retailers, such as Aéropostale. This would apply most accurately if their assortment, target market, and price structures are similar.

Table 1-3 Data

Please review the following January 2011 sales results, and answer the questions regarding 4th quarter business. The dates of these particular statistics are not important; the examples that they provide are important.

Note: Sales are shown in millions of dollars unless otherwise indicated with a "B," indicating billions of dollars.

Discount and Off-Price Retail Sales

TABLE 1-3
Discount and Off-Price Retailers, and Warehouse Clubs

Discount and Off-Price Retailers, and Warehouse Clubs	January 2011 $ Sales	January 2010 $ Sales	January Month % Change	January 2011 Comp %	YTD 2011 % Change	YTD 2011 Comp %
Stein Mart	62.8	63.8	−1.6%	−1.2%	−3.1%	−1.8%
BJ's	779.8	732.5	6.5%	2.7%	8.3%	4.4%
Costco	6.3B	5.62B	12.0%	9.0%	11.0%	7.0%
Target	4.383B	4.289B	2.2%	1.7%	3.7%	2.1%

Retail Format Comparison Questions

Answer the questions that follow by comparing the information in Table 1-3 with that in Tables 1-1 and 1-2.

15. Which retailer had the highest January 2011 sales and what are the sales?

_____

16. Which retailer had the second-highest January 2011 sales? What were their sales?

_____

17. Which retail formats appeared to have the best overall retail sales?

_____

18. If you were a designer or manufacturer, what retail stores might you target based purely on retail sales? Why? (Consider sales, % Change, and Comp %.)

_____

_____

19. What were the top seven retailers for January 2011, and what were their increases over LY? Base your decision on January % Change.

#1

_____

#2

_____

#3

_____

#4

_____

#5

_____

#6

_____

#7

_____

> **Note:** *Most of these retailers are used as benchmarks for determining overall retail performance. This means they are market leaders, and other similar retailers look to them as an indicator of how they should be performing.*

Discount and Off-Price Questions

Use only the statistics from Table 1-3 to answer the following questions.

20. Identify the top two performers, based on YTD 2011 % Change.

_____

21. Which retailer had a decrease in YTD 2011 comparative store sales?

_____

22. Which retailer had the lowest overall performance, based on comparative store sales?

_____

23. Which retailer had the highest January 2011 Comp % increase? What was the increase?

_____

24. Which retailer had the highest YTD 2011 % change, and what was the increase?

_____

25. If you have shopped at Target, list some of the strengths in their current assortment.

_____

_____

_____

_____

_____

26. If you have shopped at Costco, list some of the strengths in their current assortment.

_____

_____

_____

_____

You have now completed the retail sales analysis by vendor format.

Return on Investment

Retail sales are the most important factor in retail buying because without them the buyer is unable to buy more merchandise, and the business fails. In addition to retail sales, an adequate return on investment (ROI) is required. A retailer could have excellent retail sales, but if the cost of operating the business is too high, profit is diminished. For example, a small retailer may have expenses, such as rent and utilities, that exceed the retail sales they are able to achieve in a particular market.

In later chapters we will explore the importance of sales and how that importance is diminished if a profit is not made, or a return on investment is not obtained.

Buyer-Level Sales

The next step in the analysis of sales includes sales at the buyer level. Buyers start the day reviewing their sales for one or more departments. Store managers usually end their day reviewing and documenting daily, weekly, and monthly sales.

Percent Change Calculations

In percent change calculations, the computation still applies, but is more widely used. It can include:

- Sales by day, TY vs. LY
- Sales by week, TY vs. LY
- Sales by month, TY vs. LY
- Sales by season, TY vs. LY
- Sales by year, TY vs. LY

- Sales by location, TY vs. LY
- Sales by classification of goods, TY vs. LY
- Sales by vendor/resource, TY vs. LY

Once the % Change is determined for the above categories, buyers compare their results to that of the division and the company. These comparisons indicate if the buyer is trending above or below the company sales trend.

Merchandising Plans

In addition to LY, buyers work from a merchandising plan that includes a plan for sales, usually above LY. This is frequently broken down by department, month, week, and day. Accurate tracking and analysis of these statistics are essential to the success of a buyer.

In most cases:

- If sales are trending higher than the merchandise plan, buyers purchase more inventory.
- If sales are trending lower than the merchandise plan, buyers cancel orders, take markdowns, or negotiate a **return to vendor (RTV)**.

Sales are the number one indicator of all other actions that must be taken within a buying office.

Take a moment to review the sales for a junior denim department, shown in Table 1-4. This may be just one of several departments within a buyer's responsibility. Stores on this sales report are divided into geographic regions. Notice the differences in sales for the week and the week's % Change, as compared to the total department. (Total departmental sales and percent change are listed under total junior denim buyer, at the end of the table.)

In addition, compare total junior denim buyer statistics to those of the **ready-to-wear (RTW)** division and the total company. Once general conclusions about sales performance for the weekly sales have been made, the month and season must be compared.

Common Abbreviations		
WTD = week-to-date	MTD = month-to-date	STD = season-to-date

Sales Results

Weekly sales results are emphasized more heavily than daily sales results, because there can be greater day-to-day fluctuations in shopping patterns. This may be due to new product launches, sales events, or climate changes. Generally, the weekend has greater sales than the rest of the week.

Thus, to accurately measure sales for a period of time:

1. Examine weekly sales.
2. Analyze sales of the current month to determine how current sales compare to the sales of last year and the buying plan. Buyers have planned sales that they must make every month. If they fall short of the planned sales, they may need to take corrective action, such as reducing stock, canceling orders, adjusting orders, or taking markdowns.
3. Analyze seasonal sales. A buyer's bonus is usually based on achieving the sales plan for a six-month season. The six-month seasons include:

   February–July (Spring/Summer)
   August–January (Fall/Winter)

TABLE 1-4

Junior Denim Departmental Sales

Junior Denim	Week TY	Week LY	Week	MTD TY	MTD LY	Month	STD TY	STD LY	Season
Dept 001 Stores	$ Sales	$ Sales	% Change	$ Sales	$ Sales	% Change	$ Sales	$ Sales	% Change
Region: Northeast									
1	8.9	7.8	14.1%	18.2	16.5	10.3%	118.0	105.2	12.2%
2	5.1	4.9	4.1%	11.3	10.5	7.6%	64.5	60.1	7.3%
3	4.3	4.1	4.9%	8.4	8.0	5.0%	52.3	50.1	4.4%
5	4.6	4.3	7.0%	9.2	8.4	9.5%	60.1	55.5	8.3%
6	3.6	3.2	12.5%	7.4	6.6	12.1%	47.1	41.5	13.5%
10	2.9	2.7	7.4%	6.0	5.5	9.1%	37.5	35.1	6.8%
12	3.6	3.3	9.1%	7.1	6.4	10.9%	46.2	42.6	8.5%
13	3.4	3.1	9.7%	6.6	6.0	10.0%	42.1	38.1	10.5%
14	3.8	3.4	11.8%	8.0	7.0	14.3%	50.2	45.3	10.8%
Subtotal	40.2	36.8	9.2%	82.2	74.9	9.7%	518.0	473.5	9.4%
Region: Northwest									
18	5.0	4.7	6.4%	10.2	9.5	7.4%	64.9	60.4	7.5%
23	2.3	2.4	−4.2%	4.6	4.7	−2.1%	30.1	30.9	−2.6%
26	2.6	2.7	−3.7%	5.7	5.8	−1.7%	34.0	34.7	−2.0%
29	1.4	1.4	0.0%	2.4	2.5	−4.0%	18.4	19.2	−4.2%
Subtotal	11.3	11.2	0.9%	22.9	22.5	1.8%	147.4	145.2	1.5%
Region: Midwest									
16	2.6	2.5	4.0%	5.4	5.2	3.8%	33.9	32.4	4.6%
17	1.7	1.9	−10.5%	3.3	3.5	−5.7%	22.0	23.7	−7.2%
20	2.6	2.6	0.0%	4.5	4.6	−2.2%	31.0	31.1	−0.3%
24	3.2	3.1	3.2%	6.1	5.8	5.2%	41.9	41.0	2.2%
30	1.4	1.5	−6.7%	2.9	3.0	−3.3%	17.1	17.7	−3.4%
Subtotal	11.5	11.6	−0.9%	22.2	22.1	0.5%	145.9	145.9	0.0%
Region: Southeast									
4	5.3	5.2	1.9%	11.5	11.0	4.5%	69.0	67.6	2.1%
7	2.2	2.2	0.0%	4.6	4.7	−2.1%	28.4	28.5	−0.4%
8	4.2	4.0	5.0%	8.1	7.5	8.0%	52.1	49.2	5.9%
9	3.6	3.3	9.1%	7.2	6.4	12.5%	47.0	42.7	10.1%
11	1.8	1.7	5.9%	3.5	3.2	9.4%	23.8	22.4	6.3%
15	4.7	4.5	4.4%	9.0	8.6	4.7%	61.4	58.7	4.6%
Subtotal	21.8	20.9	4.3%	43.9	41.4	6.0%	281.7	269.1	4.7%
Region: Southwest									
19	7.0	6.1	14.8%	12.5	11.0	13.6%	91.5	81.3	12.5%
21	5.4	4.6	17.4%	10.2	8.6	18.6%	69.9	60.1	16.3%
22	5.0	4.7	6.4%	9.4	9.0	4.4%	65.0	61.9	5.0%
25	3.5	3.0	16.7%	6.4	5.7	12.3%	45.9	40.3	13.9%
27	3.0	2.8	7.1%	5.8	5.6	3.6%	39.1	37.5	4.3%
28	5.9	5.2	13.5%	11.4	10.4	9.6%	77.0	66.9	15.1%
Subtotal	29.8	26.4	12.9%	55.7	50.3	10.7%	388.4	348.0	11.6%
Total Junior Denim Buyer	114.6	106.9	7.2%	226.9	211.2	7.4%	1,481.4	1,381.7	7.2%
Total RTW Division (DMM)			6.8%			7.1%			5.2%
Total Company			5.4%			6.5%			6.1%

Table 1-4 Data

Please review the following sales for a Junior Denim Department and answer questions 27–44.

27. How do the junior denim buyer's sales compare to the RTW division and total company for the week, month, and season?

_____

28. Based on % Change, which region has the highest performance in this buyer's responsibility? What are this region's weekly, monthly, and seasonal statistics?

_____

29. If you were the buyer for this department, on which two regions would you spend the greatest amount of time and resources?

_____

30. In which stores would you most heavily invest, if you wanted to improve the lowest performing region? In other words, where would you invest based on return on investment?

_____

31. Based on volume, which are the top three stores in the Northeast region?

_____

32. Based on STD % Change, which are the top three stores in the Northeast region?

_____

33. Which is the highest performing region, based on volume? How do the stores in this region compare to the total department? Discuss overall sales and % Change for the week, month, and season.

_____

_____

_____

34. If store 17 called with a request for more stock, what might you say? Compare this store to the total department and to the rest of the stores in the region.

_____

35. "A" volume stores have the highest sales for a department. If you had to choose one store as an A volume store, which would you choose? Why?

_____

36. Which region had better sales for the week than the month, based on percentages?

_____

37. Which region does not have better increases over LY for the season or the week? Indicate % Change for both season and week.

_____

38. Usually, there is a visible difference in sales volume that moves a store from an "A" to a "B" volume category. Likewise, the same change occurs between "B" and "C" stores. Place all the stores in the department into A, B, or C store categories, based on sales. Indicate the store number on the lines provided.

A Stores =

_____

B Stores =

_____

C Stores =

_____

39. If you could eliminate four stores, which stores would you choose? Why?

_____

40. Which regions had lower season % Change, compared to the total department? What was the season % Change for those regions?

_____

41. Which regions had higher season % Change, compared to the total division? What was the season percent change for those regions?

_____

42. Which regions had a higher monthly % Change than the division?

_____

43. What are the departmental sales for the season TY, as compared to LY?

_____

44. For each region, determine which stores are performing better than the region's STD % Change and which stores are performing worse than the region's STD % Change.

Northeast	lowest:	highest:
Northwest	lowest:	highest:
Midwest	lowest:	highest:
Southeast	lowest:	highest:
Southwest	lowest:	highest:

Daily Sales

Daily sales are recorded every morning in the buying office, and are the first procedure of the day. If a buyer has more than one department, a separate daily sales record is kept for each department. A plan for daily sales is developed based on LY and total weekly sales goals, as part of the six-month business plan. The business plan is created by the buyer before the start of each season.

After recording the daily sales, a plan of action is developed based on the previous week's performance. Remember, the total week's sales are even more important than the daily sales. One great day of sales does not necessarily make the week.

Next, the buyer determines how to most effectively execute change within their department. Part of this consideration involves knowing how to get the most immediate result out of each action taken. This means breaking down your business into percentages, in order to determine where the biggest dollar returns exist. The business plan acts as an outline or a tool to guide the buyer in this process.

Most business plans ask that buyers identify their biggest strengths and opportunities, by vendor and classification of goods. Top performing vendors and classifications will be considered first, in the action plan for the week.

This is similar to the way buyers prioritize top-performing stores. In the next chapter, you will have the opportunity to break down several businesses, based on percentages.

Summary

In the Introduction and this chapter, the major responsibilities of the retail buyer were reviewed and retail buying was defined. Personality characteristics commonly found in successful retail buyers were examined. You should be able to pinpoint the characteristics that you already possess, and those that need further development. Retail formats where buying positions are typically found also were examined, and then retail sales by store format were analyzed.

Comparative sales and full-store sales were defined and compared for both the month and season. Additionally, retail sales performance was analyzed based on LY and TY sales figures. In the Junior Departmental Sales chart, department sales were broken down by store and region for comparison against a corporate division's sales and the total company.

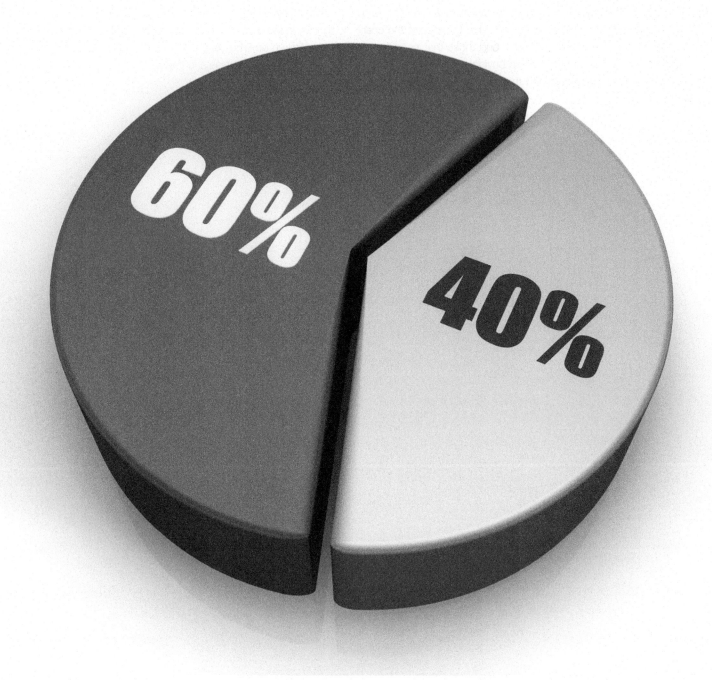

PERCENT
to TOTAL

CHAPTER OBJECTIVES

- Define *percent to total* and how it is used in retail analysis.
- Determine concentrations of business based on percentages.
- Review proper rounding procedures.
- Allocate resources based on percentage outcomes.
- Identify factors that determine the Assortment Plan.
- Recommend future purchases based on LY analysis.

2

Percent to total or **% to Total** is a common formula used in retail buying that is rarely discussed. It includes breaking a business down into smaller parts and then assessing each part's importance, as compared to the whole. In this chapter, we will use percent to total to analyze a variety of businesses and to pinpoint areas of opportunity and liability.

How Percent to Total Is Used

We will use percent to total in the analysis of:

Percent to total means taking a portion of a business and dividing it by the total business, to determine what percentage of the total it represents. In retail buying, it is typically calculated using units or dollars.

- Colors within a style
- Size breakdowns within a style
- Silhouettes within a classification of goods
- Vendors within a department
- Departments within a division

The Percent to Total Formula

$$\text{The formula for percent to total } = \frac{\text{Category of Business}}{\text{Total Business}}$$

Example

Color would be a smaller portion within a style. Therefore, you would divide the total sales for the color by the total sales for the style.

Rounding

Buyers typically round numbers to the tenth of a percent, or one place after the decimal. Rounding to a tenth of a percent is more exact than rounding to a whole number. If the number in the hundredth place is **five or higher**, add one to the tenth position. For example, you calculate a percent to total and obtain .1356 on your calculator. Move the decimal two places to the right and round to the tenth. You should get 13.6% as an answer.

In another example, you calculate a .1254 percent to total. Move the decimal two places to the right in order to convert the decimal to a percent. Next, round to the tenth of a percent. You should get 12.5%.

In yet another example, your calculator reads .2 and there is nothing after the two. In this case, you must still move the decimal two places to the right. Place a zero in the filler space. Your answer should be 20%.

Rounding Examples		
.1035 = 10.4%	.2342 = 23.4%	.0278 = 2.8%
.00123 = .1%	.4 = 40%	.064 = 6.4%

Sample Problem Set

A buyer has three colors in a basic style of socks.

Color	Units on Hand (OH)
White	5,000 units
Black	2,000 units
Blue	1,000 units
Total	8,000 units

This is how you would calculate the percent on hand by color:

Colors	Formula	% to total
White	5000/8000	62.5%
Black	2000/8000	25.0%
Blue	1000/8000	12.5%
Total	8000/8000	100.0%

Practice Problem Sets

In the following problems, add the smaller portions of the business to obtain the total sales. Next, divide the smaller portions of the business by the total sales to obtain the **% to Total**. Answer the questions that pertain to each problem set.

Problem Set 1

1. In the following problem, we need to determine what colors are the majority of our business, and where we should eliminate colors from our future reorders. In this example, the total of all colors equals one style.

Colors	Total $ Sales	% to Total
Ecru	8.6	_____
Sage	5.3	_____
Rose	2.4	_____
Sandalwood	6.5	_____
Aubergine	3.9	_____
Teal	6.6	_____
Powder	7.5	_____
Iris	4.5	_____
Melon	8.8	_____
Total $	_____	_____

1A. What are the total sales for this style? _____

_____

1B. What color or colors might you eliminate, based on % to Total? _____

_____

1C. Which two colors account for approximately 32% of this style's sales? _____

_____

1D. Which five colors account for approximately 70% of this style's sales?

_____

Successful buyers spend 90% of their time on 90% of their business!

Applying Your Knowledge

Opportunities to increase business and learn from past mistakes come from understanding where to place your buy, and knowing how to use LY history to make educated future decisions.

Part of this process includes the careful analysis of vendors, styles, colors, and size breakdowns. This is part of the assortment planning process.

The Assortment Planning Process

Buyers determine the **assortment plan** based on:

- Past sales performance
- Future availability
- Markup
- Gross margin
- Emerging trends
- Target market
- Competition

Buyers are required to anniversary last year sales. When creating the assortment plan, the buyer must look at the number of units sold and the sales that were generated last year. In many cases the buyer will buy similar items that were purchased in the past in order to anniversary those sales. Future availability of past styles becomes a crucial part of the assortment planning process. If the styles that generated significant sales last year are not available for future purchases, a new style must be found that will replace that sales volume.

Markup is a calculation that includes what the retailer pays the vendor for the product, and then what the retailer can sell it for. For the retailer, a higher markup is preferred. The retail price is always determined by the **perceived value** the consumer attaches to the product. This requires a careful analysis of each buyer's target market and what the competition is currently doing.

Gross margin (GM) is essentially a measure of profitability that includes the cost of selling the item to the consumer. If a buyer must place a product on sale multiple times during the season in order to obtain desirable sales, the gross margin is diminished.

Market Week Preparation

Market week is when the buyer visits the vendors, or manufacturers, at their showrooms and views the line for the following season.

Many buyers attend market week armed with a basic plan, which includes units by style that they plan to purchase. They have added a planned percent increase to last year's buy, and determined how many units (by style) they need to buy to make their planned sales increase. If some of these styles have basic colors that do not change from season to season, the units will be predetermined. If there are fashion colors that change from season to season, some of the units associated with last year's colors will have to be replaced by the new colors of that season.

When viewing the new fashion colors in market, buyers will determine which are having the best showing and then assign units to the colors accordingly.

Problem Set 2

In the following example, you will have the opportunity to apply LY selling history. By using last year's % to Total, you are applying lessons learned to a planned future buy. One planned future buy has already been determined for you; it is the total dollars allocated to the future purchase of the sport shirt, style #1001.

2. Determine the **% to Total** for each color in a basic men's sport shirt, style #1001. Next, break down the TY planned buy of $350.0 by color, based on the % to Total LY. White has been completed for you.

Type	Colors	LY Sales	% to Total	TY $ Buy
Basic	White	64.3	27.3% ×350 =	$95.6
Basic	Black	42.3	17.9%	$62.7
Basic	Tan	50.4	21.4%	$74.9
Fashion	Indigo	33.4	14.2%	_____
Fashion	Pewter	24.7	10.5%	_____
Fashion	Eggplant	20.6	8.7%	_____
	Total Sales	235.7	_____	_____

66.6%

33.4%

$$\frac{TY - LY}{LY} = \frac{114.3}{235.7}$$

$$= 48.5$$

2A. What are the total sales for this style LY? _____

Explanation

In the first example, *white* is responsible for 27.3% of sales. To determine white's portion of next year's buy, take the total planned buy for the style ($350.0) and multiply by white's % to Total (27.3%).

Example

Total TY planned shirt buy $350.0 × white's % to Total 27.3% = $95.6

2B. For style #1001, the basic colors are white, black, and tan. The fashion colors are indigo, pewter, and eggplant. Consider which colors are popular this season. Which colors might replace indigo, pewter, and eggplant?

> **Note:** Due to rounding, you may end up with a total purchase that is slightly higher than the plan. This is typical in retail buying. A buyer would rather estimate higher than end up short. If your total $ Buy in problem 2 was $350.2, you rounded correctly.

Problem Set 3

FIGURE 2.1
Source: © Martin Thomas Photography / Alamy

3. Four sizes of a branded logo T-shirt are carried in your department. Determine the **% to Total** for each size, based on the following sales.

> **Note:** Manufacturers frequently **pre-pack** styles using their own size distribution. Buyers must be aware of how they package styles and sizes in order to make suggestions to the manufacturer in market.

Sizes	Sales $	% to Total
Small	4.0	20%
Medium	8.0	40%
Large	6.0	30%
X-Large	2.0	10%
Total $	20.00	100%

3A. What are the total sales for the logo T-shirt? _____

3B. What percentage is each size worth in sales?

   Small _____ Medium _____ Large _____ X-Large _____

3C. In which size would you invest the most? _Medium_ _____

3D. In which size would you invest the least? _X-Large_ _____

3E. Assume that the manufacturer's pre-pack was (2S, 4M, 3L, 1XL). If the majority of sales were actually done in X-Large, was this a good manufacturer pre-pack? _no_ _____

> **Note:** The problems throughout this chapter are hypothetical and by no means represent the general population, brands, or selling statistics. They are only problem-solving sets that allow you to understand the principles behind % to Total analysis.

Other Fashion Occupations That Use Percent to Total

In addition to buyers, designers, small business owners, visual merchandisers, and account executives can easily apply these principles to their businesses. For example, **store planners** and **visual merchandisers** allocate floor space by brand and classification of goods, based on buyers' purchasing behavior.

Another example includes account executives, or vendor resources. During market week, account executives report back to the design team on what classifications of goods were most sought after. Designers, in turn, will build a larger selection of products in these key classifications. Sometimes a size request will be given to the design team, based on a retailer's sales history of selling by size. This information is given in percentages.

Small business owners, like buyers, must allocate their time based on the priorities within their businesses. This includes finding the **% to Total** of each vendor and/or classification and allocating efforts and time around the highest percentages of the business.

If all fashion professionals accurately make use of their time based on priority of business, they are more likely to succeed.

Problem Set 4

4. Three basic styles or **silhouettes** are available in a private label dress shirt collection. Based on the following information, determine how the dress shirt styles have sold **by silhouette**.

Dress Shirt Descriptions	Sales $	% to Total
White spread collar	25.8	10.3
White point collar	64.0	25.5
White button-down collar	55.1	21.9 /22
Blue spread collar	15.5	6.2
Blue point collar	48.5	19.3
Blue button-down collar	26.3	10.5
Ivory point collar	7.3	2.9
Ivory button-down collar	8.5	3.4
Total $	251	100%

4A. What are the total private label dress shirt sales? ____251____

4B. What percentage of dress shirts has sold in the **spread collar**? ___16.5___ (white + blue)

4C. What percentage of dress shirts has sold in the **point collar**? ___47.7___

4D. What percentage of dress shirts has sold in the **button-down collar**? ___35.8___

4E. If you were going to add a fashion color to this assortment, which **silhouette** would you add it to? Why?
____point collar, highest sales____

Vendor Assortment

Determining the appropriate vendor assortment is one of the most important steps in the buyer's business planning process. A vendor's **% to Total** department is based on LY sales, shipping, and profitability. New vendors that have entered the marketplace successfully may also affect the % to Total of older vendors. If the addition of new vendors does not eliminate older vendors entirely, it will inevitably change the % to Total of the low-performing vendors.

Buyers must be careful not to over-assort their department. Too many vendors within a department will result in small and insubstantial vendor presentations on the selling floor.

Problem Set 5

FIGURE 2.2
Source: © OPIS/Shutterstock

5. The denim buyer needs assistance determining his **% to Total**, based on selling so far this season.

Vendors	Sales $	% to Total
Miss Me	75.9	_____
Page Premium	145.2	_____
Volcom	89.6	_____
True Religion	182.4	_____
Hudson	36.8	_____
7 For All Mankind	136.9	_____
Joe's	22.4	_____
Lucky	46.8	_____
Burberry	106.9	_____
Levi's	120.9	_____
Total Sales	_____	_____

5A. What are the total denim sales for this department? _____
_____

5B. Which vendor could you **eliminate** without altering the department significantly? To which vendor would you direct those additional sales? _____
_____

5C. What are your top five vendors and their **combined % to Total** for the department? _____
_____

5D. What are your top two vendors and their **combined % to Total** for the department? _____
_____

Maximizing Opportunities

A buyer should consider the time spent with each vendor carefully. To maximize opportunity, buyers should spend the most time with the biggest vendors in their business. Vendors that do an independent analysis of the business and report findings to buyers are extremely valuable. These vendors are often reordered from, without hesitation.

Problem Set 6

6. The handbag buyer at an upscale department store must analyze her LY sales and determine this year's buy according to vendor. Her planned buy **this year (TY)** is **$2,050 (two million, fifty thousand)**.

Vendor	LY $ Sales	% to Total	TY $ Buy
Juicy	200.0	_____	_____
Fendi	80.5	_____	_____
Kate Spade	154.0	_____	_____
Coach	241.1	_____	_____
Burberry	37.6	_____	_____
Nine West	195.1	_____	_____
Furla	75.8	_____	_____
Lamb	61.2	_____	_____
Guess	45.2	_____	_____
Le Sport Sak	144.3	_____	_____
Total Sales	_____		

6A. What were the total department sales LY? _____

6B. If you compare this year's planned buy to last year's sales, what is the percent increase?

_____

6C. What are the **top two** vendors and their **combined % to Total**?

_____

6D. How much will the buyer spend this year on Coach, as compared to LY sales?

_____

6E. If you had to eliminate three vendors, which would they be? Why?

_____

The Right Number of Vendors

It is very easy for buyers to become over-assorted in vendors. For negotiation purposes, it is better to have fewer vendors producing more product. Reducing the number of vendors within an assortment also makes the process of buying and communication more favorable.

The questions in previous problem sets that ask you to eliminate vendors from the assortment are examples of how buyers continually question their vendor assortment. They must often eliminate a current vendor in order to make room for a new, up-and-coming vendor.

Problem Set 7

7. The buyer for women's accessories needs help determining how well each classification of goods is perform-ing. Part of this analysis includes a % to Total by classification.

Classification	Sales $	% to Total
Sunglasses	196.7	_____
Gloves	26.8	_____
Hats	48.5	_____
Wallets	56.4	_____
Belts	60.8	_____
Scarves	118.3	_____
Purses	356.8	_____
Total Sales	_____	_____

7A. What are the total sales for this department? _____

7B. If you could eliminate a classification of goods from this buyer's responsibility, what would you eliminate?

_____

7C. Which two classifications of goods make up 64.1% of this buyer's department?

_____

7D. Assume the buyer wants to purchase **$950.0** worth of merchandise next season. How would you allocate these funds if *gloves* were eliminated from the assortment? (Use the % to Total figures from Problem Set 7.)

_____

Classification	% to Total	Next Season $ Buy
Sunglasses	_____	_____
Gloves	_____	_____
Hats	_____	_____
Wallets	_____	_____
Belts	_____	_____
Scarves	_____	_____
Purses	_____	_____
Total % _____		Total $ Buy _____

Note: *The purchasing dollars allocated to next season's glove purchase must be added to one of the other classifications. A suggestion would be to add those dollars to the department's number one classification.* What is this department's top classification?

Summary

In this chapter, percent to total was defined and used in the analysis of colors, size breakdowns, classifications of goods, and vendor assortments. Assortments were analyzed to determine time priorities and future investment opportunities. Strengths in current assortments were easily assessed based on highest percentages of business. Future purchases were then allocated based on last year's performance. In addition, rounding procedures were reviewed, with examples that illustrated conversion from decimal to percentage.

Assortment planning was introduced with an emphasis on vendor assortments. We learned that buyers prioritize vendors based on their percentage of business and overall performance. Finally, we discussed how other common retail positions use percent to total to analyze their individual businesses.

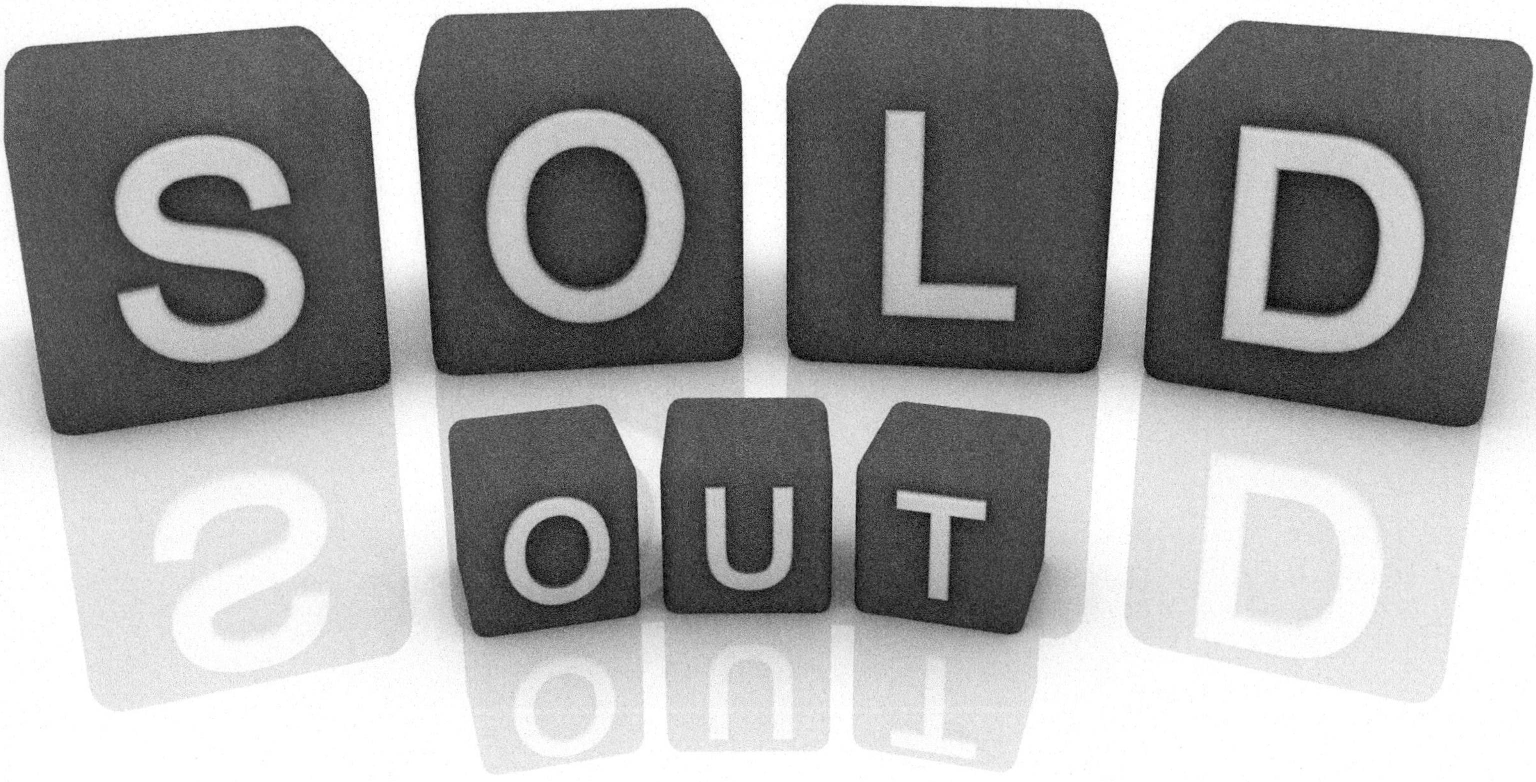

Source: MASP/Fotolia

SELL-THRU

CHAPTER OBJECTIVES

- Define *sell-thru* and how it is used in retail analysis.
- Explain good and bad sell-thru, based on time of season.
- Rank styles according to sell-thru.
- Suggest future buyer actions, based on sell-thru analysis.
- Eliminate vendors, based on poor performance.
- Describe *weeks of supply* and explain how it is used by a buyer.
- Plan future order needs based on weeks of supply.

3

Sales and **sell-thru** are important statistics that buyers use on a daily basis to determine areas of opportunity and liability. A sell-thru is calculated on styles or products, and takes into account the inventory purchased. Sell-thru takes the analysis of sales one step further; it includes what the buyer received in stock. This requires that the buyer know what he or she received in entirety, in either units or dollars.

Using *sell-thru* instead of *sell through* is common retail language. It is part of the language, or lingo, of retail buying.

The Sell-Thru Formula

Sell-thru equals the total units or dollars sold for a style, divided by the total number of units received.

$$\text{Sell-Thru} = \frac{\text{Units Sold}}{\text{Units Received}} \quad \text{or} \quad \text{Sell-Thru} = \frac{\text{Dollars Sold}}{\text{Dollars Received}}$$

The sell-thru formula in Excel is Units Sold/Units Received.

How Do Buyers Use Sell-Thru?

Buyers use sell-thru to determine the success and shelf life of styles. Retailers are most concerned with sell-thru at **full price**. A high sell-thru on merchandise that has been discounted by 50% does not tell you the success of the product at regular price. Sales naturally increase when products are promoted at less than ticket retail. This is why a **sell-thru at full price is essential**.

A built-in pricing structure is the first way to ensure adequate gross margin. In previous chapters we discussed gross margin as a measure of profitability. Once an item has been permanently reduced, the sell-thru is expected to increase if there is an adequate level of stock on hand. Once a discounted product is promoted, the profitability of the item is quickly eroded, resulting in a reduced gross margin. The buyer's top priorities are to maximize both sales and gross margin. Thus, they aim to sell all items at full price, and as many of each item as possible.

Occasionally, promotional events offering a **temporary** discount are used to drive sales and increase sell-thru. These events usually last for a short period of time. Assume that a buyer is offering a product at a 25% discount. In this instance, the buyer should have already calculated the reduction in gross margin that will occur due to this event, or asked vendors to pay for the 25%-off event. If the vendor covers the cost of the event, gross margin will not be negatively affected.

New Items on the Selling Floor

The moment a new item arrives in stores, the buyer reviews the sell-thru. Even one week of selling is indicative of how the item will sell throughout the season, assuming it has actually made it to the selling floor. A buyer may decide to take an early **permanent markdown** on an item because the sell-thru is not consistent with others within the department. If sales and sell-thru are high and the item has a place in the assortment throughout the season, a reorder should be placed.

What Is a Positive Sell-Thru?

- A sell-thru of **80%** or higher is **good**.
- A sell-thru of **90%** or higher is **great**.
- A sell-thru of 100% is the goal all retailers seek to achieve. However, the buyer must consider whether or not enough units were purchased when this occurs.

A sell-thru of **70% to 80%** needs improvement. In some cases it may indicate that too much inventory was purchased, or that it was placed in the wrong store locations. Sometimes, the product has also been priced too high; customers may be willing to purchase it at a slightly lower retail price. Further research is needed to determine *why* this merchandise does not have a higher sell-thru.

Full Price Sell-Thru

A sell-thru of 100% at full price usually indicates that with more inventory on hand, the buyer could have sold more. The buyer considers the number of weeks it took to sell this product at a 100% sell-thru, and then decides how long he/she wants to extend the selling period on that style. The next step would be to estimate the average **Units Sold** for that item per week, and then multiply it by the length of time you want the style to be available in your stores.

Example

A style sold an average of 12 units per week, and was completely sold out in 16 weeks. The buyer wants to carry the item for 20 weeks next year.

Multiply the average weekly sales, in units, by the desired selling period.

12 units sold weekly × desired selling period of 20 weeks = 240 units should be purchased

---

Best Sellers

Sell-thru also allows buyers, store managers, and sales associates to determine the best sellers within a department. Buyers record the best sellers weekly, in a report called the **Best Seller Report**. Sell-thru for the week, month, and season are calculated in this report, which goes to senior executives who strategize future business opportunities. At a lower level in the organization, buyers use this information to plan successful assortments for the coming year.

Store managers and sales associates may coordinate the same type of report for their particular store. By tracking the sales and inventory of their best sellers, they can immediately contact the buying office if they are not receiving adequate replenishment on those styles.

Buyers will also communicate what styles stores should emphasize each season. The best sellers are not always what the buying office anticipates, so communication between stores and merchants is crucial throughout the season.

Problem Sets and Formula Review

The following problems allow you to apply the sell-thru formula. Review the following information before getting started.

> **Round the result to the tenth of a percent**, or one place after the decimal point.
> For example: .8065 = 80.7%.

If Received Has Not Been Calculated

Sometimes we are given incomplete information for determining the number of units **received**. If the number of units or dollars received is not known, the formula is:

Sold + On Hand = Received

What was received has to equal what has been sold plus whatever is left on hand. This assumes that nothing has been stolen so it is not always exact.

> The formula for sell-thru equals the total units or dollars sold, divided by the total units or dollars received. Sell-thru is also expressed as ST%.

FIGURE 3.1
Source: Steve Cady/iStockphoto

1. Holiday sweaters are a popular novelty item during the holiday season in most department stores. It is now the **end of the season** and the sweater buyer must determine the **sell-thru** for the following styles. Answer the questions that follow, based on your findings.

    You do not need the On Hand column to calculate the ST% for this problem, but it has been provided to clearly demonstrate the information.

Styles	Description	Units Sold	Units On Hand	Units Received	Sell-thru or ST%
100	Singing Xmas trees	9,500	1,000	10,500	90.5%
200	Frosty the Snowman	7,580	920	8,500	89.2%
300	Singing Santa Claus	9,600	2,400	12,000	80%
400	Snowflakes	3,850	1,150	5,000	77%
500	Reindeer that light up	7,750	1,150	8,900	87.1%

1A. Which style had the highest **sell-thru** and what was the **ST%**?

_____100,___90.5%_____

1B. Units Sold + Units _____ = Units Received

1C. Units Received − Units Sold = Units _____

1D. Units Received − Units On Hand = Units _____

1E. Which style did the buyer purchase as their number one style?

300 (most)

1F. If 85% is a healthy sell-thru for the season, what were the top styles?

_100, 200, 500_

1G. If 90% was a great sell-thru for the season, what were the top styles?

1H. If this assortment was purchased to last through January and these statistics were from October, what suggestion might you have for this buyer?

Explanation

Another way of approaching question 1H is to consider if these were good sell-thrus for the first half of the season. The answer is **yes**, these are excellent. You could double these sell-thrus to estimate the total season selling. It would also indicate that the stock would be depleted before the end of the season, and a reorder should be placed.

A good sell-thru is 80%. An excellent sell-thru is 90% or higher!

Common Abbreviations	
On Hand = OH	Sell-thru = ST

Problem Set 2

2. Higher quality in sheets correlates to a higher thread count. The higher the thread count, the higher the price of the sheets. Help the sheet buyer determine the sell-thru of the various thread counts.

Sheets	Units Sold	Units OH	Units Received	ST%
250 thread count	8,000	6,600	_14,600_	_54.8%_
300 thread count	4,000	2,800	_6,800_	_58.8%_
400 thread count	2,600	3,500	_6,100_	_42.6%_
600 thread count	1,200	2,500	_3,700_	_32.4%_

2A. The first step requires that you calculate the Units Received.

How do you calculate the Units Received? _____

2B. In which thread count did the buyer purchase the most product?

_250_

2C. Based on sell-thru, are this store's customers more concerned with price or quality? Although it may be close, there is a difference in selling.

price

2D. Assume that this was the total season's selling results. How well did this category of merchandise sell?

very poorly

2E. Assume that this was halfway through the season. How well did this assortment sell?

Note: It is important when learning these formulas to learn **the formula**, not the **visual format**. Columns in some problems may be reversed.

Explanation

The answer to question 2B requires that you know that Total Received is the amount that the buyer **purchased.**

Problem Set 3

3. In cashmere sweaters, we are trying to determine the highest sell-thru by silhouette. This season's selling results can help determine the silhouettes that the sweater buyer should invest in next season.

Sweater Silhouettes	Units OH	Units Sold	Units Received	ST%
Mock Neck	1,200	6,500		
Button down Cardigan	1,325	6,500		
Crew Neck	1,550	6,500		
Turtleneck	1,435	6,500		

3A. Which silhouette had the best sell-thru, and what was the sell-thru?

_____

3B. Which silhouette had the worst sell-thru, and what was the sell-thru?

_____

3C. Assume that this was selling for the entire season. Overall, did these sweaters have a good sell-thru?

_____

3D. What was the total sell-thru for this classification of goods? (This question requires that you total each column, and then calculate sell-thru for the classification.)

_____

3E. Assume that the sales information was collected midpoint in the season. Overall, did these sweaters have a good sell-thru? Would you need to order more?

_____

3F. Use your personal knowledge of fashion for this question. What other silhouettes are popular this season? What might you add to this collection for next year?

Finding Meaning in the Results

Questions that ask you to use your knowledge of fashion trends are good examples of how a buyer thinks. While buyers analyze data on styles and collections, they are also thinking forward.

- What will the new silhouette be next year?
- What new colors will there be?
- How can I make this assortment more marketable among my target market?
- Do I have a large enough size range?
- Where could I have done better last season?

These questions also apply to store owners and designers.

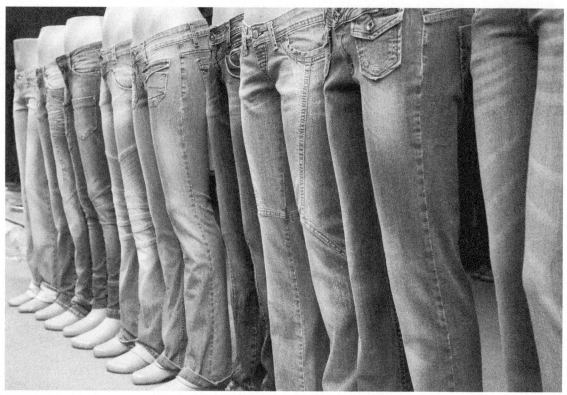

FIGURE 3.2
Source: amete/iStockphoto

4. The denim buyer needs help calculating OH, Sold, and Received. Next, determine the sell-thru for each vendor within the denim department.

Vendors	Total OH $	Total Sold $	Total Received $	ST%
True Religion	99.8		184.2	
Miss Me	90.8	99.4		
Vigoss	134.6		190.5	
Hudson	45.6	75.6		
Diesel	50.7	85.7		
Joe's		85.9	225.8	
Volcom	28.6	94.1		

4A. Which vendor had the highest sell-thru and what was it? Was it an adequate sell-thru for the entire season?

4B. Which vendor had the lowest sell-thru and what was it?

_____

4C. If you had to eliminate three vendors from this assortment **based only on sell-thru**, which vendors would you eliminate?

_____

4D. Which vendor had the most OH stock at the end of the season?

_____

4E. What was the total ST % of the department?

_____

4F. How can the buyer increase vendor sell-thru, based on these statistics?

_____

_____

Note: _When considering question 4F, think about increasing and decreasing the different column = components. Also consider vendor strengths and weaknesses._

Eliminating Vendors from the Assortment

Sometimes buyers have vendors that they would like to eliminate immediately. This is often due to the poor sales of the vendors' product lines. If the vendors continually offer a poor style selection and are unwilling to take suggestions on how they can develop more saleable styles, it may be best to remove them from your vendor assortment.

If a buyer is new to a department and a vendor's products account for a large portion of sales, it may be impossible to eliminate that vendor completely in one season. The buyer must sell down the old inventory, and replace the sales volume with another vendor.

Explanation

You should have chosen to eliminate Vigoss in question 4C, based on ST%. This vendor has $134.6 OH stock; the second highest stock of any vendor in the department. To eliminate Vigoss, the buyer must sell down on that stock and then replace the $55.9 in sales that Vigoss generated with another vendor. **That volume <u>cannot</u> be lost**. The buyer could filter those dollars into Hudson (the number 1 vendor), or add a new vendor.

Problem Set 5

Try to complete the following chart and answer all problems **without** looking back to review formulas. This will indicate what you need to study!

5. The Young Men's buyer needs to calculate sell-thru by vendor, before going to market to place next year's buy.

Vendors	Total OH $	Total Sold $	Total Received $	ST%
Claiborne	20.5	33.5		
Polo Sport	19.2		47.7	
Ralph Lauren		65.3	90.9	
Kenneth Cole	50.1		149.3	
Nautica	36.1	45.7		
Ben Sherman		88.2	138.0	
Guess	58.6		136.1	

5A. Did the vendor with the highest sales also have the highest ST%?

_____

5B. Overall, did this department have a good sell-thru for the season?

_____

5C. What was the total Young Men's department sell-thru?

_____

5D. Which vendor was left with the most inventory? What might you say to that vendor, based on sell-thru and on hands?

_____

5E. Which vendor is it unnecessary to carry, and why? Look at OH, ST %, and $ sold.

_____

Weeks of Supply

Most businesses use sell-thru to analyze selling on company-generated reports. Other companies predominantly use weeks of supply on selling reports. This can be very confusing if a buyer is used to understanding successful sales in terms of sell-thru.

Weeks of supply is more widely used in the retail industry to estimate lead time on purchases. It literally means the **weeks of supply** available in a product, based on a computation of **Sales**, **On Hand Stock**, and **On Order Stock**. When a buyer uses weeks of supply **in place of** sell-thru, it requires more working knowledge of the department for which he or she is buying.

That is why weeks of supply is introduced in this chapter. It is an **alternative analysis** when sell-thru is not available. If sell-thru is available, it may be used **in addition to** sell-thru in order to further analyze stock.

The Formula for Weeks of Supply

$$\text{Weeks of Supply} = \frac{(\text{On Hand Stock } + \text{ On Order Stock})}{\text{WTD Sales}}$$

The weeks of supply formula in **Excel** equals **(OH + OO)/WTD Sales**.

Common Abbreviations	
OH = On Hand (Stock)	**OO** = On Order (Stock)
WTD = Week-to-Date	**MTD** = Month-to-Date

What Does Weeks of Supply Analyze?

Remember that sell-thru takes sales one step further, to include a comparison to stock. Weeks of supply also includes a comparison of sales to stock. In weeks of supply, weekly selling is evaluated in either units or dollars. You compare the **WTD Sales**, in units or dollars, to **OH and OO Stock**. We assume that OO stock is in transit, or on its way to our stores, when it appears on a selling report. Thus, we add On Order stock to On Hand stock to obtain a **total stock number**. Next, we divide the total stock number by the WTD sales.

Example

A buyer sold $4.0 (or $4,000) of a denim skirt, style #201. There is OH stock of $8.0 in the denim skirt, and OO stock of $8.0. How many weeks of supply is available based on these numbers?

$$\text{Weeks of Supply} = \frac{(\text{OH } 8.0 + \text{OO } 8.0)}{\text{WTD sales } 4.0}$$

$$\text{Weeks of Supply} = 4$$

If this buyer continues to sell the denim skirt (style #201) at the same rate of sale, then based on total stock there are four weeks of supply available.

Weeks of Supply Relative to Current Sales

Weeks of supply are always relative to the current rate of sale. If sales increase on a product and stock does not, the weeks of supply quickly diminishes.

Example

The WTD sales increase to $8.0 for style #201, but the OO and OH stock stay the same. The OH stock is $8.0 and the OO stock is $8.0.

$$\text{Weeks of Supply} = \frac{(\text{OH } 8.0 + \text{OO } 8.0)}{\text{WTD sales } 8.0}$$

Based on the formula, there are now only two weeks of supply available.

Determining Inventory Needs

Although weeks of supply can be used to determine best sellers, it is more appropriately used to determine where to invest in more inventory to support sales. Weeks of supply more accurately indicates how much inventory you have left and when you need to reorder. The buyer must know the shipping standards by vendor, in order to fully utilize this concept. The buyer must know how many days it takes from transmittal of order to receipt of the goods in stores.

Assume the vendor for style #201 ships from outside of the country. The buyer knows from experience that the reorder time, from order transmittal to receipt of goods in stores, takes four weeks. Based on this information, will the buyer be out of stock in style #201 **in four weeks**?

The answer is **yes**; the buyer only has two weeks of supply available right now. The buyer should have reordered several weeks ago. This clearly illustrates how important it is to have a strong understanding of vendor lead times. Likewise, during holiday seasons the rate of sale increases very quickly. In order to use weeks of supply accurately, the buyer must be able to estimate the approximate increase in rate of sale from week to week. Some products double or triple in weekly sales during the fourth quarter (November–January).

Calculating weeks of supply is very useful if you know your product well and know exactly how long you want to have a particular style in stock. An example might be a best-selling fashion style that you want to sell completely out of by the end of the holiday season.

> **Note:** In weeks of supply, WTD may be replaced with MTD (Month-to-Date) sales, in units or dollars. MTD would not be used during a holiday period to calculate weeks of supply because the sales from week to week vary so dramatically.

$$\text{Weeks of Supply} = \frac{(OH + OO)}{WTD\ sales}$$

Problem Set 6

6. In the following example, we are determining weeks of supply based on last week's sales, by vendor, for an accessory boutique. The vendors represented in the following table are in the handbag department. This table reflects retail sales in thousands of dollars. For example, 1.6 = $1,600.00 in sales.

Vendors	WTD Sales $	OH Stock $	OO Stock $	Weeks of Supply
Furla	1.6	3.2	4.8	5.0
Lamb	4.2	12.6	4.2	4.0
Burberry	2.4	14.4	4.8	8.0
Fendi	9.2	23.0	18.4	4.5
Dooney	7.2	28.8	10.8	5.5
Betsey Johnson	5.8	17.4	2.9	3.5
Coach	3.1	10.9	9.3	6.5

Avg: 4.8

After you have calculated the weeks of supply for each vendor, answer the following questions.

The first example has been done for you. Furla has five weeks of supply based on the current rate of sale.

6A. Which vendor had the **highest** weeks of supply for this department? Did this vendor have higher or lower than average sales for the week?

Burberry, lower

6B. Which vendor had the **lowest** weeks of supply for this department? Did this vendor have higher or lower than average sales for the week?

Betsy Johnson, higher

6C. Assume that Furla ships from Europe, and that it takes **six weeks** from transmittal of a purchase order to the receipt of goods. If an order is placed today, how much stock will be left OH when the new order arrives?

0

6D. Assume that Burberry takes **four weeks** to deliver product, from transmittal of a purchase order to the receipt of goods. If an order was placed today, how much stock will be left OH when the reorder arrives?

4 weeks x 2.4 = 9.6

6E. Assume Coach takes **two weeks** to deliver from transmittal of purchase order, and we place a reorder today. How much stock will be left OH when the order arrives?

4.5 weeks x 3.1 = 13.9

6F. If Dooney doubles their WTD sales next week, how many weeks of supply will they have next week?

5.5 / 2 = 2.25

6G. If all the vendors for this department require at least **six** weeks of supply on hand, with which vendors must you place reorders today?

everyone except Burberry & Coach

6H. List the vendors from the answer in question 6G and the order needed for each to reach **six** weeks of supply. Your answer should be based on WTD Sales, or the current rate of sale.

how many weeks
short X WTD

Vendors	$ Order
1. Furla	1.6
2. Lamb	8.4
3. Fendi	13.8
4. Dooney	3.6
5. Betsy Johnson	14.5

In Chapter 13, "**Monday Morning Reports**," you will have an opportunity to review both weeks of supply and sell-thru simultaneously for several styles. Both formulas together create a dynamic analysis of selling, and ensure adequate inventory.

Summary

In this chapter, sell-thru was defined and used to determine best sellers, and a positive sell-thru was quantified through a range of percentages. You should now be able to rank styles according to sell-thru.

We learned that buyers also use sell-thru to determine weak styles within their businesses and then take appropriate action. This sometimes results in the elimination of a vendor or group of styles from an assortment.

Another method used to determine positive sales results is weeks of supply. This method of analysis is most appropriately used to determine the inventory need of a style, based on current inventory on hand. Weeks of supply varies according to sales trend and cannot be used exclusively unless the buyer has a firm understanding of the vendor's shipping standards.

Source: Kalim/Fotolia

STOCK
–to–SALES ANALYSIS

CHAPTER OBJECTIVES

- Describe the relationship of stock–to–sales.
- Apply percent to total to the analysis of stock–to–sales.
- Determine an ideal stock level based on current rate of sale.
- Recommend additions and deductions to inventory based on stock–to–sales analysis.
- Identify opportunities and liabilities in current retail assortments.
- Eliminate lower-performing vendors within a department.
- Calculate build orders by vendor, classification, and location.
- Classify stores according to LY sales volume.

4

Taking a regular inventory of **stock–to–sales** is the next step in the analysis of sales and stock. We've discussed retailer sales and how those results dictate all other procedures within a buying office. The first step in the planning process includes the development of sales plans, followed by stock plans. In following chapters we will discuss the development of these plans. Right now, we are still in the process of analyzing data and making recommendations.

Sales Relative to the Merchandise Offering

Sales are dependent on the assortment offering and thus the stock plan. Buyers must follow a merchandise plan that includes specific dollar allocations for both sales and stock. If they do not follow a merchandise plan, analysis throughout the season is irrelevant. Following a specific sales and stock plan enables a buyer to manage the most valuable aspect of the business and make adjustments as needed. It is easily compared to managing a checkbook. You must know how many dollars are coming in, and how many dollars are flowing out.

Development of the Merchandise Plan

The first two steps in the development of the merchandise plan include:

1. Developing a sales plan
2. Developing a stock plan (tied directly to the sales plan)

The development of sales and stock plans will be further discussed in Chapter 7, which guides you through the development of the merchandise plan. In the following problem sets you will analyze actual results to gain familiarity with the relationship between sales and stock.

Practice Problem Sets

In the following exercises, we will compare actual stock–to–sales results and learn how to analyze them. Buyers must first learn how to analyze sales and stock results. After the analysis is mastered, they learn how to create the actual merchandise plan.

A **stock–to–sales analysis** is only successful if the buyer has adhered to their plan. Thus, the buyer has purchased by vendor, or category, in adherence to the original merchandise plan.

Application of Percent to Total

In stock–to–sales analysis, you will expand upon the concept of **% to Total**, to include stock as well as sales. The formula for **stock–to–sales** analysis includes many steps, so it has been broken down for you, one step at a time.

For the following exercises, assume that all stock numbers are in adherence to the stock plan. The buyer has bought in accordance with his or her plan, by category or vendor. Sales may fluctuate, but the stock or inventory is purchased based on the merchandise plan.

In these exercises, the percentage comparison of stock–to–sales is most important. The goal is to have *even* or *equal* stock–to–sales percentages.

Example

"Junior denim is doing 16% sales on 16% of the stock."
If denim accounts for 16% of our business, then 16% of our stock should be denim.

This idea is commonly used in buying as a guideline to match sales trends with stock purchases by category, vendor, and location. Divisional merchandise managers use the same idea when determining how to divide purchasing dollars by buyer. If one buyer is responsible for 30% of their division's sales, then they will shift funds to that buyer to reflect 30% of the division's stock. Likewise, if a buyer is under-performing, the divisional merchandise manager may reduce dollars available for purchasing and encourage the buyer to negotiate a **return to vendor (RTV)** and/or take **markdowns**.

Return to Vendor

A return to vendor is not always easy to negotiate, but is usually approved when the merchandise is damaged or there is very poor selling on a particular assortment. Buyers will often agree to purchase the dollar amount of the RTV in another style, so it is a fair-dollar trade.

Stock-to-Sales by Store Location

When we look at stock–to–sales for retail locations, we will utilize the same concept. Instead of looking at a merchandise category, you will review an entire store's assortment in dollars and percentages. Sales and stock percentages should be equal within the store assortment. Stock–to–sales percentages are analyzed by store, and recommendations are made for either purchasing more or for reducing the inventory levels.

Flagship store locations are the exception to this rule. **Flagship stores** are located in major cities and generate a significant portion of a company's total sales. A flagship store that does 30% of a company's total business may turn very fast and warrant a significant amount of stock, but this type of store is usually unable to warehouse that level of inventory. Theoretically, when the percent of sales is this high, the store may only warrant 27% of the stock. So, as a store reaches a higher level of total sales, it may need slightly below that percentage in stock. This is something to note, but is more widely utilized in the allocation and planning department of major retailers.

Turnover

$$\text{Turnover} = \frac{\text{Total Sales}}{\text{Average Stock}}$$

For now, understand that turnover is the number of times you buy and sell thru an average amount of stock, for a season or for a year. It is a numerical value for the number of times the inventory is "turned over."

Opportunities and Liabilities

If a vendor is doing 20% of the sales on only 16% of the stock, an order is needed. This is considered an opportunity, because we can reorder. In some cases you may not be able to order more, because the vendor is out of goods. Reordering is much easier than taking markdowns and negotiating returns to vendor.

If a department is doing 15% of the sales on 20% of the stock, it is considered a liability. It means that there is unproductive stock on hand. If the 20% stock reflects stock that has arrived at the distribution center but not the stores, then the buyer would revisit these percentages after the stock has been placed on store shelves.

For the following exercises, assume that the stock is already on hand in all stores. If the 20% stock is there, the buyer considers taking a markdown after reviewing the sell thru or negotiating a return to vendor.

- Overstocked = liability (options are a markdown or RTV)
- Understocked = opportunity (option is to reorder more stock)

Transferring Merchandise

In some instances, a buyer may transfer goods from one location to another. The stock does not fall out of the buyer's inventory level; it just moves to another location. Transfers are time-consuming and require scanning the merchandise out, shipping it, and then scanning it back in. In this case, the selling period for a fashion item may be over by the time the transfer is complete. At other times, the merchandise has been on the selling floor too long, is missing tickets, or appears worn. In most cases, it is better to take markdowns on these goods and receive the benefit of sales.

Time is of great value in the buying office. Return on investment must always be considered, and that includes time invested.

Steps 1 and 2 for Completing Each Problem Set

All sales are in thousands of dollars.

Step 1: Complete the % to Total Sales for the Men's Coat Buyer

	Sales $	% to Total Sales
Sport	199.9	11.4
Suede	234.2	13.3
Leather	425.1	24.2
All-weather	188.5	10.7
Overcoats	321.4	18.3
Wool	177.7	10.1
Cashmere	210.4	12.00
Total Sales	1,757.2	100%

Step 2: Complete the % to Total Stock for the Men's Coat Buyer

	Stock $	% to Total Stock
Sport	235.9	12.7
Suede	245.3	13.3
Leather	475.6	_____
All-weather	170.8	_____
Overcoats	330.6	_____

	Stock $	% to Total Stock
Wool	204.5	_____
Cashmere	187.5	_____
Total Stock	1850.2	100%

Answers to Steps 1 and 2

Your answers should match those that follow, assuming you rounded to the nearest tenth of a percent and calculated correctly.

Sales

	Sales $	% to Total Sales
Sport	199.9	11.4%
Suede	234.2	13.3%
Leather	425.1	24.2%
All-weather	188.5	10.7%
Overcoats	321.4	18.3%
Wool	177.7	10.1%
Cashmere	210.4	12.0%
Total Sales	1,757.2	100.0%

Concern: sales higher than stock

If close, and stock is lower than sales

Stock

	Stock $	% to Total Stock
Sport	235.9	12.7%
Suede	245.3	13.3%
Leather	475.6	25.7%
All-weather	170.8	9.2%
Overcoats	330.6	17.9%
Wool	204.5	11.1%
Cashmere	187.5	10.1%
Total Stock	1,850.2	100.0%

Explanation

Sales and stock % to Total charts should be read together. For example, "sport coats are doing 11.4% of the sales in coats, on 12.7% of the stock." "Cashmere is doing 12% of the sales on only 10.1% of the stock." It is important to practice reading the stock–to–sales in this manner. In this way, you instantly know where you need more stock.

Step 3: Ideal Stock Levels

For this step you must assume that $1,850.2 ($1,850,200) is the accurate amount of coat stock this buyer should have on hand, based on the merchandise plan. Take that stock amount and multiply it by the % sales for each category of coats. We are redistributing the stock, based on how it is selling by category. This results in **ideal stock**, which is "ideally" how much stock we should have in each category, based on current sales trends.

Example

$1,850.2 total stock $\times$ sport coat sales of 11.4% = $210.9 ideal stock

> **Note:** *Remember to use the percent key on your calculator.*

In the following problem, multiply Total Stock $ by the Sales % for each category of coats.

Example

Multiply $1,850.2 times 11.4 and hit the percent key, for sport coats. Then write $210.9 in the Ideal Stock box.

	% to Total Sales	Total Stock $	Ideal Stock $
Sport	11.4%	1,850.2	$210.9
Suede	13.3%	1,850.2	_____
Leather	24.2%	1,850.2	_____
All-weather	10.7%	1,850.2	_____
Overcoats	18.3%	1,850.2	_____
Wool	10.1%	1,850.2	_____
Cashmere	12.0%	1,850.2	_____

Explanation

What does ideal stock mean? "Ideally" we should have this much stock on hand, based on current selling trends. Make sure to round the Ideal Stock $ to the **nearest tenth of a percent**, or one place after the decimal point. Notice the ideal stock for sport coats is $210.9, or $210,900 in retail dollars.

Answers to Step 3

	% to Total Sales	Total Stock $	Ideal Stock $
Sport	11.4%	1,850.2	210.9
Suede	13.3%	1,850.2	246.1
Leather	24.2%	1,850.2	447.7
All-weather	10.7%	1,850.2	198.0
Overcoats	18.3%	1,850.2	338.6
Wool	10.1%	1,850.2	186.9
Cashmere	12.0%	1,850.2	222.0

Step 4: Calculate RTV, Markdown, or Order Amounts

Compare the Ideal Stock and Actual Stock $ to get the RTV/Markdown or Order amounts.

Subtract Stock $ from Ideal Stock

Example for Sport Coats

$210.9 Ideal Stock − $235.9 Stock $ (OH) = −$25.0 RTV or Markdown

---

If you subtract in this manner, then a *positive number* indicates an order should be placed; a *negative number* implies an RTV or markdown. A return to vendor (RTV) is preferred because it does not erode profit. An RTV is harder to negotiate, so in most cases a markdown will be taken.

	Stock $	Ideal Stock $	RTV/Markdown or Order $
Sport	235.9	210.9	_____
Suede	245.3	246.1	_____
Leather	475.6	447.7	_____
All-weather	170.8	198.0	_____
Overcoats	330.6	338.6	_____
Wool	204.5	186.9	_____
Cashmere	187.5	222.0	_____
Total	1,850.2	_____	_____

Answers to Step 4

Check your answers to make sure they are correct.

	Stock $	Ideal Stock $	RTV/Markdown or Order $
Sport	235.9	210.9	−25.0
Suede	245.3	246.1	0.8
Leather	475.6	447.7	−27.9
All-weather	170.8	198.0	27.2
Overcoats	330.6	338.6	8.0
Wool	204.5	186.9	−17.6
Cashmere	187.5	222.0	34.5
Total	1,850.2	_____	_____

Analysis of Stock-to-Sales Problem Sets

The answers to the following questions can be found in the chart you just completed. You must be able to translate the information in the chart into opportunities and liabilities. You will also be required to read the sales and stock percentages together, as a unit.

Example

"Sport Coats is doing 11.4% sales, on 12.7% of the stock." This clearly indicates that Sport Coats are overstocked at this point in time.

The balance of the exercises will ask you to combine these steps in the following **stock–to–sales** charts.

Consider the strengths and weaknesses of the businesses represented by each chart. Which businesses seem small in comparison to others within a category, and might not be needed? Categories of merchandise are frequently tested and then taken out completely, based on poor sales. When considering businesses to eliminate, *do not* solely look at large RTV amounts. You must consider the Total Stock $ currently invested in a category. If the OH Stock $ are sizable compared to other categories, it may take a few seasons to get out of the merchandise. This requires a period to sell down the merchandise without reordering.

FIGURE 4.1
Source: Danish Khan/iStockphoto

Men's Coat Department stock-to-sales chart

		Sales $	% to Total Sales	Stock $	% to Total Stock	Ideal Stock $	RTV/Markdown or Order $
1.	Sport	199.9	11.4%	235.9	12.7%	210.9	−25.0
2.	Suede	234.2	13.3%	245.3	13.3%	246.1	0.8
3.	Leather	425.1	24.2%	475.6	25.7%	447.7	−27.9
4.	All-weather	188.5	10.7%	170.8	9.2%	198.0	27.2
5.	Overcoats	321.4	18.3%	330.6	17.9%	338.6	8.0
6.	Wool	177.7	10.1%	204.5	11.1%	186.9	−17.6
7.	Cashmere	210.4	12.0%	187.5	10.1%	222.0	34.5
		1,757.2		1,850.2			

8. Which department has the highest sales? 3. Leather

9. Leather goods is doing _24.2_ % Sales on _25.7_ % of the Stock.

10. What two departments have the biggest opportunities? Cashmere, All weather (largest RTV)

11. What is the total RTV needed in the Men's Coat Department, or how much is this department overstocked? −70.5

12. If an RTV cannot be negotiated, what other option is there to eliminate unproductive stock? Markdowns, promotions

The Home Furnishings general merchandise manager is checking his stock–to–sales by buyer in order to complete the open-to-buy.

Here are some of the things he is looking for:

- Do buyers with higher sales than stock percents have anything on order?
- Which buyers are overstocked compared to sales trend?
- Are the overstocked buyers planning to take markdowns or have a sale event?
- Are the overstocked buyers able to negotiate a return to vendor on unproductive stock?
- Which buyers are over their stock plans and not meeting their sales plans?
- Are there any businesses that we can live without next year?

	Sales $	% to Total Sales	Stock $	% to Total Stock	Ideal Stock $	RTV/Markdown or Order $
					ideal — what we have	
13. *Sheets*	345.7	10.4	398.7	11.6	358.5	-40.2
14. *Towels*	437.9	13.2	499.6	14.5	455	-44.6
15. *Mattresses*	820.1	24.7	750.6	21.8	851.4	100.8
16. *Comforters/Duvets*	525.2	15.8	505.4	14.7	544.6	39.2
17. *Rugs*	330.2	9.9	425.7	12.4	341.2	-84.5
18. *Bath Accessories*	287.6	8.6	295.3	8.6	296.4	1.1
19. *Home Accessories*	277.4	8.5	201.1	5.8	286.1	85.0
20. *Pillows*	302.6	9.1	370.4	10.7	313.7	-56.7
Total	3,326.7		3,446.8			

21. Which department has the most stock? mattresses

22. What is the mattress department's stock-to-sales %? 24.7% of sales on 21.8% of stock

23. Which department is the biggest liability? (largest negative number) rugs

24. If the GMM had to eliminate a department of goods, which should he eliminate? pillows and rugs

Stock-to-Sales by Location

Buyers continually analyze their business by location, in order to ensure adequate stock-to-sales in their stores. Sometimes just one store, typically a flagship store, will account for 40% of a buyer's business. A flagship store is located in a major metropolitan area and attracts both domestic and international clientele. Flagship stores turn very quickly and are often hard to keep in stock. However, if buyers focus their time and energy on these stores, they will find it nearly impossible to fall short of their sales plans. We often refer to these stores as "A stores" or even "A+ stores."

For this exercise, the buyer's top producing stores are being analyzed.

	Sales $	% to Total Sales	Stock $	% to Total Stock	Ideal Stock $	RTV/Markdown or Order $
25. **New York City**	2,546.8		2,435.7			
26. **Los Angeles**	1,234.9		1,555.7			
27. **Newport Beach**	1,098.7		1,657.9			
28. **Miami**	1,276.8		1,344.8			
29. **Boca Raton**	987.6		1,234.6			
30. **Chicago**	1,156.2		1,200.8			
31. Seattle	876.1		1,125.3			
Total						

32. Which store is the most understocked, compared to the others?

_____

33. Which store could possibly be this chain's flagship store?

_____

34. What is the total order needed to get these stores into an adequate stock position?

_____

35. Which store is in the best stock-to-sales position?

_____

Stock-to-Sales by Vendor

The buyer for Men's Casual Shoes is trying to pinpoint which vendors she should carry forward into next season and which vendors she can eliminate.

An easy way to determine next year's buy is through a stock-to-sales comparison. Find the stock and sales percentages for each vendor, and then analyze the business.

	Sales $	% to Total Sales	Stock $	% to Total Stock	Ideal Stock $	RTV/Markdown or Order $
36. *Nike*	112.5		115.4			
37. *Vans*	125.6		162.5			
38. *Fila*	46.2		90.5			
39. *Converse*	114.7		112.3			
40. *New Balance*	62.1		42.5			
41. *Airwalk*	103.5		124.4			
42. *Puma*	185.9		175.1			

43. What is the biggest opportunity for this business, based on sales and stock?

44. Where does the buyer need to allocate more dollars to stock to support sales?

45. Which vendor could the buyer eliminate, without causing a significant dollar loss that would have to be made up elsewhere?

46. What is the total RTV needed to create an "ideal stock" balance?

47. What is the total order needed to create an "ideal stock" balance?

Stock-to-sales comparisons to stock balance, by category, can be used throughout the season. This is a way of checking projected sales and stock needs, and writing build orders for those categories or vendors that are understocked. Categories or vendors that are overstocked may need a POS sale event or an RTV (return to vendor).

Stock-to-Sales by Classification

The jewelry buyer needs help analyzing a selection of her basic jewelry collection. Complete the stock-to-sales chart and then answer the corresponding questions.

	Sales $	% to Total Sales	Stock $	% to Total Stock	Ideal Stock $	RTV/Markdown or Order $
48. Earrings	46.5		55.2			
49. Bracelets	85.9		88.4			
50. Necklaces	25.7		35.6			
51. Rings	65.1		61.2			
52. Anklets	22.5		30.4			
53. Bangles	48.7		50.2			
54. Chokers	98.6		88.7			

55. Which category needs the biggest build order for an even sales to stock ratio?

56. Which category needs the second largest build order?

57. What is the biggest liability for this business?

58. Where are the biggest stock overages?

Review of Problem Set Analysis

In the previous pages you analyzed and applied the stock–to–sales concept to:

- Buyers within a corporate division
- Store locations within a corporate chain
- Vendors within a buyer's area of responsibility
- Classifications of goods within a department

In the next exercise, you will be able to read stock–to–sales, but will incorporate weeks of supply (covered in Chapter 3). This report is a small example of a "by-location report," which is commonly used in the buying office.

Supplemental Build Orders

On the next page you will determine supplemental basic build orders to ensure that this style, and all stores, are in adequate stock position, based on sales.

    Supplemental orders are written for basic styles when the automatic replenishment system fails to order up to the desired amount and rate of sale. This sometimes occurs because the replenishment analyst has not updated the profile of the basic style in the system, or because the system has not caught up to the new sales trend. When a buyer notices a basic style has a high sell thru and is low on hands, he/she writes an order to get that style up to an adequate stock level. This is above and beyond what the replenishment system will order weekly. It is also referred to as a **booster order**.

Solving the Following Problem Set

There are 20 stores total, and the report shows:

- Last week's selling (WTD)
- The month's selling (MTD)
- Stock on hand (OH)
- Stock on order (OO), but not yet received in stores

Fill in the bottom chart with a suggested basic build order for each store. Some stores will not need an order. After you have completed each store, add them together to get the total build order for the style.

    For this exercise consider only the MTD selling and assume that four weeks of supply in stock are needed.

Calculating Each Store's Build Order

Step 1: Add OH + OO = Total Stock (available for the month).

Assume OO will arrive in stores shortly.

Step 2: Total Stock − MTD Sales = the stock you have left over, or how much you need to order.

Assume MTD sales reflect how you will sell this style for the next four weeks.

- If the number is *positive*, you will have stock left over.
- If the number is *negative*, that is your build order amount.

The first two stores (stores 1 and 2) have been done for you.

Sales

Store #	WTD Sales $	WTD Sales %	MTD Sales $	MTD Sales %
1	1.8	5.9%	5.2	4.6%
2	1.5	4.9%	6.1	5.3%
3	1.1	3.6%	4.5	3.9%
4	0.7	2.3%	2.4	2.1%
5	1.6	5.2%	5.4	4.7%
6	1.3	4.2%	4.3	3.8%
7	0.8	2.6%	2.7	2.4%
8	1.4	4.6%	4.9	4.3%
9	0.9	2.9%	3.6	3.2%
10	1.6	5.2%	5.4	4.7%
11	2.0	6.5%	8.5	7.4%
12	1.0	3.3%	3.7	3.2%
13	2.3	7.5%	9.7	8.5%
14	2.5	8.1%	10.1	8.8%
15	1.6	5.2%	6.0	5.3%
16	1.2	3.9%	4.1	3.6%
17	1.4	4.6%	5.2	4.6%
18	1.1	3.6%	3.9	3.4%
19	2.1	6.8%	7.4	6.5%
20	2.8	9.1%	11.1	9.7%
Total Style	30.7	100%	114.2	100%

Stock

OH Stock $	Stock %	OO Stock $
4.5	6.2%	2.8
4.1	5.7%	0.0
2.3	3.2%	0.5
1.5	2.1%	1.2
2.7	3.7%	3.0
3.4	4.7%	2.1
3.0	4.1%	0.1
3.5	4.8%	0.0
1.8	2.5%	2.1
2.4	3.3%	3.5
4.7	6.5%	1.5
1.1	1.5%	1.3
6.2	8.6%	0.9
6.4	8.8%	5.1
5.2	7.2%	0.0
2.1	2.9%	1.0
4.2	5.8%	1.1
2.4	3.3%	2.4
4.2	5.8%	5.1
6.7	9.3%	1.9
72.4	100%	35.6

Store #	Build Order in $s
1	$–
2	$2.0
3	
4	
5	
6	
7	
8	
9	
10	
11	
12	
13	
14	
15	
16	
17	
18	
19	
20	
Total Style	

Based on the concept of weeks of supply covered in Chapter 1, determine a build order by store for this basic collection.

For this exercise, we need four weeks of supply. Use the month-to-date (MTD) selling to determine the projected sales for the next four weeks. In most cases, you would look at both WTD and MTD selling.

Consider stock on hand (OH) and on order (OO).

Example: Store #1 has MTD sales of $5.2, stock OH of $4.5, and stock OO of $2.8.

Add the **OH Stock 4.5 + OO Stock 2.8 = 7.3**.
Total stock available will be 7.3, once the OO arrives.

If projected sales for the four week period are the same as this month (MTD) at 5.2, do we have enough stock?

Total stock 7.3 − 5.2 MTD sales = 2.1.

Yes, and we have 2.1 extra! **Store #1 does not need a build order**.

Final Problem Set

The final exercise for this chapter is similar to the basic build orders just completed, but uses fashion selling history instead. In addition, it looks at **unit selling** instead of dollars and incorporates a next year **planned purchase amount**.

Use the **total received** column to determine the buyer's store modules last year. Write the store numbers on the line provided.

Example

Last year, this buyer bought 480 units of this style for "A stores."

B stores received 360 units.

C stores received 240 units.

D stores received 120 units.

Which are the A stores? _____

Which are the B stores? _____

Which are the C stores? _____

What are the D stores? _____

Next, look at the sell thru for each store. Determine if these stores really warranted the orders they received. Comment on the lines provided.

_____

_____

Steps for the Final Problem Set

Step 1   Take % to Total sales for each store from the top chart, and then rewrite them in the bottom chart under "Sales % to Total."

Step 2   Multiply the planned buy of 7,800 units for the total style by the % to Total sales for each store. Round that number to the nearest whole number, and then write it in the box titled "Next Year Unit Buy."

This is a starting point and is by no means the only way that buyers determine next year purchases. After doing this, you might consider what the natural A, B, C, and D store modules seem to be and make adjustments as needed. Buyers make many adjustments based on store closings, store openings, and management changes. Those are things you will learn in the buying office!

End of Season Selling for Fashion PJ Sets

Store #	Season Units Sold	Sales % to Total	Total Recvd	Total OH	Sell Thru %
1	158	3.6%	240	82	65.8%
2	110	2.5%	120	10	91.7%
3	107	2.4%	120	13	89.2%
4	221	5.0%	240	19	92.1%
5	254	5.8%	360	106	70.6%
6	395	9.0%	480	85	82.3%
7	104	2.4%	120	16	86.7%
8	102	2.3%	120	18	85.0%
9	301	6.8%	360	59	83.6%
10	225	5.1%	240	15	93.8%
11	341	7.7%	480	139	71.0%
12	79	1.8%	120	41	65.8%
13	206	4.7%	240	34	85.8%
14	194	4.4%	240	46	80.8%
15	456	10.3%	480	24	95.0%
16	403	9.1%	480	77	84.0%
17	77	1.7%	120	43	64.2%
18	85	1.9%	120	35	70.8%
19	388	8.8%	480	92	80.8%
20	206	4.7%	240	34	85.8%
Totals	4,412	100%	5,400	988	81.7%

Planned Future Buy

Store #	Next Year Unit Buy	Sales % to Total
1		
2		
3		
4		
5		
6		
7		
8		
9		
10		
11		
12		
13		
14		
15		
16		
17		
18		
19		
20		
Total		100%

Next Year Buy: 7,800 units

The Buyer has decided to purchase 7,800 units next year based on this year's total sell thru by style. She was pleased with the 82% sell thru, because the style arrived late and did not receive the benefit of the full selling period. Break down the order by location and consider the following:

1. Sell Thru by store

2. Stock OH

3. % sales by store

> Which of these concepts is most helpful?

Congratulations, you have completed Chapter 4! The Merchandising Math packet at the end of this chapter is meant to be a comprehensive review of Unit One, before we start pricing concepts. Try these exercises without referring to your notes and formulas. By now you should have a firm grasp of these ideas and when to use them.

Summary

In this chapter we described the relationship of stock–to–sales. The concept of % to Total was applied in the analysis of stock and sales. An ideal stock figure was determined and compared to current on-hand inventory. Build orders, markdowns, and returns to vendor were options for dealing with out-of-balance stock and sales figures. Opportunities and liabilities were determined, based on full analysis of stock–to–sales charts.

In one problem set, the concept of weeks of supply was included, which resulted in a recommendation for basic build orders, or supplemental orders, based on current stock–to–sales analysis. In the last problem set, you had the opportunity to review last year history and determine store modules for future fashion orders.

Merchandising Math Packet Review

A. **% Increase or Decrease**
    What is the formula?

(Known as % CHANGE in Retailing)

1. **Chico's FAS**

Dec '05 STD Sales	Dec '04 STD Sales	% Change
$1,314.0	$999.0	_____

2. **The Limited**

Dec '05 Sales	Dec '04 Sales	% Change
$8,961.0	$8,700.0	_____

3. **Saks Inc.**

Dec '05 Sales	Dec '04 Sales	% Change
$5,562.0	$6,000.0	_____

4. **Wilson's Leather**

Dec '05 Sales	Dec '04 Sales	% Change
$371.1	$411.0	_____

5. **Federated Department Stores**

Dec '05 Sales	Dec '04 Sales	% Change
$21,000.0	$15,000.0	_____

6. **Target Corporation**

Dec '05 Sales	Dec '04 Sales	% Change
$47,700.0	$42,600.0	_____

7. How can you double-check your answers on these problems?

_____

B. **Percent to Total**

What is the formula?

The denim buyer needs help determining % to Total for the following Denim sizes. After you have completed the chart below, answer the corresponding questions.

	Size	Sales	% to Total
8.	25	$55.4	_____
9.	26	$76.3	_____
10.	27	$61.9	_____
11.	28	$80.4	_____
12.	29	$69.1	_____
13.	30	$50.0	_____
14.	31	$39.6	_____
15.	32	$41.0	_____
16.	Total $		

17. What size would you invest the most in?

_____

18. What size would you invest the least in?

_____

19. What three sizes are worth 47.7% of this business?

_____

20. If you had to get rid of one size what would it be based on % to Total?

_____

21. Is it a sound business decision to get rid of the size mentioned in question #20? Why or why not?

_____

22. You have **$600.0** to invest in these sizes next year. How will you invest those dollars?

Size	LY Sales	Planned $ Buy
25	$55.4	_____
26	$76.3	_____
27	$61.9	_____
28	$80.4	_____
29	$69.1	_____
30	$50.0	_____
31	$39.6	_____
32	$41.0	_____

The fine jewelry buyer needs help determining the % to Total for the following styles in her ring collection. Please determine the % to Total for each style and then answer the questions below.

	Style #	Description	Sales	% to Total
23.	6100	Platinum diamond band	$ 158.4	_____
24.	6101	White gold diamond band	$ 149.2	_____
25.	6102	Silver diamond band	$ 78.3	_____

	Style #	Description	Sales	% to Total
26.	6103	Platinum ruby and diamond band	$149.5	_____
27.	6104	White gold ruby and diamond band	$141.1	_____
28.	6105	Silver ruby and diamond band	$117.4	_____
29.	6106	Platinum sapphire and diamond band	$172.0	_____
30.	6107	White gold sapphire and diamond band	$128.6	_____
31.	6108	Silver sapphire and diamond band	$104.4	_____
		Total $	_____	_____

32. What five styles are responsible for approximately 64% of this business?

_____

33. What two styles are worth 27.5% of this business?

_____

34. What color setting above do you think this buyer could live without? Platinum, white gold, or silver?

_____

35. Based on the type of stone used, what is the top seller? Ruby and diamond, sapphire and diamond, or diamond only?

_____

36. Based on current trends in settings and stones, what might the buyer add to this assortment to make it more appealing?

_____

_____

B.   **Percent to Total applied to a purchase**

The men's Divisional Merchandise Manager needs help determining the % to Total, by department, within his division.

	Men's departments	LY Sales	% to Total
37.	Sport coats	$98.9	_____
38.	Suits	$489.0	_____
39.	Pants	$300.4	_____
40.	Shoes	$256.1	_____
41.	Shirts	$312.6	_____
42.	Golf	$64.3	_____
43.	Coats	$111.2	_____
44.	Big & Tall	$148.9	_____
	Total Dept	_____	_____

The men's denim buyer needs help determining her % by vendor for last year.

		LY Sales	% to Total
45.	AG Jeans	$128.4	_____
46.	Ben Sherman	$100.2	_____
47.	Chip & Pepper	$210.4	_____
48.	Diesel	$112.9	_____
49.	G-Star	$198.6	_____
50.	Lacoste	$142.1	_____
51.	Lucky	$169.3	_____
52.	Quicksilver	$86.4	_____
	Total Dept	_____	_____

The men's denim buyer has $1,500 to spend on purchases for next season. Break down the order in dollars by vendor, based on last year's % to Total.

		LY Sales	Next Year Buy
53.	AG Jeans	$128.4	_____
54.	Ben Sherman	$100.2	_____
55.	Chip & Pepper	$210.4	_____
56.	Diesel	$112.9	_____
57.	G-Star	$198.6	_____
58.	Lacoste	$142.1	_____
59.	Lucky	$169.3	_____
60.	Quicksilver	$86.4	_____

C.   Sell Thru

What is the formula?

The children's buyer nees help determining the Sell Thru's for last season in her novelty slipper collection. Some slippers included a sound chip, as noted in the description.

	Style	Description	Units Sold	Units Recvd	% Sell Thru
61.	100	Frogs	8,542	10,800	
62.	101	Ducks that quack!	9,750	10,800	
63.	102	Pigs	7,420	10,800	
64.	103	Dogs that bark!	10,013	10,800	
65.	104	Monkeys	8,890	10,800	
66.	105	Cats that meow!	9,856	10,800	

67. If these were Sell Thru's for the season, were they acceptable? Why or why not?

_____

68. What could you add more of to the assortment next year, based on this information?

_____

The women's hosiery buyer needs help determining Sell Thru's for third quarter of the fall season, in her sock department. Start by calculating Units Received.

	Class	Description	Units Sold	Units OH	Units Recvd	ST%
69.	2	Basic socks	10,010	14,562		
70.	4	Athletic socks	6,112		6,112	
71.	6	Fashion socks	8,450	5,510		
72.	8	Knee highs		6,100	6,100	

73. Are these good Sell Thru's for third quarter, considering there are 3 months left in the season?

_____

74. Why might basic socks have a below average Sell Thru but such a large amount received? Did the buyer forget to review LY history?

_____

D. **Stock–to–Sales**

What is the formula?

The buyer for the Men's Casual Shirt Department would like to know if his stock levels are consistent with his sales volume by department.

	Sales $	% to Total Sales	Stock $	% to Total Stock	Ideal Stock $	RTV/Markdown or Order $
75. *Long-sleeve sport*	64.5		120.1			
76. *Short-sleeve sport*	180.4		164.8			
77. *Polo*	160.5		135.2			
78. *Tropical*	45.3		65.8			
79. *Stripe*	55.4		75.8			
80. *Basic solid*	204.6		236.5			
81. *T-shirt*	356.8		300.1			

82. Which classification has the most stock?

_____

83. Basic Solid Shirts are doing _____% of the sales on _____% of the stock.

_____

84. Which classification is the biggest liability?

_____

85. What is the total department order, based on this analysis?

_____

86. If you had to eliminate a classification from this assortment, what would it be?

_____

Better and Best Price

MARKUP
and MARKDOWNS

CHAPTER OBJECTIVES

- Define *markup* and perform markup calculations.
- Explain how the markup of an item is determined.
- Describe the relationship of private label, exclusives, and retail format to markup.
- Differentiate usage of *point-of-sale* and *permanent markdowns*.
- Identify markdown allowance and when it is used.
- Calculate and compare markdown rate to plan.

5

Markup

Markup is the foundation of assortment planning, and if properly planned, ensures profit. It requires a solid understanding of the retail company's target market. The buyer plans the product assortment based on an average **markup** plan for the department or store.

In large retail stores, a planned markup may be given to the buyer for each season. The buyer is required to meet this plan, and strives to beat the specified markup. Small business owners will also use a markup plan to guide them in their purchasing decisions. Properly used, it is a roadmap to achieving a desired gross margin. You will recall from earlier chapters that gross margin is the first measure of profitability.

The two components that derive markup are:

1. Cost—the price paid by the retailer for the goods
2. Retail—the ticket price of the goods to the consumer

Markup Formula

$$\text{Markup} = \frac{\text{Retail} - \text{Cost}}{\text{Retail}} \qquad \text{Also known as MU\%}$$

The markup Excel formula is: = (Retail − Cost)/Retail.

Pricing Merchandise

Buyers shop the market for the best price available on their merchandise. Whether they are buying from well-established designer lines like Calvin Klein, or buying directly from manufacturers and placing their own label on the products, the cost is crucial to their bottom line. Determining whether a cost is favorable involves a thorough investigation of the products needed and the perceived value of the products, among other things.

Perceived value is the most important factor when determining the cost and retail of a product.

Unless an in-depth analysis of the competition and target market is conducted, the retailer does not know the perceived value of the product. Retailers often underestimate a product at the start of a season if it is new to the market. If sales are much higher than planned, they soon realize they have "**undersold**" the product. Changing the retail price of the product at this point is risky. Increasing the ticket retail is a sure way to irritate the loyal consumer who regularly shops in your stores.

Conversely, retailers often **overprice** the product at the start of the season. If competing retailers have the same product at much lower prices, the retailer will lose a substantial amount of business. This is important, because it is far more expensive to generate new customers than to retain existing customers. Once the buyer realizes that the product is overpriced, it may be too late to adjust pricing, and the selling window may be nearly closed.

As you can see, setting the retail price too high or too low can negatively affect sales. That is why a thorough analysis is needed to determine both the desired cost and acceptable retail of all products in a retailer's assortment.

How Do Buyers Determine Price?

Buyers decide what cost and retail to place on merchandise by:

1. Looking at past selling history (LY)
2. Reassessing the target market
3. Creating a desirable assortment plan

4. Developing and adhering to a gross margin plan
5. Shopping a wide variety of resources
6. Determining whether the product should be purchased from a well-known designer or developed as a private label
7. Estimating the number of markdowns that will be taken in order to sell thru the product
8. Continually assessing the consumers' perceived value of the product
9. Continuing to scour the market for the best prices and quality
10. Reviewing selling information as soon as new products arrive on the selling floor, and then taking appropriate action

Private Label and Exclusives

Markup is the difference between the cost and retail of an item for which there is a **desired range**, based on retail store format and product type. Markup differs among different categories of merchandise within a store. **Private label** and **exclusive** merchandise tends to have higher markup structures than fashion items or merchandise sold in many retail stores.

Private label brands are in-house brands. Retailers work directly with manufacturers to develop a line of goods and then place their own name, or a specially created brand name, on the product label. Private label brands are usually easy to detect within retailers. An example of a strong "in-house" or private label brand is I.N.C. at Macy's. Another example is the Home brand at Target, which includes a wide variety of products, from sheets to towels. These brands are expected to raise the overall markup of the store because the buyer works directly with manufacturers, is not going through a middleman, and is not paying a higher price for a brand name.

FIGURE 5.1 *Buyers work with manufacturers to develop private label*
Source: Digital Vision/Thinkstock

If customers catch on to the brand, it can be a huge success for the retailer and increase overall markup and gross margin. The other benefit is that private label brands provide an assortment that can only be found at the store where they are offered. The retailer does not have to worry about the competition selling the exact style and brand at a lower price.

- The approximate markup range for private label brands is from 55% to over 65%.

Exclusives include brands with the attachment of a celebrity or designer and are only offered at one retailer. An example is the Missoni collection at Target. This fun collection was designed by Missoni to be sold exclusively at Target. Another example would be a designer denim line with one exclusive style of embellished denim for Bloomingdale's. Retailers benefit from this addition to their assortment in the same ways they benefit from private label. They are the only stores carrying the line, which makes them stand out against the competition. Exclusives do not always have the higher markup associated with private label, but the uniqueness of the product catches the attention of the consumer.

Store Formats and Markup

Many strategies are used by the various store formats to generate sales. Some of the stores have a much higher markup than others, due to their unique strategies.

Most retailers can be categorized as **volume driven** (sales driven) or **gross margin driven**. Some retailers are a combination of both.

Volume driven businesses focus on selling as many items as possible. The emphasis is not on markup as much as it is on setting a retail price that will produce the largest quantity of sales.

A **gross margin driven** business focuses on the markup of each individual style. The emphasis here is on getting the highest markup on each product without setting the retail price too high, or beyond the perceived value of the customer.

Walmart is more volume driven than Neiman Marcus. Neiman Marcus is more gross margin driven. Some retailers have **specific categories** within their assortment that are more gross margin driven, and other categories that are more volume driven.

Remember that gross margin results from a variety of factors, but high markup is a major contributor to high gross margin. This assumes you do not have to take a large number of markdowns in order to sell the product. Understanding the retail format is the key to understanding the desired markup structure.

Department stores usually have an average markup, but **private label** collections have higher than average markup. An estimated markup range is from low 50% to over 60% in private brands.

Specialty stores usually have a high markup because they produce their own merchandise or develop **exclusive** merchandise with their manufacturers. An estimated markup range is from mid 50% to high 60%. Luxury goods retailers who are first to capitalize on a unique fabrication or style can have a markup as high as 70%.

Discounters and **warehouse clubs** negotiate deep discounts on items because they buy in bulk, or economies of scale. In turn, they offer deep discounts to the customer. Their markup varies according to classification of goods, but is usually average. An estimated markup range is from 50% to mid 50%.

Off-price retailers sell merchandise at deep discounts, but they buy at an even deeper discount. The merchandise they buy is at the decline stage of the fashion life cycle. They tend to have high markup. For example, the Dollar Stores retail items at $1.00, but they expect to pay only $.30 per item. This is a 70% markup.

Setting the markup on a product or assortment is first based on the goals of the retail format. After that has been established, the target market, resources, assortment plan, and competition must be taken into account. The goal of all retailers is to exceed sales history and increase market share. Strategies for achieving a higher than

FIGURE 5.2 *Department stores have well developed private label assortments*
Source: © Philip Lange/Shutterstock

average markup include the addition of private label brands and negotiation of exclusives. A retailer that is the first to receive a new product or unique fabrication has the advantage. As the first to receive a new and unique item, you gain the ability to set your own profitable pricing structure.

Practice Problem Sets

In the following examples, you will practice the markup formula in a variety of formats. In the past, a popular way of describing a basic **50% markup** was to call it **keystone**. Many manufacturers still refer to markup as above or below keystone. The desired markup is above keystone.

An example of a keystone markup:

$$\text{The formula is} \quad \frac{\text{Retail} - \text{Cost}}{\text{Retail}} \quad \frac{(\$100 - \$50)}{\$100} = 50\% \text{ Markup}$$

FIRST MARKUP FORMULA

$$\text{Markup} = \frac{\text{Retail} - \text{Cost}}{\text{Retail}} \quad \text{Also known as MU\%}$$

Formula in Excel: = (Retail − Cost)/Retail

Example

Retail = $50.00

Cost = $25.00 ($50.00 − $25.00)/$50.00 = 50% Markup

Remember in this answer to move the decimal two places to the right, and round to the nearest tenth of a percent.

WHEN DO I USE THIS FORMULA?

This computation is commonly used to find the markup of an item within a department or when completing a purchase order. It is also used when recording vendor purchase orders and determining each vendor's purchase order markup.

1. Retail = $85.00
   Cost = $30.00   MU% __64.7%__

2. Retail = $195.00
   Cost = $120.00   MU% __38.4%__

3. Retail = $60.00
   Cost = $35.00   MU% _____

4. Retail = $75.00
   Cost = $35.00   MU% _____

5. Retail = $285.00
   Cost = $85.50   MU% __70.2%__

6. Retail = $500.00
   Cost = $150.00   MU% _____

7. What would the retail be on an item with a cost of $1,200.00, if the vendor said the markup was at keystone?

SECOND MARKUP FORMULA

In the following examples, you are given the cost and the markup and must find the retail price.

WHEN DO I USE THIS FORMULA?

This computation is commonly used when the manufacturer's price and the departmental markup are known. The buyer in this example may know what cost they need to find in the marketplace to reach their departmental markup plan. They must also know what the perceived value of the merchandise is in order to determine the retail.

$$\text{The formula is R} = C/(1 - MU)$$

or

$$\text{Retail} = \text{Cost}/(1 - MU)$$

You can always double-check yourself by calculating $\dfrac{(\text{Retail} - \text{Cost})}{\text{Retail}}$

Example

Cost $50.00
Markup % = 60%   (1 − 60%) = .40
$50.00 Cost/.40 = $125.00 Retail

Write down the exact retail you find when calculating the formula, including dollars and cents. Keep in mind that retailers commonly round off odd-ending numbers. For example, if the retail after doing the formula is $119.67, they will round it to $120.00.

---

8. Cost   = 35.00
   Markup % = 60%   Retail _87.5_

9. Cost   = 85.00
   Markup % = 65%   Retail _____

10. Cost   = 20.00
    Markup % = 55%   Retail _$44.44_

11. Cost   = 195.00
    Markup % = 60%   Retail _____

12. Cost   = 18.00
    Markup % = 45%   Retail _$32.73_

THIRD MARKUP FORMULA

In the following examples, you are given the retail and the markup %. You must find the cost.

WHEN DO I USE THIS FORMULA?

This computation is used when the buyer has determined the retail and the departmental markup structures. The desired cost is calculated, and the buyer then shops the market to find a manufacturer that can produce the goods at the desired cost.

This is important, because buyers frequently replace old styles with new and better versions, and may shop the marketplace for a better price. If the buyer has already determined the perceived value of an item and his/her markup plan or goal, then he/she is ready to go shopping!

Designers or vendors may also use this formula when they are trying to position a product to meet a specific retailer's expectations. They may ask the buyer what kind of markup and retail they are looking for, and then see if they can make the product within those guidelines.

The formula is C = R × (1 − MU%)

or

Cost = Retail × (1 − MU%)%

You can always double-check yourself by using the formula $\dfrac{(Retail - Cost)}{Retail}$

Example

Retail $100.00
Markup % = 60%   (1 − 60%) = .40
$100.00 Retail × .40 = $40.00 Cost

13. Retail   = 175.00
    Markup % = 66.5%   Cost _58.63_

14. Retail   = 99.00
    Markup % = 50%   Cost _____

15. Retail   = 45.00
    Markup % = 45%   Cost _24.75_

16. Retail   = 19.99
    Markup % = 65%   Cost _____

17. Retail   = 67.00
    Markup % = 58%   Cost _28.14_

WHICH FORMULA DO I USE?

These questions ask you to choose which formula from the preceding lessons must be used in order to solve the problem.

18. Cost = $9.99

    Markup % = 50%   Retail _$19.98 ____ *PP PP*

19. Retail = $300.00

    Cost = $150.00   MU% _50%___

20. Cost = $59.00

    Markup % = 57%   Retail _$137.4___

21. Retail = $149.00

    Markup % = 54%   Cost _$68.54___

Review these formulas frequently and understand how they are applied.

In later chapters we will discuss in detail how markup and markdowns affect the Profit and Loss Statement and how they directly contribute to gross margin.

Markdowns

Even a high markup obtained on merchandise from the point of negotiation can be quickly diminished by an abundance of **markdowns**. Markdowns quickly erode gross margin and should be dealt with financially as they occur. Avoiding them entirely would be favorable, but highly unlikely. A store like Victoria's Secret recognizes the necessity of markdowns at the end of each season, but has trained their customers to *expect* a sale only twice a year.

In the following pages we will review the standard markdowns taken within a retail buying office, and why it is necessary to take timely markdowns.

Questions Regarding Markdowns

- Why are markdowns taken if they erode gross margin?
- How can an excessive number of markdowns be avoided?
- Why are buyers not better able to project the wants of their customers and avoid the accumulation of unproductive stock?

Two Markdown Types

1. **Permanent markdowns** occur when the actual owned retail price of an item is reduced "permanently." The moment this type of markdown is processed, the markdown accumulates based on the ownership of the item at that time. Some retailers will print a new ticket, but it usually appears in red (or another bright color) to tell the customer that the item has been reduced. If you were to peel off the red ticket, you would find the original ticket retail underneath.

2. **Point–of–sale (POS) markdowns**—A temporary promotion or sale of an item that does not permanently change the retail value of the item in the retailer's computer system. These markdowns accumulate only if the item is sold during the promotional period.

FIGURE 5.3 *Promotion*
Source: © Talaj/iStockphoto

Example

A store decides to have a 25% off sale on back-to-school merchandise. Signs are hung throughout the stores, but no merchandise tickets are changed. If someone buys the item, the price rings in the system at 25% off the ticket price, and the markdown accrues. If nothing sells during this sale period, no markdowns accrue. The retail item in the system is not permanently reduced.

FORMULA FOR FINDING PERMANENT MARKDOWN $ (ONE UNIT)

To find the markdown dollars for **one unit**, follow this formula:

Original Ticket Retail − Reduced Ticket Retail = MD

FORMULA FOR FINDING MARKDOWN $ (MANY UNITS)

To find the markdown dollars for **many units**, follow this formula:

Units × MD$ = Total MD$

PROBLEM EXAMPLE (PERMANENT MARKDOWN)

A dress shirt has a ticket and owned retail of $120.00. The buyer decides to permanently reduce it to $79.99. He owns 1,200 units. The markdown is entered in the computer system and store employees "Red Tag" the item.

PROBLEM SOLUTION

Original Ticket Retail − Reduced Ticket Retail = MD$
($120.00 − $79.99) = $40.01 MD$
Units × MD$ = Total Markdowns
1,200 units × $40.01 = $48,012 Total MD$

EXPLANATION

The total cost of the markdown based on the current on-hand stock in the dress shirt style is $48,012. The markdown dollars for one unit are $40.01. **Red Tag** occurs when a permanent markdown has been taken and the ticket retail of an item is crossed out with a red pen. The new reduced price is written in red.

FORMULA FOR FINDING POS MARKDOWN $ (ONE UNIT)

To find the markdown dollars for **one unit**, follow this formula:

$$\text{Original Ticket Retail} \times \% \text{ Off} = \text{MD\$}$$

FORMULA FOR FINDING POS MARKDOWN $ (MANY UNITS)

To find the markdown dollars for **many units**, follow this formula:

$$\# \text{ Units Sold} \times \text{MD\$} = \text{Total MD\$}$$

PROBLEM EXAMPLE (POS MARKDOWN)

The children's buyer decides to have a 25% off sale on back-to-school sweatshirts. The original ticket retail price of the sweatshirts is $35.00. The store sells 1,300 sweatshirts at the 25% off promotion. What is the markdown cost on one unit, and the total markdown cost for the department?

PROBLEM SOLUTION

$$\text{Original Ticket Retail} \times \% \text{ Off} = \text{MD\$}$$
$$\$35.00 \times 25\% \text{ off} = \$8.75 \text{ MD\$}$$
$$\text{Units Sold} \times \text{MD\$} = \text{Total MD\$}$$
$$1,300 \text{ Units Sold} \times \$8.75 = \$11,375$$

EXPLANATION

In a POS sale event, markdowns only accrue on those items that sell while the promotion is on. The total department markdown was $11,375 based on the 1,300 units that sold at a reduced retail price of $26.25. The value of the markdown on one unit was the difference between the ticket retail of $35.00 and the promotional retail of $26.25, which equals $8.75.

Taking Timely Markdowns

Buyers have to buy a certain quantity to offer variety to the customer. They want to have an adequate selection of merchandise available in the right sizes and colors. They also use selling history and intuition to predict future best sellers. If they can predict best sellers, they will dominate the marketplace and enjoy the benefits of being the first to have the new item on hand. Even if an item is a best seller, there is a point at which the style becomes broken in size and cannot be properly housed on the selling floor. The style loses significance on the selling floor. At this time, it is most appropriate to take a permanent markdown.

WHEN DO I TAKE A PERMANENT MARKDOWN?

1. Fashion styles that have become broken in size (or do not have a full size range available) and have lost significance on the selling floor. No future reorders have been planned.
2. A style has poor selling from its arrival on the selling floor. The buyer has checked with the store to make sure it has definitely been on the selling floor.

3. A style is placed in a department that frequently changes its assortment, such as the junior department. It has been bought for a short selling window, and will soon be replaced by something new.

4. A style is reduced to make room for more merchandise. This is not a wise idea, unless the style has been selling poorly. The buyer wants the benefit of full price and a higher markup for as long as the style is selling adequately. A markdown is not the answer to a floor space issue.

5. A style is seasonal or holiday related and has a very short selling window. For instance, Halloween candy and Christmas cards.

6. Private label styles are being updated, replaced, or deleted from the assortment.

A common rule in department stores is to take a permanent markdown on fashion goods after three months on the selling floor, if the styles have not been marked down before that.

If the styles have poor selling from their arrival, markdowns should be taken as soon as the buyer can afford to do so. The merchandise plan includes a plan for markdowns, so adherence to the plan is crucial for success.

Summary of Merchandise Categories

Fashion goods are those styles bought for a season that are in line with current trends. They are bought to sell out of, not to be replenished or reordered. On occasion, fashion styles may be reordered if they are very popular and continue as best sellers.

Holiday or seasonal goods are bought for an even shorter selling period than fashion styles. They are items associated with a particular holiday or season that usually sell very well, but for a short period of time. They are usually not reordered and must be permanently marked down as soon as the selling window closes.

Basic goods are classic in detail and silhouette and are reordered on a continual basis through an automatic replenishment system. They may include anything from basic socks to a basic dress shirt. Buyers will occasionally promote them with a POS markdown. They do not take a permanent markdown until the basic goods are replaced with new styles or taken completely out of the assortment.

Fashion goods usually have both POS and permanent markdowns. Buyers negotiate POS sale events with vendors, for fashion goods that are very popular. An example is the Calvin Klein Semi-Annual Intimate Apparel sale at major department stores.

Markdown or Vendor Allowance

Buyers partner with vendors on markdowns so that the vendors will help cover the markdowns accrued from sale events. When a vendor covers the cost of a markdown, it is called a **markdown** or **vendor allowance**.

Basic Replenished Goods

Basic goods do not usually have a permanent reduction in retail ownership until the buyer is ready to update the style, or get rid of it completely. If styles within a basic assortment are being changed or updated, a buyer will turn off automatic replenishment and sell down the style at full price. When the style becomes broken in size, a permanent markdown will be taken. When the old style has sold out, the buyer will bring in the new replacement style. Unless the style of the replacement looks dramatically different, the buyer does not want the old version and the new version on the selling floor at the same time. This is often referred to as duplication of a style.

Jobbers

If the old style sells down to a point that it is almost, but not completely, gone, the buyer may sell the remaining pieces to a **jobber**. A **jobber** is a company that buys old or discontinued merchandise from retailers and sells the merchandise to off-price retailers, such as Ross or Marshall's. Buyers avoid this option if possible, because jobbers typically pay for merchandise by the pound. The retailer takes a significant loss on these goods.

When to Take a Point-of-Sale (POS) Markdown

- To launch a new collection of basics or styles
- During a big, storewide event when traffic is high
- During changes in seasons or holidays

Some basics are purchased as promotional vehicles with the intention to have POS sales frequently on these goods. This strategy is commonly used during the holiday season.

When there is a high markup structure on a style or collection, buyers are able to promote more frequently. This is because a higher markup allows buyers to financially afford more markdowns. Private label collections are an example of this concept. Some private label collections are used primarily as promotional vehicles to generate excitement in the department and direct mail advertising.

In the following pages, there are a variety of problems that ask you to identify the markdown type, original retail price, promotional retail price, MD$, Total MD$, and markdown percent.

Markdown Percent

Markdown percent is a new formula that requires a comparison of Total MD$ to Total Sales $ generated from the sale.

Review of Formulas for POS Markdowns

The following example problem includes the new formula for **markdown percent**.

Step 1 Original Ticket Retail × % Off = MD$

Step 2 Units sold × MD$ = Total MD$

Step 3 Total Sales $ = Total Units Sold × Original Ticket Retail

Step 4 Markdown Percent $= \dfrac{\text{Total MD\$}}{\text{Total Sales\$}}$

Example Problem

The buyer for the Children's Department has decided to promote all stuffed animals at 25% off during a customer appreciation event. The event lasts three days and she projects to sell 200 items. The original ticket retail of the stuffed animals is $20.00.

Step 1 Original Ticket Retail $20.00 × 25% off = MD $5.00

Step 2 Planned Units Sold 200 × MD $5.00 = Total MD $1,000

Step 3 Planned Units Sold 200 × Original Ticket Retail $20.00 = Total Sales $4,000

Step 4 $\dfrac{\text{Total MD } \$1,000}{\text{Total Sales } \$4,000}$ = 25% Markdown Percent

Review of Formulas for Permanent Markdowns

This example problem includes the new formula for **markdown percent**.

Step 1 Original Ticket Retail − Reduced Ticket Retail = MD$

Step 2 # Units × MD$ = Total Markdowns

Step 3 Total Sales $ = Total Units Sold × Original Ticket Retail

Step 4 Markdown Percent = $\dfrac{\text{Total MD\$}}{\text{Total Sales\$}}$

Example Problem

A buyer for novelty sweaters has 5,000 units on hand and wants to permanently reduce them from $50.00 to $25.00 before the end of the holiday season. Assume that she sells all 5,000 units after the reduction.

Markdown Type	Perm
Original Retail	$50.00 for one
Promotional Retail	$25.00 for one
MD$	$25.00
Total Units	5,000 units
Total MD$	$125,000
Markdown Percent	50%

Problem Sets

2. The buyer for men's coats is planning a 25% off sale that will last two weeks. He projects to sell 1,254 units in his $450.00 leather coats. Assume he meets the projection. What will the markdown be?

Markdown Type	POS (temporary)
Original Retail	$450.00
Promotional Retail	$337.50
MD$	$112.50
Total Units	1,254
Total MD$	$141,075
Markdown Percent	25%

3. A specialty music store is promoting $2.00 off every CD in the store for a week, to generate extra traffic. CDs are regularly priced at $14.99. The store projects to sell 10,050 units. What will the markdown be?

Markdown Type	
Original Retail	
Promotional Retail	
MD$	
Total Units	
Total MD$	
Markdown Percent	

4. The women's shoe buyer is reducing her summer flip-flops from $20.00 to $12.99 to make room for new fall merchandise. She has 5,600 pairs left on hand. Assume she sells all units. What will the markdown percent be?

$20 \times 5600 = 112,000$

$\dfrac{39,256}{112,000} = 0.3505$

Markdown Type	permanent
Original Retail	$20
Promotional Retail	$12.99
MD$	$7.01
Total Units	5,600
Total MD$	39,256
Markdown Percent	35.1%

5. The private label collection in the Women's Casual Wear Department is being revamped, so the old styles will need to be marked down. Determine the markdown for each style, and then the total collection markdown. If all units are sold at the reduced price, what would the markdown percent be?

35.56% Style 1000 – Reduced from $45.00 to $29.00 – 2,300 OH

29.1% Style 1001 – Reduced from $55.00 to $39.00 – 2,500 OH

24.62% Style 1002 – Reduced from $65.00 to $49.00 – 4,500 OH

$45 \times 2300 = 103,500$
$55 \times 2500 = 137,500$
$65 \times 4500 = 292,500$
$533,500$

Markdown Type	permanent
Total Units	9,300
Total MD$	$148,800
Markdown Percent	27.89%

$\dfrac{148,800}{533,500}$

6. A new sleepwear vendor has agreed to promote its pajama sets at 40% off for a pre-Thanksgiving sale. The store owns 6,500 units at $49.99 ticket retail. If the store sells all the units, what will the markdown percent be?

Markdown Type	Temporary
Original Retail	$49.99
Promotional Retail	$29.99
MD$	$20.00
Total Units	6500 units
Total MD$	$130,000
Markdown Percent	40%

$\dfrac{130,000}{324,935}$

Now that you have reviewed markdown types and the application of formulas to actual units and dollars, you are ready to look at the total departmental view of markdowns and markdown percent.

Markdown Planning

Markdown planning from the larger perspective involves a careful analysis of last year (LY) history. This includes a promotional advertising plan that reflects last year, but may incorporate new vendor and company-wide events. It is extremely important to keep a detailed record of all advertising and promotional events, so that you can easily recall why you had peaks and valleys in sales. For buyers who are new to a particular department, it becomes a guessing game if accurate records are not kept. Most buyers will keep copies of all advertisements and a recap of the sales generated in units and dollars for all promotional sales.

The following is an example of planning markdowns by week, when you have last year's history to consult. The planning of markdowns by day follows the same concept, and will be further discussed in Chapter 13.

November 2004 Last Year History

	Markdown $	Sales $	Markdown Percent
Week 1	4.4	87.0	5%
Week 2	9.5	95.0	10%
Week 3	16.3	125.0	13%
Week 4	28.1	165.0	17%

472   *45*

November 2005 Plan

	Markdowns $	Sales $	Markdown Percent
Week 1	8.8	93.0	9.5%
Week 2	6.3	90.0	7%
Week 3	21.8	145.0	15%
Week 4	32.3	190.0	17%

518   *48.5%*

In the 2005 plan, some adjustments have been made. The first and most obvious is a planned sales increase. Even though the planned markdown percent for week 4 of Nov 2005 is the same as last year, the increase in sales affects the projected markdowns. The buyer for this area plans to take a few more pre-Thanksgiving markdowns in 2005 versus last year. Thus, the markdown percent for week 3 in 2005 is 15% versus last year at 13%.

A sale event took place in week 2 of last year, but shifted into week 1 in 2005. This accounts for a shift in both sales and markdowns for weeks 1 and 2. November 2005 has greater sales and markdowns in week 1 due to the sale. November 2004 has greater sales and markdowns in week 2, due to the placement of the sale that year.

Markdown planning involves some markdowns that are predictable and others that are less predictable. In Chapter 8 we will discuss employee discount in detail. Employee discount is expressed as a percentage of sales that can be projected similar to markdowns. It is based on last year's employee purchases within a specific department. Most large retailers will give the buyer a projected employee discount percent for each department.

Difficult Markdowns to Predict

- Direct mail coupons (typically for 10–20% off)
- Credit card holder discounts
- Additional percentages off already reduced red tag

When we revisit markdown planning in Chapter 13, we will discuss ways to predict accurate markdowns that account for all of these factors.

Now that you have applied both types of markdowns and understand when they are used, we can review **markdown planning** as it applies to the merchandise plan.

Markdown percent, also known as the **markdown rate**, is frequently calculated and analyzed when reviewing the open-to-buy. Markdowns are always measured as a percentage of sales. This is because as sales increase markdowns can as well, as long as the percentage stays within plan. This is more easily understood when you can view each component of gross margin.

PROBLEM EXPLANATION

In the following example, calculate the markdown percent for each month in the six-month buying cycle. Total the sales and markdowns for the season and then calculate a markdown percent based on the season totals. You cannot simply add all the items in the markdown percent column.

FORMULA REVIEW

$$\text{Markdown Percent} = \frac{\text{Total MD\$}}{\text{Total Sales\$}}$$

Months	Sales $	Markdown $	Markdown %
FEB	125.7	8.8	
MAR	145.9	10.2	
APR	189.6	9.5	
MAY	190.5	19.1	
JUN	210.6	20.0	
JUL	175.4	31.6	
TOTALS			

7. What are the total season's sales, markdowns, and markdown percent?

_____

8. What month has the highest markdown rate, and what is the markdown rate?

_____

9. Why might June and July have such high markdowns? Do they also have the highest sales?

_____

For the next exercise, take the same concept and back into Markdowns by applying the percentage to the sales by month.

Months	Sales $	Markdown %	Markdown $
AUG	210.2	9%	
SEPT	227.9	7%	
OCT	235.4	8.5%	
NOV	255.7	10%	
DEC	350.3	25%	
JAN	289.6	35%	
TOTALS			

Now that we have reviewed markdowns by month for both buying seasons, let's look at the total season numbers.

For the fall season, we have total sales of $600.0 and a markdown plan of 10% or $60.0. We end the season with a markdown rate of $90.0 or 15%.

We are 5% over our plan.

Vendor and Markdown Allowance

In order to reduce our markdown rate to the planned 10%, and meet our gross margin goals, we must pay for the **extra $30.0** in markdowns.

We can pay for those markdowns by negotiating a **vendor or markdown allowance** that will pay for mark-downs taken throughout the course of the season. A **vendor allowance** is money paid to the retailer, by the vendor or manufacturer, to cover markdowns accrued in the process of selling that vendor's goods.

If we wait until the end of the season and ask a vendor to write us a check for $30.0, chances are that we will not get it. One way to avoid this situation is to take timely markdowns and pay for them as they accrue. A good negotiator can negotiate more allowance than needed to meet the 10% markdown plan, and will reap the rewards in gross margin.

Assume for this exercise that we are passing a vendor allowance with one vendor.

VENDOR ALLOWANCE

Authorization # 3469005

Date   October 25, 2011   Vendor # 466

Dept #   246

Class	Total Retail	Total Cost	Markup%
25	$30,000	$13,800	54%

Reason: 25% POS sale event on basics and Perms on old basic collection styles being discontinued.

Buyer Signature: _____

DMM Signature: _____

The allowance must be written at the **cost and retail**. Vendors deal in cost values, while retailers mostly deal in retail values. Thus, both values must be passed in the allowance, similar to the taking in and returning of merchandise.

The allowance must be passed at the typical vendor or **departmental markup**.

You will be asked to pass it under a **specific classification**. If the markdown is taken on basic goods, then the allowance should be passed in the basic classification. If it is taken on fashion goods, then the allowance should be taken in the classification for fashion that most closely represents the styles included in the markdown.

The buyer and the divisional merchandise manager's **signatures are required**.

The **authorization code** is obtained from the vendor. If this code is not obtained, the retailer's accounting department will not approve the allowance.

These exercises have demonstrated how markdowns relate to sales, and will be revisited when we review the merchandise plan. We plan markdowns at the departmental level and then break them down by classification, vendor, or style. If proper records are kept every season, last year's performance can be reviewed when projecting markdowns this year. This becomes extremely useful when there are large sale events at the same time every year, or there are vendor sale events that are similar from year to year.

It is very important to keep track of shifts in the retail fiscal calendar from year to year, because these shifts can affect the placement of markdown projections. A copy of the retail fiscal calendar is provided in Chapter 13, where we plan markdowns by day. To obtain a current fiscal calendar, you can always go to the National Retail Federation's website (www.NRF.com).

Keeping accurate records will not only help with the planning process; it will ensure you are well prepared for end-of-season negotiations.

Successful Record Keeping

1. **Markdown history**—includes plans by day, and actual numbers by season, month, and week. The sales plan and actual sales for the month should be included as well.

2. **Vendor allowance**—includes a "by month" summary of vendor markdowns accrued and allowances passed. This should also include vendor allowance information with authorization numbers, total retail and cost passed, and items promoted.

3. **Advertising and sale event calendar**—includes month, week, and day summaries of sale events by vendor and style, as well as the advertising medium used. Copies of all advertisements should be filed by month. Advertising allowances should be recorded by vendor. This is the same concept as a markdown allowance, but the dollars are passed through advertising.

4. **Fashion and basic style notes**—these should reflect the buyer's plans to roll out collections, test new styles, revamp basic styles, add colors, and so on.

Summary

In this chapter, markup was defined and several formulas for deriving markup were calculated. We learned that the single most important factor when pricing an item is the customer's perceived value. Determining the right markup was also described in context of various retail formats and merchandise categories.

Permanent and point-of-sale (POS) markdowns were identified as the two major markdown types used by retailers. Criteria for determining when to use each of these markdown types was established, and applied through several problem sets. Markdown rate was described as a percentage of sales, and this was demonstrated in a comparison of sales and markdowns for the week and the month.

A vendor/markdown allowance was the result of a proactive buyer negotiation that reduced total markdowns, and thus markdown percent. It is evident that vendor negotiations should be conducted as markdowns accrue, rather than waiting until the end of the season. You should also have a clear understanding of how important it is to keep accurate records.

6 Purchase Orders

7 The Six-Month Merchandise Plan

8 Profit and Loss Statement

9 Cooperative Advertising

MANAGING
the Business

UNIT 2

PURCHASE
ORDERS

CHAPTER OBJECTIVES

- Explain the importance of accurate UPC management.
- Label and calculate components of the purchase order.
- Define standard industry dating and shipping terminology.
- Describe purchase order tracking and record maintenance.
- Compare purchase order markup to departmental markup plan.
- Summarize the key importance of the purchase journal.

6

Purchase Orders and UPC Management

Purchase orders are one of the most important aspects of buying because they involve the inventory. Without inventory, there are no sales. New buyers should immerse themselves in the management and tracking of purchase orders. One of the first responsibilities often given to an assistant buyer, and sometimes to an intern, involves the management of purchase orders. This includes setting up styles, linking **UPC codes**, and tracking deliveries. Keeping an organized purchase order book or file is very important. An Excel spreadsheet that includes vendor shipping statistics is also very useful for future negotiations. On the following pages, a few examples have been given to visually represent the kind of organization necessary, and the information needed by buyers, to support their businesses.

A **UPC code** is formally called a **unit product code** and is located underneath the bar code of retail products. It is a 13-digit number that consists of a vendor's DUNS number, vendor style number, and one check digit of little significance. It is how the retailer and vendor link their style identification numbers to one another.

> **Note:** DUNS stands for "Data Universal Numbering System." It is a unique nine-digit numbering system that is used to identify a business.

After Market Week

After the completion of market week, the buyer returns with planned buys in hand. He/she may already have given placement units to the vendor at appointments. This is the most efficient method of placing orders during market week. The urgency to link those placement units to a purchase order begins upon the buyer's return back home. In the event that a vendor runs out of goods, the first orders in usually receive highest priority.

Assistant buyers may be responsible for setting up the styles. This means that they will either have the vendor send a list of UPC codes or look them up in the **UCC catalog**. The UCC catalog is a universal catalog on which vendors post their UPC codes, by season. It is extremely important to properly set up each style. If a style is linked to the wrong UPC code, it will ring up at the wrong price on the selling floor.

For example, an assistant buyer mistakes a down comforter for a duvet cover in the UCC catalog. The $250.00 down comforter scans at $49.00 when a customer purchases it. Ouch! In another example, a buyer sets up fall styles for the Coat Department. The vendor faxes them a list of UPC codes and the corresponding style numbers for the fall coat collection. When the $450.00 leather coat arrives in stores, it scans at $1.99. Why?

UPC codes are recycled once the style they first represented is long gone. In this example, the UPC code was improperly linked to the leather jacket by the vendor. In fact, it is a very old style that is now marked obsolete by the retailer.

Obsolete Merchandise

Obsolete, to most large retailers, is merchandise that shows no selling and has not been marked down for over thirteen months. In short, the merchandise is considered to have very little financial value because it is old and no action has been taken on it. Buyers usually receive a list of items that are being considered obsolete by the planning office. These items will be taken to a drastically low price point, sometimes as low as $1.99. If buyers have taken no action on these styles but own a lot of stock in them, this can be a very substantial, unplanned markdown. This is why it is very important to take timely markdowns and to know every style in your assortment.

The UPC code links the vendor style number to the retailer's style number, sometimes referred to as the **mark style**. It also holds the information for the cost, retail, markup, and description of an item.

The retailer should be strategic about how they set up new style numbers. If a retailer wants to look back on Mother's Day selling, it may set up all Mother's Day styles under style numbers in the 6000's—6001…6002…6003…6004…6005, and so on. This makes it very easy to refer back to Mother's Day history. In some retailers, a query may be compiled (on one page) that pulls styles from all vendors with digits in the 6000's.

Style Descriptions

It is also important to set up a proper description. In most cases, color is very important, and selling history that does not include it can be useless. The description portion of the style is limited to a few spaces, so start with color. For example, *Brwn long slv leather coat* means brown long sleeve leather coat. Come up with descriptions that are easily deciphered by future buyers of this area.

If UPC codes are improperly set up or information changes, there are forms usually available on the retailer's intranet system that can be completed. They are usually called **UPC add** and/or **UPC change** forms.

Computerized Purchase Orders

Purchase orders are virtually all online today and available on the retailer's intranet. Some require divisional merchandise manager approval if they are over a specified amount. If they do not require approval, they transmit directly to the vendor upon completion. Some systems will allow you to work on them, save them, and come back to them without transmitting.

Online purchase orders are easy, because the vendor information appears on the screen, once you enter the vendor number. This leaves the buyer with only the order and shipping information to input.

A very small boutique may still write a paper purchase order that has duplicated copies.

The vendor's **DUNS number** is a universal identification code that is used for billing and payment. It holds the vendor's personal information including address, phone number, contact information, and so forth. If a vendor is not currently in the retailer's system, a **vendor add** form must be completed.

It is important to regularly update vendor information including phone numbers, contact names, and addresses through a form called a **vendor change** form. If this information is not updated, shipments may be delayed. At the distribution center, there may be issues with a shipment that require the center to contact the vendor. If the vendor information linked to the DUNS number is incorrect, the shipment will sit, untouched, until the issue is resolved.

These procedures should be followed to ensure the smooth input of purchase orders and the flow of goods to stores. Success is often in the details. Headaches can be avoided with attention to these details.

In Chapter 7, we will discuss where the budget for writing purchase orders comes from. In short, it is a month-to-month budget that depends on sales. Orders will have to be cancelled if sales are not met, or if markdowns and returns to vendor are poorly projected.

Both basic and fashion orders are planned based on LY history and projected plans for this year.

Automatic Replenishment

The planning and allocation offices run the automatic replenishment systems for basic goods. This is by no means a fail safe system, however, and should be monitored by the buyer. There are two basic types of replenishment systems, and more complex systems are currently being developed. One system requires that the buyer and planner input a minimum unit requirement and an order-up-to point, by store.

Example:

Style 100 should never have fewer than 12 units on hand in store 1. This style is pre-packed in sixes, so you must order in multiples of six. The system will not order until the units on hand fall to 12, and at that point it will order six. The order-up-to point is 18.

In another system, seasonality and trends in selling are taken into account based on LY information or several years of selling history. Selling peaks and valleys are accounted for. The system will order based on the time of year and past year information.

Both systems require constant maintenance and system manipulation based on calendar shifts, changes in styles and trends, and sales event changes.

More advanced systems allow a buyer to borrow selling history from a past style and use it as a model for the setup of a new style. In addition, a buyer may be able to take a style to selling trend based on selling for the last four weeks or even two months. To take a style to trend, the computer application looks at past sales compared to the original projection of sales, and then projects a new sales plan based on the difference.

All of these manipulations to the system can take place if the buyer is invested in the business and works with the replenishment analyst. This involves weekly meetings with the analyst to review orders, updates, and actions to be taken. It is important to update analysts on styles that are being turned off and marked down, as well as on those being added.

On the following pages, forms have been provided for tracking purchase orders in the buying office. The first form is used for basic replenished goods. It could be placed in a file online that is accessible to the buying office and the replenishment analyst. It requires that the analyst or the buying office input the orders that generate weekly, by vendor.

Controlling Vendor Shipping

A buying office with excellent control of its orders will contact the vendors weekly to make sure they received the orders and are in the process of working on them. Good buyers train their vendors to ship on the ship date, rather than waiting until the cancel date to ship.

Ship date—The first day the retailer can technically receive the merchandise and the first day the vendor actually ships the merchandise. The vendor may wait until the cancel date to ship if not properly trained to ship on this date.

Cancel date—The last day the vendor can ship the merchandise and the retailer can receive the merchandise. As long as it goes into transit on this day, the vendor has made the ship/cancel window.

ASN (advanced shipping notice)—A notification of when a basic order will be shipped. It includes a projected ship and received date. Once the merchandise has actually been shipped, it will include a carton count and more detailed information about what was actually shipped.

Assistant buyers are usually responsible for completing and tracking ASNs. A sample form is provided on the next page.

Buyers would like all orders to be shipped 100% complete. However, colors and sizes sell out, or vendors have issues with their manufacturers. Generally, orders that are shipped at 90% complete are sufficient. Anything below this percent complete rate may be used in vendor negotiations at the end of each season. We will discuss this concept further in Chapter 11.

It is important that buyers use their budget wisely and order from vendors that ship promptly and completely. The sales plan is tied to the stock plan. Each month's sales plan is contingent on receiving *that month's* allotted stock. Orders should be written so that they are received *the first week of each the month*, so they get the benefit of selling for the entire month.

Record Keeping for Automatic Replenishment

DEPT # _____448_____   **MONTH AND YEAR**

VENDOR _____Fun Denim_____

PO#	COMMENTS	STYLES	SHIP DATE	CANCEL DATE	ASN? Y OR N	EXPECTED SHIP	EXPECTED ARRIVAL	$ RECVD	SHIP %
8156035	late due to hurricane	1001, 1002, 1003, 1004	25-May	1-Jun	Yes	28-May	5-Jun		
8156036	reorder	2005, 2006	25-May	1-Jun	Yes	25-May	1-Jun	$98.2	98%

In the first order tracking form for basic replenished goods, each page is allocated to a different vendor. The vendor name is placed at the top of the page. The first example is of a purchase order that is late due to hurricane activity. Notice the $ received and Ship % cannot be filled in yet, because the shipment is in transit. Once it arrives at the retailer's distribution center, this information can be completed. This order may need an extension due to the delay in shipping. In the second purchase order, the order has shipped on time. The $ received is filled in, and the Ship % is excellent.

This may be filed in a binder next to copies of the actual purchase orders. If swatches or pictures of the merchandise are available, they may be placed here for reference as well.

Record Keeping for Fashion Orders

On the second form, the same information appears, but in a different format. Notice that several vendors can be recorded on one page. The larger sheet is organized by month. There are usually more basic orders than fashion orders because they are run weekly. When tracking fashion orders, it is important to ensure that they ship whole and on time.

Each month is of great importance, because holiday merchandise has a short selling window. If it is planned to arrive in October, it must. If it is late, it may arrive at a markdown or be on the selling floor for a very short period of time before it is marked down. This is a sure way to erode gross margin.

Review the order tracking form for fashion merchandise below.

Dept # _____   **MONTH AND YEAR**

VENDOR	PO#	STYLES	SHIP DATE	CANCEL DATE	ASN? Y OR N	EXPECTED ARRIVAL	$ RECVD	COMMENTS	SHIP %

Dating Terms (Dating the Order)

Dating is the amount of time a retailer has to pay for the goods it received from the vendor. In some cases, a vendor that has great confidence in a new retailer may extend the dating, allowing extra time for the retailer to sell the merchandise before having to pay for it.

In some department stores in Japan, where floor space is extremely valuable, retailers do not pay for their goods until they sell them. This is the same idea as a consignment agreement.

An **invoice** for the order is sent out, either by mail or electronically, to the accounting office of the retailer. The invoice is sent when the purchase order ships from the vendor.

The **Date of Invoice (DOI)** is regular dating that starts with the invoice date, or when the order actually ships.

Example: 4/8, n/30

This means the retailer receives a 4% discount on the order if it is paid for within 8 days of shipping. Otherwise, the entire balance is due within 30 days of shipping.

Receipt of Goods (ROG)—The retailer does not pay until the goods are actually received. This is very common dating.

Example: 2/10, n/30 ROG

This means that the retailer receives a 2% discount on the order if it is paid for within ten days after the receipt of goods. Otherwise, the entire balance is due within 30 days of the receipt of goods.

Most large retailers take full advantage of opportunities to receive a discount, because they have the funds available to pay early. Most large retailers also have standard terms they use with almost all vendors. Buyers for these stores spend less time on the actual dating of the order.

FIGURE 6.1

Source: © gilles lougassi/iStockphoto

They may frequently negotiate a **discount** based on late shipping of an order. The distribution center may charge the vendor for late shipments or for poor attention to shipping standards. This is called a **chargeback**. A **chargeback** is a fee charged to the vendor for violation of a shipping standard.

With a **Collect on Delivery (COD)**, payment is received at the point of actual delivery. This is often used for small stores that have a rush delivery in small quantities. Cash or a certified bank check may be required.

Shipping Terms

Freight on Board (FOB)—The freight is in the process of transit or shipment. The question of when it changes ownership is explained in the following FOB types.

FOB 50/50—Splitting the freight charges equally between vendor and retailer.

FOB Los Angeles—The vendor agrees to pay until it arrives in Los Angeles, then the freight charges become the responsibility of the retailer. Los Angeles may be replaced by *any city*.

FOB Shipping Point—The retailer pays all freight charges. In some cases, a retailer may have a consolidator that picks the merchandise up from the vendor.

FOB Store—The vendor pays all freight charges to the retailer's store or distribution center. This type of agreement may be made if the vendor is late on very important merchandise. In this instance, direct ships to stores are designated.

Directions for Completing Purchase Orders

On the next page, you will be given information to apply to the following purchase order. Pay attention to all details and find the placement on the actual order form. For most retailers, entering the DUNS number for the retailer will pull up their information on the electronic order. If you are handwriting an order, you must include the vendor's number, name, address, phone number, and fax number. The same retailer information must also be provided. Shipping locations for stores and/or warehouses are also necessary. The purchase orders provided are typical of retailer order forms used when planning the order.

Purchase Order #10568800

Entry Date: January 5, 2012
Ship Date: March 28, 2012
Cancel Date: April 5, 2012

Shipping and Dating: 2/10, n/30 ROG
FOB New York

Dept # 100
Vendor # 345678
Departmental Markup Plan: 50%

Store # – all units are going to only one store. Write #1 in the first box provided that says Store # on the order. The other three boxes will not be completed.

Order:
Style 100 – Brown suede pant, Cost per unit: $75.00, Retail per unit: $160.00
Units ordered 1,200

Style 101 – Brown suede jacket, Cost per unit: $234.00, Retail per unit: $420.00, Units ordered 2,250

Style 102 – Citron blouse, Cost per unit: $35.00, Retail per unit: $75.00,
Units ordered 1,600

FOR ALL ORDERS:

In the SIZE box write **Asst.** (This means the size breakdown is pre-packed.)

Total Cost = Units Ordered × Unit Cost

Total Retail = Units Ordered × Unit Retail

Add down the Total Cost and Total Retail columns and write the answers under Total Order Retail and Total Order Cost at the bottom of the page. Determine the Markup of the order.

STORE NAME IN FANCY FONT

PO# 10568600

Date Entered: 5-Jan-12

Dept # 100

Ship Date: 28-Mar-12

Vendor # 345678

Cancel Date: 5-Apr-12

Shipping Terms: 2/10, N30 ROG

FOB New York

QTY	Style #	DESCRIPTION	SIZE	COLOR	Unit COST	Unit RETAIL	Store #	Store #	Store #	Store #	Store #	Total UNITS	Total COST	Total RETAIL
1,200	100	Brown suede pant	Asst.	Brown	75.00	160.00	1					1,200	90,000.	192,000
2,250	101	Brown suede jacket	Asst.	Brown	234.00	420.00	1					2,250	526,500	945,000.0
1,600	102	Green blouse	Asst.	Green	35.00	75.00	1					1,600	56,000.0	120,000.0

Total Order COST 672,500

Total Order RETAIL 1,257,000

Order Markup % 46.5 %

Planned Dept. Markup % 50%

Purchase Order #10568801

Entry Date: February 5, 2012
Ship Date: April 28, 2012
Cancel Date: May 5, 2012

Shipping and Dating: 8/10, n/30 EOM
FOB 50/50

Dept # 200
Vendor # 345690
Departmental Markup Plan: 57%

Store # – all units are going to only one store. Write 1 in the first box provided that says Store # on the order. The other three boxes will not be completed.

Order:
Style 200 – Multi stripe shirt, Cost per unit: $42.00, Retail per unit: $108.00
Units ordered 4,300

Style 201 – Black leather jacket, Cost per unit: $210.00, Retail per unit: $535.00, Units ordered 2,700

Style 202 – Dark denim pant, Cost per unit: $95.00, Retail per unit: $210.00,
Units ordered 5,500

FOR ALL ORDERS:

In the SIZE box write **Asst**. (This means the size breakdown is pre-packed.)

Total Cost = Units Ordered × Unit Cost

Total Retail = Units Ordered × Unit Retail

Add down the Total Cost and Total Retail columns and write the answers under Total Order Retail and Total Order Cost at the bottom of the page.
Determine the Markup of the order.

STORE NAME IN FANCY FONT

PO# 10568801

Dept # 200

Vendor # 345600

Shipping Terms: 8/10, N/30 EOM

FOB 50/50

Date Entered: 5-Feb-12

Ship Date: 28-Apr-12

Cancel Date: 5-May-12

QTY	Style #	DESCRIPTION	SIZE	COLOR	Unit COST	Unit RETAIL	Store #	Store #	Store #	Store #	Store #	Total UNITS	Total COST	Total RETAIL
4,300	200	Multi Stripe Shirt	Asst.	Multi	$42.00	$108.00	1					4,300	180,600.0	464,400.0
2,700	201	Black leather jacket	Asst.	Black	$210.00	$535.00	1					2,700	567,000.0	1,449,500.0
5,500	202	Dark Denim Pant	Asst.	Dk. Denim	$95.00	$210.00	1					5,500	522,500.0	1,155,000.0

Total Order COST $1,215,500

Total Order RETAIL $2,923,500

Order Markup % 58.4%

Planned Dept. Markup % 57.0

Purchase Order #10568802

Entry Date: March 5, 2012
Ship Date: May 28, 2012
Cancel Date: June 5, 2012

Shipping and Dating: 3/10, n/30 ROG
FOB Chicago

Dept # 220
Vendor # 345700
Departmental Markup Plan: 60%

Store # – all units are going to only one store. Write 1 in the first box provided that says Store # on the order. The other three boxes will not be completed.

Order:
Style 300 – Olive corduroy pant, Cost per unit: $37.00, Retail per unit: $85.00
Units ordered 6,500

Style 301 – Natural long sleeve knit, Cost per unit: $45.00, Retail per unit: $95.00, Units ordered 3,400

Style 302 – Olive turtleneck, Cost per unit: $12.00, Retail per unit: $35.00,
Units ordered 5,000

Style 303 – Rust v-neck top, Cost per unit: $15.00, Retail per unit: $45.00, Units ordered 7,000

FOR ALL ORDERS:

In the SIZE box write **Asst.** (This means the size breakdown is pre-packed.)

Total Cost = Units Ordered × Unit Cost

Total Retail = Units Ordered × Unit Retail

Add down the Total Cost and Total Retail columns and write the answers under Total Order Retail and Total Order Cost at the bottom of the page. Determine the Markup of the order.

STORE NAME IN FANCY FONT

PO# _____   Date Entered: _____

Dept # _____   Ship Date: _____

Vendor # _____   Cancel Date: _____

Shipping Terms: _____

QTY	Style #	DESCRIPTION	SIZE	COLOR	Unit COST	Unit RETAIL	Store #	Store #	Store #	Store #	Total UNITS	Total COST	Total RETAIL

Total Order COST _____

Total Order RETAIL _____

Order Markup % _____

Planned Dept. Markup % _____

Purchase Order #10568803

Entry Date: April 5, 2012
Ship Date: June 28, 2012
Cancel Date: July 5, 2012

Shipping and Dating: 2/8, n/30
FOB Factory

Dept # 230
Vendor # 345850
Departmental Markup Plan: 55%

Store # – all units are going to only one store. Write 1 in the first box provided that says Store # on the order. The other three boxes will not be completed.

Order:
Style 400 – Black long skirt, Cost per unit: $67.00, Retail per unit: $145.00
Units ordered 3,300

Style 401 – White blouse with detail, Cost per unit: $30.00, Retail per unit: $65.00, Units ordered 4,550
Style 402 – Black jacket, Cost per unit: $75.00, Retail per unit: $178.00, Units ordered 4,800
Style 403 – Red scarf, Cost per unit: $17.00, Retail per unit: $40.00, Units ordered 5,000

FOR ALL ORDERS:

In the SIZE box write **Asst.** (This means the size breakdown is pre-packed.)

Total Cost = Units Ordered × Unit Cost

Total Retail = Units Ordered × Unit Retail

Add down the Total Cost and Total Retail columns and write the answers under Total Order Retail and Total Order Cost at the bottom of the page.
Determine the Markup of the order.

STORE NAME IN FANCY FONT

PO# _____   Date Entered: _____

Dept # _____   Ship Date: _____

Vendor # _____   Cancel Date: _____

Shipping Terms: _____

QTY	Style #	DESCRIPTION	SIZE	COLOR	Unit COST	Unit RETAIL	Store #	Store #	Store #	Store #	Store #	Total UNITS	Total COST	Total RETAIL

Total Order COST _____

Total Order RETAIL _____

Order Markup % _____

Planned Dept. Markup % _____

Questions Regarding Purchase Orders

Now that you have completed the purchase orders, answer the following questions regarding the purchase order markup versus the planned departmental markup.

1. Which orders had a favorable order markup compared to the departmental markup plan?

_____

2. Which orders did not meet the departmental markup plan?

_____

3. How could you alter the purchase order markup on the orders that did not meet the departmental markup plan?

_____

4. Based on your answer for question 3, alter one of the purchase orders to meet the departmental markup plan. You cannot eliminate any styles on the order completely.

_____

_____

_____

_____

Refer back to the purchase orders to review how you obtained total costs and retails for the order. This is referred to as **extended cost and retail**. This means that we extend the cost and retail to apply to the total units being ordered, by style. It is simply multiplying the units by the cost and retail for each style.

It is extremely important to write purchase orders that are at or above a buyer's departmental markup plan. Adherence to this concept will help to ensure optimum gross margin results. If you must order something below the markup plan for the department, offset it with merchandise at a higher markup than the department plan. In most cases, buyers will not purchase merchandise below their plan. They will instead hunt the market place for a better deal.

The Purchase Journal

The **purchase journal, or the PJ**, is a report that lists all purchase orders and purchase order information. It is typically available for a department on a weekly basis. It shows total dollars received on the order and the status of the order. One of the most important features is the brief, one-line summary of an order with the purchase order markup. Scanning the PJ for markups that seem out of place will ensure easier inventory reconciliation at the end of each season.

Reasons for Low Markup on Purchase Orders

1. The buying office marked down basic styles without telling the replenishment analyst. Marked down basics were reordered automatically.
2. A UPC used for a new style is actually linked to an old style that is marked down.
3. Incorrect entering of a purchase order.
4. The buyer had to purchase something below the markup plan and could not offset the order with other styles.

Buyers tend to off put checking the purchase journal, but in just a few minutes it is easy to pinpoint problems so they can be resolved quickly.

Now that we have finished purchase orders, we are ready to review the entire budget. In chapter 7, we will learn the formulas used in the calculation of the merchandise plan and analyze existing merchandise plans.

Review all formulas before starting the next chapter. Many of them will be repeated in the merchandise plan.

Summary

In this chapter, we discussed all aspects of the purchase order. This included management of the UPC code and the proper input of style descriptions. Buyers who are the first to place orders are given priority in shipping. Successful buyers maintain strict control of the timely shipping of orders, realizing that sales are directly tied to their stock investment. Shipping and dating terminology was defined and applied to the purchase order.

The total, or extended cost and retail, were calculated for each purchase order and then markup for the order could be determined. Markup on each order was compared to the buyer's departmental markup plan. The purchase journal was emphasized as a resource used by the buyer to review details of the purchase order including cost, retail, and markup.

Marketing business sales

Source: © Robert Mizerek/Fotolia

THE SIX-MONTH
MERCHANDISE PLAN

CHAPTER OBJECTIVES

- Define all components of the Six-Month Merchandise Plan.
- Explain the importance of adherence to the Six-Month Merchandise Plan.
- Describe how inventory additions/subtractions affect open-to-buy.
- Calculate appropriate beginning-of-month (BOM) stock levels relative to sales.
- Complete a merchandise plan for fall and spring seasons based on given information.
- Create a merchandise plan using LY history as a reference.
- Assess the strengths and weaknesses of a merchandise plan.
- Reforecast the open-to-buy based on weekly business results.
- Update vendor-specific open-to-buy based on business results.

7

The Six-Month Seasons

Retailers break the twelve-month calendar year into two six-month seasons in order to prepare business plans and manage the daily business. The two seasons are:

Fall/Winter—includes the months of August through January

Spring/Summer—includes the months of February through July

Quarters

Additionally, retailers break each season into three-month quarters in order to discuss business results for periods of time. The three-month quarters are:

Quarter 1 (Q1) = February, March, and April

Quarter 2 (Q2) = May, June, and July

Quarter 3 (Q3) = August, September, and October

Quarter 4 (Q4) = November, December, and January

Based on this quarter breakdown, we can make deductions about peak business. For example, Q4 typically has the highest sales, due to the holiday season. Q3 is usually a peak selling period for Back-to-School, and Q2 is the summer selling period. Being able to recognize which months each quarter represents is important in retail, because sales results and industry articles often refer to these selling periods.

The end of one full year of business for most retailers concludes with January figures. After January's figures have been recorded, annual reports are published for the completed year. Thus, the retail buyer completes one full year of business each January.

The Six-Month Plan

The buyer creates a business plan for each of the six-month seasons that includes projected sales, markdowns, and inventory needs. This business plan is called the **Six-Month Merchandise Plan**.

The Six-Month Merchandise Plan consists of additions and subtractions to the buyer's stock value, or inventory, in dollars. It is essentially the buyer's month-to-month checkbook. When you think of calculating your checkbook, there are both deposits and withdrawals. This concept is similar. When we calculate the additions and subtractions to the inventory, we are constantly comparing the actual results to our merchandise plan. A buyer's success depends on adherence to the merchandise plan and the ability to forecast in light of new information and results.

When Do Buyers Develop the Six-Month Plan?

The timing of the development of the merchandise plan depends on the type of retail format. Buyers who work for department stores tend to prepare the Six- Month Merchandise Plan a full six months to one year before the season for which it is being developed. In a specialty retailer that primarily carries an in-house brand or private label, the merchandise plan may be prepared over a year in advance. This is because the buyer for this type of format is working directly with manufacturers to develop new products. In this situation, the buyer must have a skeletal plan conceived before he/she can give specifications to the manufacturer. In either case, a great deal of planning and reference to last year's statistics goes into the development of the plan.

Open-to-Buy

When a buyer uses current statistics to update the merchandise plan, he or she is calculating the **open-to-buy**. Open-to-buy is the amount of money available to purchase new inventory based on current business trends.

A buyer will update the merchandise plan, and thus calculate the open-to-buy, on a weekly and monthly basis. This process results in a comparison of the original merchandise plan to current trends in business. The buyer may also change future month projections, based on current information.

The buyer's success depends on this accurate, ongoing forecast. If he/she does not adjust the merchandise plan as statistics change, he/she cannot take full advantage of the open-to-buy dollars allocated each month for purchases. For example, if sales increase, as compared to the original plan, there will be an opportunity to purchase more merchandise. If this additional inventory is not purchased, the buyer's department may be grossly understocked, resulting in a loss of sales. Likewise, if sales decrease, the open-to-buy dollars decrease, resulting in an overstocked position unless the buyer reduces purchases.

The Plan at Retail

All dollars on the Six-Month Merchandise Plan are at retail value. This means that all purchases, when received, are recorded by the retailer at the retail price. That is why we learned in the previous chapters the importance of ensuring that orders are at, or above, the planned departmental markup.

Another source for verifying the cost value of our inventory and markup is the Purchase Journal. Other reports may also apply, depending on the specific retailer. The **Purchase Journal (PJ)** is a record of all purchase orders. It includes the total retail, cost, and markup of every order. It also includes the date the order was received by the retailer.

Additions and Subtractions to the Merchandise Plan

The merchandise plan includes components that either increase the retail inventory value or decrease it. Additions to a buyer's inventory value include:

1. Orders
2. Increase in retail, or the markup in ownership, of particular styles

Reductions to a buyer's inventory value include:

1. Sales
2. Markdowns
3. Returns to vendor (RTVs)
4. Employee discount
5. Shortage or shrink

These components affect the open-to-buy dollars in the same way. The information on the following pages mimics the order that a buyer would follow in the stages of the planning process. Some of the above items will not be discussed further until after you have the opportunity to complete the sample merchandise plans.

Merchandise Planning Methods

There are two basic methods for creating the merchandise plan each season: top-down and bottom-up.

Company → GMM → DMM → Buyer → Dept → Class → Vendor → Style

1. **Top-down planning**—Starts with the retailer's overall sales increase for the season, based on last year performance. The company plan is then broken down by the general merchandise manager (GMM). Each GMM breaks down his/her specific sales goal by divisional merchandise manager (DMM), based on last year's sales performance. Each DMM breaks down his/her individual plan by buyer. Each buyer breaks down his/her plan by department, classification, vendor, and style. In addition, each buyer plans each style by color and size, if applicable.

   The top-down plan is usually the least time-consuming process, because you can easily see the big picture and base projections on last year percentages. Most large retailers use this method for planning. In most instances, this results in a very realistic plan. Once sales are calculated, the other components of the merchandise plan are determined. The disadvantage to this plan can be overlooking the statistics at the style, color, and size level, with too much emphasis on the larger picture.

   The second procedure for creating the Merchandise Plan is the bottom-up planning method.

SKU → Class → Vendor → Dept → Buyer → Division → GMM → Company

2. **Bottom-up planning**—Starts with a SKU-level analysis of last year sales, and then builds into classification plans, vendor plans, department plans, buyer plans, and eventually the total company plan.

   The bottom-up method of planning is very time-consuming and is usually used by smaller retailers or individual stores. It often results in inflated plans that are not viable, due to the lack of a larger perspective. It is important to see the total company and department goals, not just issues of size and color. If a buyer can see where he/she is going, it is easier to get there. This includes the overall plan for increasing or decreasing vendors. Imagine looking at only the smallest detail and projecting from that direction. Inevitably, you will end up with an inflated plan. If, however, you have very few styles in only one store, this may create a very precise plan.

   In both methods of planning, the buyer has an opportunity to discuss the plan with his/her immediate boss, usually a DMM. In some cases, the buyer may be able to have the company plan for his/her department adjusted down, if a strong enough argument is presented.

Example

The coat buyer had an amazing +18% sales increase last season, due to an unseasonably cold winter. This year, the coat department is planned up 10%. In the past five years, this buyer has typically increased sales over the previous year by 4% to 8%. This buyer knows it will be impossible to make the 10% increase, and will be lucky to make last year's sales figures. A well-presented history of this department persuades the DMM to reduce the coat buyer's sales plan to +5%. This is still an aggressive plan, but better than the original +10% planned increase.

Outline of the Merchandise Plan

Before starting the formulas on the merchandise plan, let's review an outline of what the merchandise plan entails. This gives you the overview of the major components. You will usually see six months at a time, but here the example shows only August and September to make it more manageable.

The following merchandise plan is a month-to-month flow of the topics listed.

	August	September
1. BOM Stock	$270, 400	$297,200
2. Purchases	$70,000	$84,000
3. Total Stock	$340,400	$381,200

	August	September
4. Markdowns	$1,200	$3,200
5. Sales	$42,000	$80,000
6. Total Deductions	$43,200	$83,200
7. EOM Stock	$297,200	$298,000

The following is a brief description of components 1 through 7, listed in the outline of merchandise plan above.

1. **BOM stock (beginning-of-month stock)** is the stock value on hand, in dollars, at the start of each month, thus, the beginning of month stock. It is usually the second item planned in the merchandise plan.
2. **Purchases** include the amount of inventory the buyer can bring into the store each month. The amount is determined by all other factors plus the target EOM stock for each month.
3. **Total stock** is simply the BOM stock plus the purchases. It is the total amount of stock available each month for sale. This is why it is crucial for all planned purchases to arrive the first week of the month, if possible. As you can see, the sales for the month are based on that total stock value.
4. **Markdowns** are the total amount of markdowns, in dollars, accrued each month. Recall that these come from a POS sale event or permanent reduction in the ticket retail of a style.
5. **Sales** are the dollar amount of the inventory that sold each month.
6. **Total deductions** are sales plus markdowns. More elaborate merchandise plans may also include returns to vendor, shortage, and employee discount. These all reduce the inventory value in the merchandise plan. They will be discussed in detail later in this chapter.
7. **EOM stock (end-of-month stock)** is the stock value, in dollars, that should be on hand at the end of each month. It is a target that the buyer aims to achieve by manipulating the other factors. This stock is carried to the next month; it becomes the next month's BOM stock.

Explanation

In the merchandise plan above, the August EOM stock of $297,200 is carried over and becomes the BOM stock for September. The total deductions are calculated by adding the sales and markdowns. The total stock is calculated by adding the BOM stock and the purchases. The purchases are the last figure to be calculated, and are based on all other components. When we start to calculate an entire merchandise plan, this will become clear. Note that the sales and markdowns figures are just an example and are slightly exaggerated. It would be highly unlikely for a store to double its August sales in September.

Planning Sales

The first step in planning is to accurately plan sales. All other factors are based on this calculation. Last year history is extremely important for this step in planning, and the buyer will plan one six-month season at a time. Please review last year's sales.

Last Year's Sales						
AUG	SEPT	OCT	NOV	DEC	JAN	SEASON
$112,450	$129,000	$129,500	$134,500	$150,423	$167,300	$823,173

The total season sales are calculated by adding all six months for the fall/season together. After examining the high and low points in sales for the season, calculate the **monthly sales percent (% Sales by Month)** to total.

Monthly Sales % = Monthly Sales divided by Season Sales

or

$$MS\% = \frac{MS\$}{SS\$}$$

Example

August Sales 112,450 ÷ Season Sales 823,173 = 13.7%

In this example, August represents 13.7% of the sales for the fall season.

Complete the monthly sales percent for each month using the sales listed here.

Monthly Sales %						
AUG	SEPT	OCT	NOV	DEC	JAN	SEASON
13.7%						100%

Last Year's Sales						
AUG	SEPT	OCT	NOV	DEC	JAN	SEASON
$112,450	$129,000	$129,500	$134,500	$150,423	$167,300	$823,173

This is the first step in the analysis of last year's performance. Now consider applying a planned percent increase to last year's sales for the season.

If the Planned Sales for next year are + 4% over LY, or + 4% over $823,173, what are next year's planned sales?

In the last question, if you took season sales of $823,173 + 4%, you should have calculated **$856,100** for next year's planned sales.

Now we will take the concept of monthly sales percent and apply it to next year. When we do this, we are creating the plan. Use the buyer's notes concerning last year's business to plan your sales and monthly sales percent. The result is the sales plan for the next fall season.

These are the buyer's notes from last year:

- Should have slightly higher sales in August. Were short shipped a few August orders last year.
- October should be a higher % to Total this year. Last year was an unusually slow month.
- November should have similar sales results this year as compared to last year.
- Should have higher sales in December than January this year. Last year received December deliveries late!

Last Year's Sales						
AUG	SEPT	OCT	NOV	DEC	JAN	SEASON
$112,450	$129,000	$129,500	$134,500	$150,423	$167,300	$823,173
Planned Sales						
AUG	SEPT	OCT	NOV	DEC	JAN	SEASON
						$856,100
Monthly Sales %						
AUG	SEPT	OCT	NOV	DEC	JAN	SEASON
						100%

One way to approach this problem is to write down the monthly sales percent last year in the spaces provided. Next, break down the new season sales of $856,100 using those percentages. This assumes the same flow of sales TY versus LY. The same flow will probably not happen, but this is a *starting point*. The flow for next year will change, based on the *buyer's notes* about what did or didn't happen last year. Now, consider the buyer's notes and make adjustments to sales where appropriate.

Example

The first bullet point states that August sales should be higher next year. In this plan, increase the monthly sales percent for August vs. last year, and change the dollars accordingly.

This is an example of what you might have come up with.

Planned Sales						
AUG	SEPT	OCT	NOV	DEC	JAN	SEASON
$120,000	$135,600	$139,500	$140,600	$165,000	$155,400	$856,100

Monthly Sales %						
AUG	SEPT	OCT	NOV	DEC	JAN	SEASON
14%	15.8%	16.3%	16.4%	19.3%	18.2%	100%

The chart above will be used in the calculations for the next exercises in the Merchandise Plan.

Planning Stock

The second step in the planning process is the development of stock plans that are tied to the sales plans. Specifically, we are trying to determine the BOM stock for each month, tied to the sales plan for the same month. As we learned in previous chapters, sales are dependent on the inventory that is available. If too little stock is available, it will be impossible to meet the sales plan. A very simple way to develop stock plans is using the **Basic Stock Method**, which requires that you have planned sales and turnover figures.

Many retailers who follow top-down planning will give the buyer these planned figures to achieve. The planning division is usually responsible for determining a turnover goal for each department. **Turnover** is the number of times you buy and sell thru your inventory within a certain period of time.

- Turnover is calculated for a season and/or a year.

$$\text{Turnover} = \text{Season Sales} \div \text{Average Stock}$$

or

$$\text{Turnover} = \frac{\text{Season Sales}}{\text{Average Stock}}$$

The Basic Stock Method

In this example, the given information is turnover and season sales.

$$\text{Turnover} = 2.85$$
$$\text{Season Sales} = \$856,100$$

1. Determine **average monthly sales** by dividing season sales by six, the number of months in each buying season.

$$\frac{\text{Season Sales } \$856,100}{6 \text{ months}} = \$142,683 \text{ Average Monthly Sales}$$

2. Determine **average stock at retail** by dividing season sales by turnover.

$$\frac{\text{Season Sales } \$856,100}{2.85 \text{ Turnover}} = \$300,386 \text{ Average Stock at Retail}$$

3. Subtract average monthly sales from average stock at retail.

Average Stock at Retail $300,386 − Average Monthly Sales $142,683 = $157,703

4. The last step is to add **$157,703** to each month's sales in the following chart. The answer will be placed under BOM Stock.

	AUG	SEPT	OCT	NOV	DEC	JAN	SEASON
BOM Stock							
Sales	$120,000	$135,600	$139,500	$140,600	$165,000	$155,400	$856,100
Turn							2.85

BOM stock is the amount of total inventory at retail that you have at the beginning of the month. This is carried over from the previous month. Any inventory that is not sold, returned to vendor, or stolen within a month continues to the next month.

This method of planning BOM stocks is very accurate because it increases BOM stock based on increases in sales. It says that, in a month when higher sales are planned, higher BOM stock is required to fulfill those planned sales. Notice the number that you are adding to the sales each month is the same. It is **$157,703**. The sales are what change each month, thus increasing the BOM stock level from month to month.

This is what you should have calculated for the BOM stocks from the previous data.

	AUG	SEPT	OCT	NOV	DEC	JAN	SEASON
BOM Stock	$277,703	$293,303	$297,203	$298,303	$322,703	$313,103	
Sales	$120,000	$135,600	$139,500	$140,600	$165,000	$155,400	$856,100
Turn							2.85

BOM and EOM Stock

In the following example you will see the BOM stocks calculated previously, compared to the EOM stock. What is important here is how they flow from one month to the next. We can derive the EOM stock based on the BOM stocks just calculated, when we used the Basic Stock Method.

EOM stock is the amount of inventory you are left with at the end of each month. It is the last stock calculation done before the end of the month. The EOM for a month becomes the BOM for the following month. In the following example, recognize that where we end August must be where we start September, the next month in the season. The inventory does not disappear; it continues to the next month.

	AUG	SEPT	OCT	NOV	DEC	JAN	SEASON
BOM Stock	$277,703	$293,303	$297,203	$298,303	$322,703	$313,103	
EOM Stock	$293,303	$297,203	$298,303	$322,703	$313,103	$300,385	

Once BOM stocks are calculated, EOM stocks can be established by simply taking the next month's BOM stock and placing it in the previous month's EOM stock. This has been done in the previous chart.

At the end of each season, the EOM for the last month of the season becomes the BOM for the start of the new season.

$$\text{JAN EOM Stock} = \text{FEB BOM Stock}$$

FEB BOM Stock has been calculated for you. In order to figure this out, you must know the sales plan for the spring season, and the planned turnover for the spring season.

This flow of stock from one month to the next makes the importance of taking timely markdowns, each season, abundantly clear. Even taking monthly markdowns in a timely manner is important. In this way a buyer can resolve issues as they occur, instead of waiting until the end of the season.

Late deliveries of goods create the same issues. A delivery that is planned for January but does not arrive until February throws off the start of the entire spring season. In this case, the buyer should immediately ask the vendor to pay for a markdown on the late goods. The goods probably would not sell without a 50% markdown, if they were planned for January.

Stock-to-Sales Ratio

Another method for planning BOM stocks relative to sales uses a history of **stock-to-sales ratios**.

$$\text{Stock-to-Sales} = \text{BOM Stock divided by the same Month's Sales}$$

Example

$$\text{BOM Stock for December} = \$298,000$$
$$\text{December Sales} = \$120,000$$
$$\frac{\text{December BOM Stock } \$298,000}{\text{December Sales } \$120,000} = 2.5 \text{ Stock-to-Sales Ratio}$$

This new formula tells you the amount of BOM stock needed to make the sales for the same month. According to the plan, in December, you need 2.5 times sales in BOM stock, in order to support those sales. This is a helpful figure when planning next year's BOM stock levels. However, if mistakes were made last year, this ratio is detrimental.

	AUG	SEPT	OCT	NOV	DEC	JAN	SEASON
BOM Stock	$30,000	$32,000	$36,000	$40,000	$54,000	$48,000	
Sales	$10,000	$12,000	$16,000	$20,000	$34,000	$28,000	$120,000
Stock-to-Sales	3.0	2.7	2.3	2.0	1.6	1.7	

In this example, the month of December has the lowest stock-to-sales ratio. This is because the sales that are done in December are due to the holiday season. A large portion of your BOM stock (and total stock) will be sold in this month. In months where a retailer is building stocks in anticipation of future business, the stock-to-sales ratio will be much higher. In this example, August has the highest stock-to-sales ratio, at 3.0. This could be due to the addition of new fall receipts and "Back to School" sales. Clearance months like January and July also have lower stock-to-sales ratios than other months in the season, due to the amount of clearance merchandise that is being sold in preparation for the next season.

Now apply last year's stock-to-sales ratio to a new sales plan for future business. August has been calculated for you using the new sales plan and the LY stock-to-sales ratios to generate the BOM stock for August.

AUG BOM Stock = AUG Sales $12,000 × AUG Stock-to-Sales Ratio 3.0

When you have the sales plan for the month and the stock-to-sales ratio, you can calculate the BOM stock using the following formula.

BOM Stock = Monthly Sales × Monthly Stock-to-Sales Ratio

	AUG	SEPT	OCT	NOV	DEC	JAN	SEASON
BOM Stock	$36,000						
Sales	$12,000	$16,000	$18,000	$25,000	$43,000	$38,000	$152,000
Stock-to-Sales	3.0	2.7	2.3	2.0	1.6	1.7	

Complete the rest of the BOM stock calculations using the same formula. These are the answers that you should have calculated.

	AUG	SEPT	OCT	NOV	DEC	JAN	SEASON
BOM Stock	$36,000	$43,200	$41,400	$50,000	$68,800	$64,600	
Sales	$12,000	$16,000	$18,000	$25,000	$43,000	$38,000	$152,000
Stock-to-Sales	3.0	2.7	2.3	2.0	1.6	1.7	

Advantages and Disadvantages of Stock-to-Sales Ratio

Planning stock using this method has advantages and disadvantages. A buyer who has a full year of history within that same department can use these statistics. I highly recommend *not* using this method for planning stocks if you were not working in the department when the ratios occurred. Imagine that last year the buyer did not receive the majority of planned purchases for November until December. The vendor shipped late. If you planned future seasons based on inaccurate stock-to-sales ratios for both November and December, you would hurt future business and the plan would be inaccurate. This is an example of reliving someone else's buying mistakes. Of course, a mistake that is made in November and December is much easier to pinpoint through history than a mistake that was made regarding a few smaller deliveries. This is where this method of planning based on someone else's history of stock-to-sales ratios can be very risky.

Computerized Logarithms

Most computer logarithms that buyers use to build their merchandise plans have a built-in range for BOM stock values based on the stock-to-sales ratio idea. The built-in range might say that November BOM stock must fall between 2.0 and 2.5. Based on the sales for that month (input by the buyer), the computer will accept or decline the buyer's BOM stock for that month. The computer will either indicate "out of range" or too high/too low. This logarithm is basing the acceptability of the BOM stock on the desired range and the sales input.

A buyer for a small store may find it easier to use the Basic Stock Method for planning stocks, although many large chain buyers use it as well. It is a preference for how one plans stocks, but the history of last year performance must be accurate and fully understood.

Planning Markdowns

The next step in the planning process is to estimate markdowns based on LY markdowns and their percentage of sales. Markdowns are shown as a dollar amount and a percentage, and are always based on sales. If sales go up, markdowns can also be higher. Markdown % is also called **Markdown Rate**.

$$\text{Markdown\%} = \text{Monthly Markdowns} \div \text{Monthly Sales}$$

or

$$\text{MD\%} = \frac{\text{Month MD\$}}{\text{Month Sales\$}}$$

Example

$$\text{August Markdowns } \$10,354 \div \text{August Sales } \$120,000 = 8.6\%$$

$$\text{Markdown\%} = 8.6\%$$

or

$$\frac{\text{August MD } \$10,354}{\text{August Sales } \$120,000} = 8.6\% \text{ MD}$$

In the following chart, calculate the markdown rate based on sales. August has been calculated for you. Round to one place after the decimal point, or to the tenth of a percent.

	AUG	SEPT	OCT	NOV	DEC	JAN	SEASON
Sales	120,000	135,600	139,500	140,600	165,000	155,400	856,100
Markdowns	10,354	8,246	7,980	13,452	23,453	35,000	98,476
Markdown%	8.6%						

The season's markdown rate also needs to be calculated using the same formula, but applying it to the season's figures.

Using LY Markdown Rate

When using last year history to plan future sales, the markdown rate from last year can be a basis for following seasonal plans. In order to be profitable, most retailers have a season markdown rate that they must meet. Any markdowns accrued that fall above this rate for the season will negatively affect profitability. If the season markdown rate comes in above the plan, the buyer may negotiate with vendors to cover more of the markdowns taken for that season. A better way to handle this problem is to negotiate markdown coverage every month, in order to meet the planned markdown rate each month. Vendors appreciate such effort, and are more likely to partner with buyers who conduct business in this manner.

These are the answers for the previous chart.

	AUG	SEPT	OCT	NOV	DEC	JAN	SEASON
Sales $	120,000	135,600	139,500	140,600	165,000	155,400	856,100
Markdown $	10,354	8,246	7,980	13,452	23,453	35,000	98,476
Markdown %	8.6%	6.1%	5.7%	9.6%	14.2%	22.5%	11.5%

Explanation

The Markdown % (markdown rate) for the season came in at 11.5% of sales. December had a higher than average markdown rate due to the holiday selling period. If retailers are not making the fall season's sales plan, they usually take deeper markdowns in the fourth quarter to drive volume. As you can see, the month of January had an exceptionally high markdown rate, at 22.5% of sales. This is often the case in the last month of the season, when fall/winter merchandise must be sold in order to make room for the spring/summer season. It would be advantageous for the buyer in this case to resolve monthly markdowns with vendors in the month that they accrued. Imagine that a buyer waited to negotiate markdowns until the end of this season. If the planned markdown rate was **6% of sales** for the total season, the buyer would have to find a way to pay for any markdowns that came in above **$51,366**.

Season Sales $856,100 × 6% = $51,366 Season Markdown Plan

Actual Markdowns $98,476 − Markdown Plan $51,366 = $47,110 Excess

The buyer in this case generated **$98,476** in markdowns, or **$47,110 above** the markdown plan. If this buyer waited until the end of the season, he or she would have to scramble in January to negotiate **$47,110** from vendors.

Complete the next example using the formula for Markdown %, then check your answers given below. Remember to calculate the season markdown rate.

	AUG	SEPT	OCT	NOV	DEC	JAN	SEASON
Sales $	40,000	47,000	42,000	80,000	120,000	85,500	414,500
Markdown $	3,000	1,600	1,200	3,200	15,000	11,000	35,000
Markdown %	7.5%						

Notice that if you were given the markdown rate and the sales for each month, you could calculate the markdown dollars. Multiply the sales dollars by the markdown rate and you are left with markdown dollars.

AUG Sales $40,000 × AUG Markdown Rate 7.5% = $3,000 AUG Markdowns

Here are the correct answers for the preceding exercise.

	AUG	SEPT	OCT	NOV	DEC	JAN	SEASON
Sales $	40,000	47,000	42,000	80,000	120,000	85,500	414,500
Markdown $	3,000	1,600	1,200	3,200	15,000	11,000	35,000
Markdown %	7.5%	3.4%	2.9%	4%	12.5%	12.9%	8.4%

If the planned markdown rate for the fall season was 5% of sales, by how many dollars is this buyer over the markdown plan?

Later in this chapter, you will review an entire Six-Month Merchandise Plan for the fall season. The top portion of the spreadsheet is the actual merchandise plan. It includes the following headings:

BOM Stock

Purchases

Total Stock

Markdowns

Sales

Total Deductions

EOM Stock

The bottom half of the spreadsheet includes the computations that go with the merchandise plan. These computations include:

Monthly Sales %

Markdown Rate

Stock-to-Sales Ratio

Average Stock

Turnover

Formula Review

Please review the formulas for monthly sales percent, stock-to-sales ratio, and markdown rate before continuing.

What is the formula for monthly sales percent?

_____

_____

What is the formula used to find the stock-to-sales ratio?

_____

How can you determine the monthly and seasonal markdown rate?

monthly markdowns ÷ Monthly sales

The additional formulas you must know before reviewing the full merchandise plan are *Average Stock* and *Turnover*.

Average Stock

Average stock, or average inventory, means the typical amount of stock that was held in inventory for a specific period of time. Average stock is calculated for each season and also for the total year.

$$\text{Average Stock} = \frac{\text{(All BOM Stocks} + \text{EOM Stock for the last month in the period)}}{7 \text{ (the number of stocks being added)}}$$

If average stock was being calculated for the fall season, you would add the BOM stocks for August though January, plus the EOM stock for January. Next, divide by seven, the amount of stocks that you added together.

	AUG	SEPT	OCT	NOV	DEC	JAN
BOM Stock	$277,703	$293,303	$297,203	$298,303	$322,703	$313,103
EOM Stock						$300,385

$$\text{Average Stock} = \frac{(\$277,703 + \$293,303 + \$297,203 + \$298,303 + \$322,703 + \$313,103 + \$300,385)}{7}$$

$$\text{Average Stock for fall} = \$300,386$$

This means that, on average throughout the fall season, this department had about $300,386 in BOM stock on hand.

Let's try another example of average stock for the spring season.

	FEB	MAR	APR	MAY	JUNE	JULY
BOM Stock	$70,160	$69,960	$70,660	$75,160	$79,560	$79,560
EOM Stock						$77,900

What is the average stock for the spring season? _____

Now look at each month and determine which BOM stocks are above the average stock number for the season. Record those months on the line provided.

_____

In which months are the BOM stock values below the average stock for the season?

_____

If you wanted to determine average stock for an entire year, you would add the BOM stocks for February through January, plus the EOM stock for January. Next, you would divide by thirteen, because there are twelve months in the year, plus the EOM stock for the end of the year. The answer for the average stock is **$74,709**.

Determine the average stock for this example, and then add the concept of turnover to this calculation.

	AUG	SEPT	OCT	NOV	DEC	JAN
BOM Stock	$80,000	$69,500	$77,300	$80,820	$92,620	$88,520
EOM Stock						$70,160

What is the average stock for this season? _____

Turnover

Turnover (or Turn) is the number of times a department has replenished and sold-through an average amount of inventory for a period of time. Turnover is calculated for both the season and the year.

$$\text{Turnover} = \text{Season Sales\$} \div \text{Average Stock\$}$$

or

$$\text{Turnover} = \frac{\text{Season Sales\$}}{\text{Average Stock\$}}$$

In the previous example, the average stock is $79,846. Find the turnover for that season, if the season sales are $160,000. The turnover in the previous example is 2.00.

$$\text{Turnover } 2.00 = \frac{\text{Season Sales \$160,000}}{\text{Average Stock \$79,846}}$$

Turnover is shown to the hundredth place, or two places after the decimal point, due to the size of the number. It is a very small number that holds great significance. If a buyer had a planned turnover of 2.50 and the actual turnover came in at 2.56, but turnover was only calculated to the tenth position, you would not see the difference, which is significant.

Rounded to one place after the decimal, these numbers look the same.

2.5	2.5
2.56 Actual Turnover	2.50 Planned Turnover

Find the turnover in the following problems, making sure to round to two places after the decimal point.

Average Stock = $145,600   Season Sales = $407,680

What is the season turnover?   _____

Average Stock = $1,245,000   Season Sales = $4,565,000

What is the season turnover?   _____

Average Stock = $202,309   Season Sales = $809,234

What is the season turnover?   _____

Entire Seasonal Merchandise Plan

On the following page is an entire merchandise plan for the fall season. Some of the information has been filled in for you. The actual merchandise plan is the top portion of the spreadsheet, with the bottom portion containing the formulas that are part of the merchandise plan. Try to find the calculations without using the formulas provided.

The only calculation that we have not reviewed is purchases. You must calculate total deductions **before** you can find the purchases.

Purchases = (EOM Stock + Deductions) − BOM Stock

You only need to find the *season totals* for purchases, markdowns, sales, and markdown rate.

In the previous exercise, you had the opportunity to apply formulas previously learned to the completion of a seasonal merchandise plan. Check your answers on the previous page, before continuing.

Merchandise Plan

	AUG	SEPT	OCT	NOV	DEC	JAN	FALL SEASON
BOM Stock	277,703	293,303	297,203	298,303	322,703	313,103	
+ Purchases							
= Total Stock							
Markdowns	10,345	8,246	7,980	13,452	23,453	35,000	98,476
+ Sales	120,000	135,600	139,500	140,600	165,000	155,400	856,100
= Total Deductions							
EOM Stock	293,303	297,203	298,303	322,703	313,103	300,385	

	AUG						FALL SEASON
% Sales by Month	14.0%						100.0%
Markdown Rate	8.6%						
Stock-to-Sales	2.3%						
Average Stock							
Turnover							

Formula Review:

% Sales by Month = Monthly Sales ÷ Season Sales

✗ Markdown Rate = Monthly Markdowns ÷ Monthly Sales

Stock-to-Sales Ratio = BOM Stock ÷ Monthly Sales

✗ Average Stock = All BOMs + Jan EOM ÷ 7

✗ Turnover = Season Sales ÷ Average Stock

Total Stock = BOM Stock + Purchases

Total Deductions = Sales + Markdowns

Purchases = (EOM Stock + Total Deductions) − BOM Stock

Answers to Merchandise Plan

	AUG	SEPT	OCT	NOV	DEC	JAN	FALL SEASON
BOM Stock	277,703	293,303	297,203	298,303	322,703	313,103	
+ Purchases	145,945	147,746	148,580	178,452	178,853	177,682	977,258
= Total Stock	423,648	441,049	445,783	476,755	501,556	490,785	
Markdowns	10,345	8,246	7,980	13,452	23,453	35,000	98,476
+ Sales	120,000	135,600	139,500	140,600	165,000	155,400	856,100
= Total Deductions	130,345	143,846	147,480	154,052	188,453	190,400	
EOM Stock	293,303	297,203	298,303	322,703	313,103	300,385	

	AUG	SEPT	OCT	NOV	DEC	JAN	FALL SEASON
% Sales by Month	14.0%	15.8%	16.3%	16.4%	19.3%	18.2%	100.0%
Markdown Rate	8.6%	6.1%	5.7%	9.6%	14.2%	22.5%	11.5%
Stock-to-Sales	2.3	2.2	2.1	2.1	2.0	2.0	
Average Stock							300,386
Turnover							2.85

Junior Department Seasonal Merchandise Plan

FIGURE 7.1 *Florida Palm Beach Gardens. The Gardens Mall Nordstrom department store business retail fashion upscale shopping display juniors*
Source: © Jeff Greenberg/Alamy

In the following exercise, you will complete an entire fall and spring season merchandise plan for the junior department. As you will see from the format, the entire year is broken down into two merchandise plans. The connecting piece between the two plans is the EOM stock value for January, which becomes the BOM stock value for February. Use the information on page 131 to complete and calculate the merchandise plans. After you are finished, use the bullet points below to assess the strengths and weaknesses of this buyer's merchandise plan.

- Back to School sales are important to this department and the bulk of these sales should occur in the month of August.
- Holiday includes November and December, with the bulk of purchases received in these two months.
- Holiday inventory levels build incrementally each month, starting with the month of September.
- January is reserved as a markdown month to clear through merchandise that did not sell during the holidays. Some receipts may be received in this month to transition into the spring season.
- February is the start of the spring season. Most of holiday and winter merchandise should be sold through prior to this month.
- June is an important swimwear month for this department.
- July should end at relatively low stock levels, to make room for Back to School received at the beginning of August.

Use these notes to analyze monthly sales percent, markdown rate, purchases, stock-to-sales ratio, average stock, and turnover for each season. You will be required to answer questions regarding these topics after completing the merchandise plan.

Fall information			
	BOM Stock	Markdowns	Sales
AUG	150,000	8,000	58,000
SEPT	130,000	6,000	55,000
OCT	175,000	7,500	60,000
NOV	190,000	8,800	70,000
DEC	220,000	23,000	120,000
JAN	175,000	35,000	90,000

Spring information			
	BOM Stock	Markdowns	Sales
FEB	140,000	10,000	33,000
MARCH	110,000	3,000	28,000
APRIL	115,000	2,800	30,000
MAY	118,000	4,100	36,000
JUNE	125,000	6,000	46,000
JULY	118,000	14,000	43,000
JULY EOM Stock = 125,000			

Complete the merchandise plan and answer the questions on the following pages, using the history you've calculated.

Merchandise Plan for Junior Department

	AUG	SEPT	OCT	NOV	DEC	JAN	FALL SEASON
BOM Stock							
+ Purchases							
= Total Stock							
Markdowns							
Sales							
Total Deductions							
EOM Stock							
% Sales by Month							
Markdown Rate							
Stock-to-Sales							
Average Stock							
Turnover							

	FEB	MARCH	APRIL	MAY	JUNE	JULY	SPRING SEASON
BOM Stock							
+ Purchases							
= Total Stock							
Markdowns							
Sales							
Total Deductions							
EOM Stock							
% Sales by Month							
Markdown Rate							
Stock-to-Sales							
Average Stock							
Turnover							

1. In the fall season, which month had the highest markdown rate, and what was it?

   _____

2. In the spring season, which month had the highest markdown rate, and what was it?

   _____

3. In the fall season, which month had the lowest % Sales, and what was the percentage?

   _____

4. How could you increase turnover in the spring season?

   _____

   _____

5. Based on markdown rate, how could you improve the plan for next fall and spring seasons?

   _____

   _____

   _____

   _____

6. How did you determine the EOM stock for the month of January?

   _____

7. Based on purchases, how could you improve the flow of goods for both the fall and spring seasons?

   _____

   _____

   _____

   _____

8. What percentage of sales is the fall season worth, compared to the total year of sales?

   _____

9. What percentage of sales is the spring season worth, compared to the total year of sales?

   _____

10. Using the stock-to-sales ratio and peak selling periods, what months should have higher and lower stock-to-sales ratios?

   _____

   _____

   _____

Returns to Vendor

After sales, stock, and markdowns are planned, the buyer plans any **returns to vendor (RTVs)** he/she can estimate for the season. An RTV occurs when the vendor or designer agrees to take back a damaged or unsuccessful style or group of merchandise.

An RTV is fairly difficult to negotiate, unless the merchandise is damaged or the fit and color is not up to standards. Returns are usually difficult to estimate in advance because they occur during the season, although some items are negotiated up front during market week. If a vendor would like a retailer to add or test a new collection, the buyer might negotiate a return up front, in the event that the merchandise does not sell. Returned merchandise leaves a buyer's inventory at the retail it is marked at in the POS system when it is returned. Markdowns directly affect gross margin, so negotiating a return is always more favorable.

A return may also be suitable when a private label assortment is being updated. At this point, the buyer will stop replenishing the assortment and sell down on it at full price. The vendor will usually return the old private label styles and then quickly replace them with new, updated styles. This avoids duplication and customer confusion on the selling floor.

Buyers will also trade inventory. If a vendor is pressuring a buyer to order a new line, the buyer may agree only after negotiating a return on a poor selling group or classification of goods. In this way, both retailer and vendor work together to create mutually rewarding business opportunities.

Fragrance Department Merchandise Plan

FIGURE 7.2 *Florida Palm Beach Gardens. The Gardens Mall Saks Fifth 5th Avenue business retail fashion upscale luxury high-end department store*
Source: © Jeff Greenberg/Alamy

The following information is provided for the fragrance department of a large retailer. Peek holiday selling includes Valentine's Day, Mother's Day, Father's Day, Christmas, and Hanukkah. Returns on special promotional gift sets have been negotiated up front. These returns appear under the **RTV line** of the merchandise plan. The line provided in this merchandise plan for RTV is figured into the total deductions calculation.

$$\text{Total Deductions} = \text{RTV} + \text{Markdowns} + \text{Sales}$$

In addition, the purchase section of the merchandise plan has been expanded to include both basic and fashion purchases.

$$\text{Total Purchases} = \text{Basic Purchases} + \text{Fashion Purchases}$$

$$\text{Total Stock} = \text{Total Purchases} + \text{BOM Stock}$$

Total stock describes the amount of stock the buyer has on hand for each month's sales. This is why we learned in Chapter 6 the importance of monthly receipts arriving the **first week of the month**.

You will start with the spring season in this exercise. Remember that the EOM stock value for July becomes the BOM stock value for August, and starts the fall season. This is an example of how the spring season leads into fall. After you have completed the fragrance merchandise plan, critically assess its strengths and weaknesses. Use statistics to defend your assessment.

Fragrance Department

Spring information			
	BOM Stock	**Markdowns**	**RTVs**	**Sales**
FEB	330,000	14,500	8,000	135,000
MARCH	340,000	10,400	0	170,000
APRIL	355,000	11,200	0	155,000
MAY	375,000	16,700	17,000	175,000
JUNE	400,000	33,600	0	225,000
JULY	320,000	20,100	25,000	115,000

Fall information			
	BOM Stock	**Markdowns**	**RTVs**	**Sales**
AUG	320,000	14,500	12,400	145,000
SEPT	345,000	8,000	0	190,000
OCT	375,000	7,500	0	225,000
NOV	450,000	16,700	0	290,400
DEC	508,000	66,700	0	345,600
JAN	410,000	75,000	66,000	275,600
JAN EOM Stock = 350,000				

Six-Month Merchandise Plan for Fragrance (Spring)

	FEB	MAR	APR	MAY	JUN	JULY	SPRING SEASON
BOM Stock							
Basic Purchases	119,000	125,300	119,720	83,480	63,440	120,125	631,065
Fashion Purchases	48,500	70,100	66,480	150,220	115,160	39,975	490,435
Total Purchases							
Total Stock							
RTV's							
Markdowns							
Sales							
Total Deductions							
EOM Stock							

% Sales by Month			
Markdown Rate			
Stock-to-Sales			

Average Stock	
Turnover	

Six-Month Merchandise Plan for Fragrance (Fall)

	AUG	SEPT	OCT	NOV	DEC	JAN	FALL SEASON
BOM Stock							
Basic Purchases	98,100	83,000	72,500	68,400	78,000	141,200	541,200
Fashion Purchases	98,800	145,000	235,000	296,700	236,300	215,400	1,227,200
Total Purchases							
Total Stock							
RTV's							
Markdowns							
Sales							
Total Deductions							
EOM Stock							

% Sales by Month							
Markdown Rate							
Stock-to-Sales							

Average Stock							
Turnover							

Calculating the Open-to-Buy

Open-to-Buy is the amount of money available to purchase inventory at any given time.

Now that you have experience planning and critiquing the merchandise plan, we will practice calculating the open-to-buy. The merchandise plan is a guideline. Competent buyers are able to predict performance very close to actual results. Based on a number of outside influences, components of the merchandise plan fluctuate.

Most buyers calculate current open-to-buy on a weekly basis. This usually occurs on a Monday morning, after sales and stock reports for the previous week are received.

Rolling Forecasts

Most substantial retailers require buyers to do a rolling open-to-buy forecast every two to four weeks. This usually includes updating the merchandise plan and forecasting the open-to-buy for the entire season, based on current information. Remember that as sales results and inventory change, so do all other factors on the merchandise plan.

Example

If a buyer is trending at –4% for the month in sales, it may be wise to calculate the next few months down 4% in sales from the original sales plan. The buyer must consider other factors as well. If there is an event or holiday in the next few months, the buyer may know that they can make up lost sales. Another issue might include late inventory on hot-selling items. The buyer may know that an opportunity exists to make up lost sales when the stock arrives.

August/September Rolling Forecasts

In the example on page 000, the actual results are recorded in boxes labeled **ACTUAL** for each component of the merchandise plan. The original plan precedes each **ACTUAL** box. The act of filling in these **ACTUAL** boxes is calculating the open-to-buy. Stock flows from one month to the next, so all months in the season are affected by changes in any **ACTUAL** month's results.

Both August and September have been shown in the example. Buyer notes are provided next to the month of September for many categories to clearly illustrate how the numbers were decided upon. Note that the starting BOM stock for the month of August was $319,000, compared to the original plan of $320,000. In the next category, notice basic purchases at $125,000, compared to an original projection of $98,100.

Estimating Returns in Rolling Forecasts

Returns to vendor are projected based on the system on hands for the styles being returned. It is very common for the stores not to pick every item the first time the RTV is submitted to the stores. Merchandise may be misplaced in the stock room, or the store may miss the RTV altogether. Very often the buying office must reissue the RTV the following month to ensure the entire chain complies. This directly affects the buyer's open-to-buy and EOM stock value. The buyer relies on those dollars being taken out of inventory in the month that the RTV is projected. If the stores do not meet expectations, the buyer could end up **overbought**. Compare August's **ACTUAL** RTVs to the original merchandise plan. Notice the projection for September, based on a resubmittal of the RTV for the balance missed by stores.

What is the amount over the estimated EOM stock projection for August?

The amount over the estimated EOM stock for August was **$39,000**. This is not a huge amount to be over, and the buyer may have another department that can be under in stock to offset this overage. However, if all the buyers within a division were over in similar amounts, the divisional merchandise manager (DMM) would have quite an issue. It is important for buyers to clearly communicate these changes with their superiors. One way to do this is through the accurate update of the open-to-buy forecast. Like buyers, DMMs and GMMs are responsible for their departments adhering to the merchandise plan. It is adherence to the merchandise plan, including accurate projections and rolling forecasts, that make or break retailers.

Use this snapshot of a buyer's open-to-buy to fully understand the additions and reductions to stock that affect the merchandise plan. Think of how you can increase or decrease different components on the plan to meet the EOM stock goals for each month.

On page 000, you will have the opportunity to input a projection, or update the open-to-buy, for the month of October. You will complete this based on September results and your own creative ideas. Make sure to end this month aligned with the plan projection of $450,000 in EOM stock.

Rolling Open-to-Buy Forecast

	AUG	SEPT	
BOM Stock	320,000	345,000	
ACTUAL BOM Stock	319,000	384,000	Ended over EOM plan in August due mostly to sales.
Basic Purchases	98,100	83,000	
ACTUAL Basic Purchases	125,000	83,000	Keep the same, cannot starve basics to make plan.
Fashion Purchases	98,800	145,000	
ACTUAL Fashion Purchases	99,100	94,520	Will have to cancel $50.5 in fashion orders.
Total Purchases	196,900	228,000	
ACTUAL Purchases	224,100	177,520	
Total Stock	516,900	573,000	
ACTUAL Total Stock	543,100	561,520	
RTV's	12,400	-	
ACTUAL RTV's	10,500	2,000	Resubmit RTV's to stores, they missed a lot last month.
Markdowns	14,500	8,000	
ACTUAL Markdowns	15,600	10,100	Vendor agreed to pay for additional markdowns.
Sales	145,000	190,000	
ACTUAL Sales	133,000	174,420	Projecting the same percentage down (−8.2%) as Aug.
Total Deductions	171,000	198,000	
ACTUAL Total Deductions	159,100	186,520	
EOM	345,000	375,000	
ACTUAL EOM	384,000	375,000	

Rolling Open-to-Buy Forecast

	SEPT	OCT
BOM Stock	345,000	375,000
ACTUAL BOM Stock	384,000	365,000
Basic Purchases	83,000	72,500
ACTUAL Basic Purchases	81,000	
Fashion Purchases	145,000	235,000
ACTUAL Fashion Purchases	95,000	
Total Purchases	228,000	307,500
ACTUAL Purchases	176,000	
Total Stock	573,000	682,500
ACTUAL Total Stock	560,000	
RTV's	–	–
ACTUAL RTV's	1,500	
Markdowns	8,000	7,500
ACTUAL Markdowns	9,500	
Sales	190,000	225,000
ACTUAL Sales	184,000	
Total Deductions	198,000	232,500
ACTUAL Total Deductions	195,000	
EOM	375,000	450,000
ACTUAL EOM	365,000	

In the following example September "Actual" figures, are actually what occurred for the month of September. We are using September's statistics to project the entire month of October. First, calculate the PERCENT CHANGE for September.

Sept Sales Plan $190,000 − Sept Actual Sales $184,000 = $6,000
$6,000/190,000 Sales Plan = **−3.2%**

When you compare the sales for the original plan to what actually occurred, You will determine what this department is trending at. Either a percentage over or below the plan. Apply this percent to next month's (OCT) projection. Fill in your October projection under the "Actual" boxes. This is very similar to how you would reproject your Open-to-Buy in a corporate forecasting system. Although in actuality, you may need to do this reprojection for the <u>entire season</u>, every two to four weeks.

Employee Discount

Employee discount is the amount of the reduction in an employee-generated retail sale for which a percentage off was applied. It is a dollar amount and is recorded as a percentage of retail sales.

In the Six-Month Merchandise Plans from this chapter, shortage and employee discount were not included. In most retailers both shortage and employee discount are based on past year's percentages by department. They are always recorded as a percentage of sales.

Example

Based on several years' statistics, the Coat Department has an average employee discount that is 1% of sales. That means that 1% of sales in coats per season are typically employee purchases, for which an employee discount applies.

If the sales plan for coats equals $500,000, what is the season's estimated employee discount? _____

In the merchandise plan, another row under deductions would be added for employee discount. Each month, 1% of sales would be allocated to employee discount. This 1% at first glance seems insignificant, but for the season may be somewhat sizable, based on sales. In Chapter 11, you will have the opportunity to see how employee discount figures into the calculation of gross margin, in preparation for vendor negotiations.

The correct answer for the Coat Department's seasonal employee discount is **$5,000**.

Shortage

Shortage, or shrink, is also based on a percentage of sales and is estimated based on previous year's actual results. **Shortage** is the difference between a retailer's physical inventory and book inventory, when the physical count is lower than the system on hands (or the book inventory).

It is a reduction to the merchandise inventory. A coat is not something that is typically easy to steal. For this department, we have sales of $500,000 and a planned shortage of 1.1%.

What is the estimated shortage for the coat department? _____
You should have **$5,500** for the estimated Coat Department shortage.

Another row under the heading Deductions in the merchandise plan would reflect this shortage plan of 1.1%. For each month of the season, 1.1% of sales would be taken out to cover projected shortage.

Inventory

Retailers typically take inventory twice a year, or once every quarter. The smaller the store, the more likely they are to take a physical inventory every quarter. **Inventory** is a physical, hand count of the merchandise in a store.

All stores are scanned, or physically counted, and the results are compared with the book inventory. Buyers then reconcile the differences in a week-long process of comparing and hunting for paperwork errors or obvious miscounts. Shortage includes theft, but also includes paperwork errors. This is why it is extremely important to review the Purchase Journal and actual purchase orders every week throughout the season. In addition, quick resolution of UPC issues can avoid many shortage issues.

Merchandise Overage

In some rare instances, merchandise overages occur. This is the difference between physical and book inventory, when the physical inventory is higher than the on hands (or the book inventory).

When overages occur, the store or department is usually asked to scan each section again to make sure this was not a simple scanning error. At the end of inventory reconciliation, the book inventory is adjusted to the physical inventory. Overages will usually create an overbought situation going into the next season. Likewise, if the buyer had lower than anticipated shortage, they may end up overbought. This is why it is very important to have an accurate shortage projection for each season, based on several years' history. When we discuss vendor negotiations, you will see how shortage directly affects vendor gross margins.

Now that we have completed the merchandise plan, you will have the opportunity to review Profit and Loss Statements. You will see many of the merchandise plan components again on the Profit and Loss Statement. Take a few moments to review the merchandise plans you have created in this chapter, before continuing to the next chapter.

Summary

In this chapter you learned the calculations and the meaning of the different components on the merchandise plan. You should have a thorough understanding of the steps that a buyer takes in completing the merchandise plan, and the necessity of accurate last year history. We also discussed different approaches to planning that included the top-down and bottom-up perspectives.

Additions to inventory levels include purchases and sometimes merchandise overage. In the Fragrance Merchandise Plan, you saw how purchases could be divided into basic and fashion purchases. Deductions on the merchandise plan, or subtractions to inventory, included: sales, markdowns, returns to vendor, shortage, and employee discount. Most of these deductions were also calculated as a percentage of sales, which makes estimating future seasons much easier.

You should recognize that inventory issues must be dealt with in a timely manner, because each season's inventory is carried over to the next season. The rolling forecast and calculation of the open-to-buy gave specific examples of how projections change and, in light of new information, how the merchandise plan must be re-forecasted weekly and monthly.

PROFIT
and LOSS STATEMENT

CHAPTER OBJECTIVES

- Create a skeletal outline of the Profit and Loss Statement from memory.
- Define *gross margin* in accounting terminology.
- Explain all components of cost of goods sold.
- Provide examples of direct and indirect expenses.
- Plot key elements of the merchandise plan within the framework of the Profit and Loss Statement.
- Analyze the Profit and Loss Statement and make recommendations to improve performance.
- Develop a Profit and Loss Statement for a hypothetical business.

The daily operations of a retail business require detailed merchandise planning. Adherence to the merchandise plan is reflected in the Profit and Loss Statement, often referred to as the P&L or Income Statement. It is a tool for businesses and also a method for evaluating the previous year's performance against a plan or outline. The **Profit and Loss (P&L) Statement** is a financial summary of a business that reflects its overall health.

This statement is one of a series of statements that summarizes a year of business activity. Most retailers release the Profit and Loss Statement publicly and to their shareholders after they close their books at the end of January. It is essentially a recap of major financial components and it is also used as a guideline for entrepreneurs.

8

Profit and Loss Outline

Before viewing the Profit and Loss Statements on the following pages, review the skeletal outline that follows. Think about the parts of the summary that were mentioned in previous chapters.

> **Gross Sales**
> **− Returns and adjustments**
> **= Net Sales**
> **− Cost of Goods Sold (COGs)**
> **= Gross Margin (GM)**
> **− Operating Expenses**
> **= Net Profit or Loss**

Major Categories on the P&L

It is important to recognize that not all components of the merchandise plan are easily recognized on the Profit and Loss Statement. The major categories on the statement include:

1. Sales
2. Cost of Goods Sold
3. Gross Margin
4. Expenses
5. Net Profit or Loss

Sales

Sales are broken down into gross sales and net sales. Net sales is the most important to the retailer, and is used as a basis with which to compare other components on the Profit and Loss Statement. As you will see on the following statements, gross margin and profit are compared to net sales in the same way that markdowns was compared to sales on the merchandise plan. The question is always, "What percentage of sales are these other components on the P&L Statement?"

Gross sales are the total company sales before any returns and credits are calculated. Net sales are the sales that are left after returns and adjustments are calculated. It is now obvious why net sales are most important to the retailer. Selling something does not matter if the customer ends up returning it.

$$\textbf{Gross Sales} - \textbf{Returns and Adjustments} = \textbf{Net Sales}$$

RETURNS AND ADJUSTMENTS

Returns and adjustments are not easy to estimate if you are a relatively new retailer or business owner. Once a retailer has a history of business activities over a few years, returns can be estimated based on past percentages. Returns are a tangible dollar amount, but are also viewed as a percentage of gross sales. You might ask, "What percentage of my gross sales were returned?"

$$\frac{\textbf{Returns/Adjustments \$}}{\textbf{Gross Sales \$}} = \textbf{Return \% of Gross Sales}$$

If a small business had gross sales of $250,000 and 5% of gross sales were returned, what was the return in dollars? _____

The answer is **$12,500** was returned.

Retailers will look at return percentages over several years and estimate this percentage going forward. If a retailer had a return percent between 3% and 6% over a five-year period, they might estimate future business at a 5% return rate. If this retailer's gross sales projection for the same time period was $430,000, their projected returns would be $21,500.

Planned Gross Sales $340,000 × 5% Planned Returns = $21,500 Returns

After returns are subtracted from gross sales, we are left with net sales. Now the retailer compares net sales to the costs associated with selling that merchandise. Net sales are compared to the cost of goods sold.

Cost of Goods Sold

Cost of goods sold (COG) includes expenses associated with the actual sale of the merchandise. They include the actual stock cost (purchases), freight, cash discount, and workroom expenses.

Let's look at an example of the elements that are calculated to find the total cost of goods sold. Note that on P&L the following factors are all at the cost value. The merchandise plan is at the retail value, however, and this makes it necessary for the retailer to convert those retail figures to the cost equivalent.

Opening Inventory	144,000
+ Purchases	725,000
+ Freight	6,000
= Total Goods at Cost	875,000
− Closing Inventory	175,000
= Gross Cost of Goods Sold	700,000
− Cash Discounts	36,000
Net Cost of Goods Sold	664,000
+ Alterations/Workroom	2,500
Total Cost of Goods Sold	666,500

The **opening inventory** is what the retailer started with for the period of time the Profit and Loss Statement reflects. This is usually one full year, ending in January. For an entrepreneur writing a business plan, the opening inventory is the BOM stock for the first month of business. However, this number is at cost. At a 50% markup, the BOM stock at retail would equal $288,000. You would need to use the markup formula to back into the cost, or the opening inventory, on the P&L.

The next heading is **Purchases**, and it reflects the entire year's purchases at cost. To find this at-cost number, the retailer must determine the departmental or total company markup and convert it to the cost equivalent.

Freight is the total cost of shipping the merchandise to the store. As discussed in previous chapters, this depends on the retailer and vendor agreements. Freight can be compared to total purchases and/or a percentage of cost of goods sold. To estimate freight on the Profit and Loss Statement a retailer will also use a history of freight percentages. For a new entrepreneur to estimate this figure, he/she could look at other Profit and Loss Statements from similar businesses, in addition to his/her own summary of their agreements with all vendors. Again, the percentage to total is the most important factor when creating a plan for future business.

Total goods at cost is the first subtotal in this category.

Opening Inventory + Purchases + Freight = Total Goods at Cost

Closing inventory is the amount of stock on hand when the Profit and Loss Statement is configured. It is a cost value and must be backed into, based on the current department or company markup at the time the statement is being created. The markup at that moment is called **maintained markup**. Maintained markup is the final cost and retail at a given point in time. It reflects any permanent markdowns that may have been taken.

For a company that is using the P&L to reflect a one-year period that ends in January, it would use the EOM stock value for January as the closing inventory. On the merchandise plan, this value would be at retail and would need to be converted to a cost value. This is where maintained markup comes in. If any of the styles in that closing inventory have already had a permanent markdown, the entire markup for that group of merchandise will be reduced from the initial markup. **Initial markup** is the original cost and retail of the merchandise before any reductions have occurred.

The next heading is a subtotal called **Gross Cost of Goods Sold**.

$$\text{Total Goods at Cost} - \text{Closing Inventory} = \text{Gross Cost of Goods Sold}$$

After gross cost of goods sold is calculated, any cash discounts that have been applied to purchases are subtracted. **Cash discount** is a reduction (usually a percentage) applied to purchases for paying the invoice early.

$$\text{Gross Cost of Goods Sold} - \text{Cash Discount} = \text{Net Cost of Goods Sold}$$

This reduction can positively reduce the cost of goods sold on the P&L, and therefore should be aggressively sought by the buyer.

Remember, an example of cash discount is 2/10 N30. This means that if the retailer pays the invoice for the purchase order within 10 days, he/she will receive a 2% discount on the purchase order. Otherwise, the balance of the invoice is due within 30 days.

The next item under COGs includes all **workroom and alteration** fees associated with the inventory. Large retailers over the last decade have pressured manufacturers to ship merchandise ready for display. This includes shipping merchandise on hangers with loss prevention tags. These fees negatively affect cost of goods sold, so negotiating with resources to ship ready for display is highly favorable.

$$\text{Net Cost of Goods Sold} - \text{Alterations/Workroom fees} = \boxed{\text{Total Cost of Goods Sold}}$$

Total Cost of Goods Sold (COG) is a major category on the Profit and Loss Statement that can be compared to net sales. It is a dollar amount and a percentage of net sales.

$$\frac{\text{Cost of Goods Sold \$}}{\text{Net Sales \$}} = \text{COG \% of Net Sales}$$

When planning this total category, entrepreneurs can compare their percentage of net sales to other, similar businesses when planning future business or making projections.

MARKDOWNS AND SHORTAGE

Some items are included under the heading Costs of Goods Sold, but are harder to pinpoint. Examples of this are shortage and markdowns. For example, the closing inventory value for the period may reflect shortage. If the merchandise was not sold and is not accounted for in the closing inventory, shortage has occurred. It may have been stolen, misplaced, or a paperwork error might have occurred. Additionally, any stock included in the closing inventory that received a permanent markdown is reflected in the value of that closing inventory. Any markdowns that were applied to the sale of the merchandise are accounted for in the gross and net sales figures. This is visible through the application of the markup to these categories.

Gross Margin

Gross margin (GM) is one of the first measures of profitability and is derived by subtracting cost of goods sold from net sales. It is a dollar figure (GM $) and a percentage of net sales (GM %).

$$\text{Net Sales} - \text{Cost of Goods Sold} = \text{Gross Margin}$$

$$\frac{\text{Gross Margin \$}}{\text{Net Sales \$}} = \text{GM \% of Net Sales}$$

The formula alone implies that increasing sales or decreasing the cost of goods sold will positively affect gross margin. The higher the gross margin, the more profitable the first half of the Profit and Loss Statement. This explains a retailer's incentive to find merchandise at the best possible prices when sourcing. Consider all factors that contribute to cost of goods sold. A high initial markup on goods can be quickly eroded by not attending to slow selling merchandise in a timely manner.

Questions for Review

Take a moment to answer the following questions regarding the first half of the Profit and Loss Statement.

1. How can retailers increase gross margin? _____
   _____
   _____

2. How can retailers increase net sales? _____
   _____
   _____

3. For a retailer that closes the period at the end of January, what figure is closing inventory on the merchandise plan? _____
   _____
   _____

4. Are purchases at cost or retail on the P&L Statement? _____

5. What is opening inventory? _____
   _____

6. What is an example of cash discount, and what does it mean? _____
   _____
   _____

7. Does freight positively or negatively affect gross margin? _____

8. Does cash discount positively or negatively affect the total cost of goods sold? _____

9. Do alterations and workroom costs increase or decrease gross margin?
   _____

10. Is gross margin compared to net sales or to gross sales? _____

11. If gross margin dollars were $220,000 and net sales were $500,000, what is the GM %? _____

_____

12. If cost of goods sold (COG) is $345,000 and net sales are $725,000, what is the COG % of net sales?

_____

If you found the questions difficult, take a moment to carefully review each topic before continuing.

Expenses

The second half, or bottom portion, of the Profit and Loss Statement consists of expenses. There are two types of expenses:

1. **Direct expenses** are the costs that directly affect the department of interest. They include such things as salaries, travel, advertising, supplies, and any other expense that directly impacts the department.
2. **Indirect expenses** are the costs that are related to the operation of the entire company. They include such things as rent, utilities, physical facilities (warehouse or distribution centers), insurance, security, taxes, depreciation, repair and maintenance, telephone or satellite communications, accounting and legal services, and bank fees.

EXAMPLES OF DIRECT AND INDIRECT EXPENSES

In large companies, direct expenses include salaries for the department but not salaries for positions that oversee the big picture for the company. For example, the Human Resource division would fall under indirect expenses, while the buyer for a specific department would fall under direct expenses. Likewise, travel for the buyer(s) of the department would be included under direct expenses. The divisional merchandise manager's travel expenses would appear under indirect expenses. A clerical or secretary who works for only one department would appear under that department's direct expenses on the Profit and Loss Statement.

The number of separate headings under direct and indirect expenses depends on the retailer. A new entrepreneur may have a simpler expense breakdown than a large corporate chain. As a business grows and becomes complex, so does its Profit and Loss Statement.

CONTROLLABLE EXPENSES

When retailers' comment on controllable expenses, they are referring to direct and indirect expenses. In light of recent technology and increases in utilities, many retailers are becoming more environmentally friendly and experimenting with new building materials. One example is the use of longer lasting lightbulbs and the inclusion of skylights in stores. This may, in turn, decrease the total utilities bill for a retailer and decrease the indirect expenses.

Another example would be using alternative building materials in the physical store structure, which might include fixtures that are more durable and depreciate less quickly than other choices. This reduction in expenses would appear under indirect expenses, under depreciation, and reflect a smaller percentage of depreciation than in past years, if compared. Typically, a reduction in building materials, fixtures, or utilities includes the discovery of new technology that results in increased efficiency.

Other drastic measures include reductions in actual jobs. Unfortunately, one of the most controllable expenses is salary. This also includes health care benefits and pension plans. If you think about the activity that surrounds big industry consolidations, there is usually some discussion of reduction in health care benefits, pension plans, and/or freezes on wage increases.

Net Profit or Loss

The last section of the Profit and Loss Statement is considered the bottom line. It is the total company net profit or loss for a period of time. Net profit/loss is a dollar figure and also a percentage of net sales.

$$\frac{\text{Net Profit/Loss \$}}{\text{Net Sales \$}} = \text{Profit/Loss \% of Net Sales}$$

After all revenue and expenses are considered and everyone has been paid, what dollars are left? **Net profit** is the positive dollar amount that is left after all company revenue and expenses are considered. **Net loss** is a negative balance after all company revenue and expenses are considered.

IN THE RED OR BLACK

In the past, retailers have been known to operate in the red for the majority of the year. Black Friday, or the day after Thanksgiving, got its name from this concept of being in the black (profit), or in the red (loss). Many retailers operate in the red until Black Friday, when they shift into the black, or to profit. Thus, Black Friday is the name given to the day after Thanksgiving that symbolizes a shift on the P&L to profit.

Some of the new retail formats have been successful by not reinvesting as much initially, but instead waiting to build value and revenue over a period of time. An example of this would be warehouse clubs that offer a large assortment, but in a basic warehouse format with minimal visual costs. They have traditionally operated on the fringe of major trading areas. It is only now that they are starting to build stores in more urban locations, where real estate is more expensive. Over time, they have built strong brands with relatively low expenses for their large format stores.

Questions for Review

Now consider warehouse clubs (Costco, Sam's Club) and how they have strategically increased gross margin. Consider their merchandising strategies.

13. How have the merchandising strategies of warehouse clubs positively affected the top portion of the Profit and Loss Statement?

_____

_____

14. How have warehouse clubs controlled expenses on the Profit and Loss Statement? _____

_____

_____

15. How have the merchandising strategies of department stores negatively affected the top portion of the Profit and Loss Statement? _____

_____

16. What heading under the heading Indirect Expenses makes up the highest percent of indirect expenses for department stores? _____

Review of P&L Major Headings

Now that we have reviewed the basic components of the Profit and Loss Statement, you will have the chance to review one below. Consider it carefully, and then answer the questions that follow. Make sure to review all of the components that are based on a percentage of total net sales. The percentages appear in the far right column. Each section has been numbered to specify the portion of the income statement to which it corresponds.

> 1 = Sales (Gross and Net)
> 2 = Cost of Goods Sold (at Cost)
> 3 = Direct Expenses (for the department)
> 4 = Indirect Expenses (for the total company)
> 5 = Profit or Loss (the bottom line in dollars)

Profit and Loss Statement

		COST		RETAIL	% OF SALES
1	Gross Sales			1,250,000	
	Returns			70,000	5.6%
	NET SALES			1,180,000	
2	Opening Inventory	144,000			
	+ Purchases	725,000			
	+ Freight	6,000			
	= Total Goods at Cost	875,000			
	− Closing Inventory	175,000			
	= Gross Cost of Goods Sold	700,000			
	− Cash Discounts	36,000			
	Net Cost of Goods Sold	664,000			
	+ Alterations/Workroom	2,500			
	TOTAL COST OF GOODS SOLD	666,500	COGs	666,500	56.5%
			GM	513,500	43.5%
3	Direct Expenses				
	Buying Salaries	90,000			
	Selling Salaries	115,000			
	Advertising	37,000			
	Travel	13,000			
	Supplies	5,000			
	TOTAL DIRECT EXPENSES	260,000		260,000	22.0%
4	Indirect expenses				
	Rent	110,000			
	Utilities	30,000			
	Repair & Maintenance	28,000			
	Depreciation	15,000			
	TOTAL INDIRECT EXPENSES	183,000		183,000	15.5%
			Total Expenses	443,000	37.5%
5	PROFIT OR LOSS?		Net Profit/Loss	70,500	6.0%

The following questions reflect statements regarding the Profit and Loss Statement on the previous page. Please answer the questions below.

17. What percentage of gross sales is returns and adjustments worth?

_____

18. If gross sales increased to $1,500,000, what would net sales and gross margin be? Is this a positive effect?

_____

19. What is cash discount, and how does it affect the cost of goods sold?

_____

20. What might be a reason for alterations or workroom costs? Why does it increase the cost of goods sold?

_____

21. Do selling salaries under the heading Direct Expenses include selling associates for the entire company?

_____

22. What percentage of net sales is rent?

_____

23. What are this department's gross margin dollars and GM %?

_____

24. Did this department have a profit or a loss? What was it? What was the percentage of sales?

_____

25. What are the total expenses for this department?

_____

26. What percentage of net sales is utilities?

_____

27. What percentage of net sales is travel expenses?

_____

28. If the opening inventory increased to $244,000, what would the total cost of goods sold be? What would the COG percentage of sales be?

_____

29. Under which category heading is depreciation found?

_____

Profit and Loss Statement

	COST		RETAIL	% OF SALES
Gross Sales			650,000	
Returns			25,000	3.8%
NET SALES			625,000	
Opening Inventory	160,000			
= Purchases	250,000			
+ Freight	4,500			
= Total Goods at Cost	414,500			
− Closing Inventory	75,000			
= Gross Cost of Goods Sold	339,500			
− Cash Discounts	12,000			
Net Cost of Goods Sold	327,500			
+ Alterations/Workroom	1,700			
TOTAL COST OF GOODS SOLD	329,200	COGs	329,200	52.7%
		GM	295,800	47.3%
Direct Expenses				
Buying Salary	55,000			
Selling Salaries	60,000			
Dept advertising	15,000			
Travel	6,000			
TOTAL DIRECT EXPENSES	136,000		136,000	21.8%
Indirect expenses				
Allocated rent	100,000			
Utilities	30,000			
Maintenance	14,500			
Other	10,000			
TOTAL INDIRECT EXPENSES	154,500		154,500	24.7%
		Total Expenses	290,500	46.5%
PROFIT OR LOSS?		Net Profit/Loss	5,300	0.8%

The following questions reflect statements regarding the Profit and Loss Statement above.

30. If returns was reduced to 1.5% of gross sales, what would returns be? How would this reduction affect net sales and gross margin?

_____

_____

31. If purchases was reduced to $150,000, how would this affect cost of goods sold and gross margin?

_____

32. What percentage of purchases is allocated to freight?

_____

33. If the cash discount increased to 2.5% of net sales, what would the cash discount be, and how would it affect the gross margin?

_____

_____

34. If there were no workroom/alteration costs, would the gross margin be affected positively or negatively?

_____

35. How would a decrease in selling salaries affect the bottom line?

_____

36. Does this department show an overall profit or loss? What is the profit or loss?

_____

37. If the buyers' salary increased to $75,000, how would the bottom line be affected?

_____

38. If allocated rent increased to $110,000, how would the profit or loss be affected? What would the new percentage of net sales become?

_____

39. Is direct or indirect expenses more favorable on this Profit and Loss Statement? Why?

_____

40. If there was no cash discount, how would the gross margin be affected? What would the gross margin percent become? _____

_____

Profit and Loss Statement

	COST		RETAIL	% OF SALES
Gross Sales			375,000	
Returns			12,500	3.3%
NET SALES			362,500	
Opening Inventory	60,000			
+ Purchases	135,000			
+ Freight	3,500			
= Total Goods at Cost	198,500			
– Closing Inventory	45,000			
= Gross Cost of Goods Sold	153,500			
– Cash Discounts	7,900			
Net Cost of Goods Sold	145,600			
+ Alterations/Workroom	3,500			
TOTAL COST OF GOODS SOLD	149,100	COGs	149,100	41.1%
		GM	213,400	58.9%
Direct Expenses				
Buying Salary	65,000			
Selling Salaries	37,000			
Dept Advertising	14,000			
Travel	8,000			
TOTAL DIRECT EXPENSES	124,000		124,000	34.2%
Indirect expenses				
Allocated rent	72,000			
Utilities	15,500			
Maintenance	6,700			
Other	4,500			
TOTAL INDIRECT EXPENSES	98,700		98,700	27.2%
		Total Expenses	222,700	61.4%
PROFIT OR LOSS?		Net Profit/Loss	(9,300)	–2.6%

41. Analyze the Profit and Loss Statement above, and then compare it to the two previous income statements. Assess the strengths and weaknesses of the statement, comparing percentages of net sales for the major sections of the statement. Identify ways in which the bottom line might be improved.

_____

_____

_____

_____

_____

_____

_____

_____

Summary

In this chapter you had the opportunity to evaluate and analyze different Profit and Loss Statements. You were asked to determine how different components of the Profit and Loss Statement affect the gross margin and the bottom line. We evaluated how changes to minor subheadings directly affect all other factors.

An entrepreneurial approach to planning the Profit and Loss Statement for a start-up business was discussed. You should understand how historical data and percentage of net sales can be used to plan future business. It is the categorical percentage breakdown that is most important when comparing Profit and Loss Statements.

The cost of goods sold and the inventory on this statement were at cost, as compared to the merchandise plan where inventory is at the retail value. Opening and closing inventory figures can be easily found on the merchandise plan. The gross margin was described as the first layer of profitability. Direct and indirect expenses were deducted from the gross margin, leaving the actual profit or loss of the business. Direct expenses included costs paid out for the benefit of the department, while indirect expenses included costs associated with the larger company.

COOPERATIVE
ADVERTISING

CHAPTER OBJECTIVES

- Define *cooperative advertising* and its importance to the retailer's bottom line.
- Describe the buyer's role in advertising.
- Analyze the strengths and weaknesses of direct mail and ROP advertising.
- Illustrate the relationship between advertising and markdown allowance.
- Plan sale events for a year using a given sum for advertising and markdown allowance.

9

Cooperative advertising is a necessary negotiation for retailers in a saturated market. In light of recent mergers in the retail industry, cooperative advertising is essential to the big business procedures of major retailers.

Cooperative advertising (Ad Co-op) includes vendor contribution or partnership on expenses related to advertising. In the past, cooperative advertising meant a 50/50 or equal sharing of advertising expenses by vendor and retailer. Today, cooperative advertising includes any contribution made by a vendor or designer to the cost of advertising.

Vendor Support of Advertising

Manufacturers and designers have felt the increase in competition alongside retailers and have become more willing to contribute to advertising expenses. They see the benefit in supporting an advertisement that may increase both the retailer's sales and their own. This is not a method of negotiating that is limited to big business. Smart entrepreneurs also ask their resources to share advertising expenses. Manufacturers see the benefit of placing an advertisement in local media, especially when they are paying for only part of the actual advertisement.

As we have seen in previous chapters, reducing advertising expenses directly affects the bottom line. For a retailer with substantial orders and promotional opportunities, cooperative advertising negotiations should be aggressive and well planned. The first step is understanding promotional periods and key volume drivers. This includes the buyer's decision as to which styles will be bought in depth and advertised during major holidays or vendor promotions (sales).

Advertising as a Percentage of Purchases

Department stores have many promotional catalogs and storewide events that drive volume through markdowns and advertising. Many vendors are willing to share in advertising expenses or to contribute a percentage of total purchases to advertising expenses. In this way, retailers are rewarded for increasing purchases with particular vendors.

Example

Calvin Klein agrees to contribute **5%** of a retailer's total purchases to cover advertising expenses. If the buyer purchases $250,000 worth of merchandise, the amount given to the retailer for advertising would be

$$\$250{,}000 \times 5\% = \$12{,}500$$

Or, if the buyer purchases $400,000 worth of merchandise, the amount given to the retailer for advertising would be

$$\$400{,}000 \times 5\% = \$20{,}000$$

Manufacturers usually prefer this method of contributing to advertising expenses because there is a clear guideline established. The manufacturer expects that the retailer will not ask for more advertising money during the course of the season. Manufacturers who have not established advertising contribution as a percentage of purchases often convert to this method after continually going back and forth with the retailer over the amount of advertising contribution. This can become quite frustrating for the manufacturer. Remember that the buyer's job includes getting as much help with expenses as he/she can muster from his/her vendors in order to increase gross margin.

Incremental Sales

It is advantageous for both the retailer and vendor to support advertising of specific styles and programs, because it often results in incremental sales. If a buyer is willing to allocate one page of their department's space within a Christmas catalog to a specific vendor, that vendor can generate a considerable amount of sales. The vendor is usually willing to support this advertisement by paying for the entire advertisement, or a portion of it. Additionally, the vendor may agree to pay for the markdowns that accrue if the advertisement included merchandise at a promotional price point.

Advertising Media

There are several types of advertising, but the two major categories used by large retailers are ROP and direct mail. **ROP (run off press)** means ads that are placed on the pages of a newspaper. They are widely circulated, easily visible, and offer shorter deadlines than other advertising options. They can range in size from a small portion of a page to a full-page ad. The benefit of ROP advertisement is that it reaches customers outside of the typical target market for a retailer, and it has a wider audience of readers.

Direct mail includes company-generated catalogs, postcards, or advertisements that appear in color or black and white. They take longer to orchestrate than ROP advertisements, and are mailed directly to the customer's home.

Direct mail advertisements are commonly used by department stores, and are distributed several times throughout the course of the season. The advantage of direct mail is that it is specifically mailed to credit card holders (customers), and often appears in color. It may also include inserts that are hard to miss, as they fall out when you open the direct mail catalog. For customers who shop sales, these are an important advertisement and retailers must have depth in inventory to support the ad, or customers will be displeased.

Other Advertising Media

Other advertising media include television and radio spots, which may be used for specific promotional events and new product launches. These types of advertising are expensive and are most often used by larger retailers. Postcards are often used by the smaller retailer or starting entrepreneur because of the size and cost-efficient pricing. Customers are also able to place these on their refrigerator as a reminder of an upcoming trunk show or sale. Art galleries often use this method to advertise new gallery openings, and this has increased their upscale appeal. A trunk show is a private screening of a vendor's seasonal collection. They are often held at high-end department stores and boutiques.

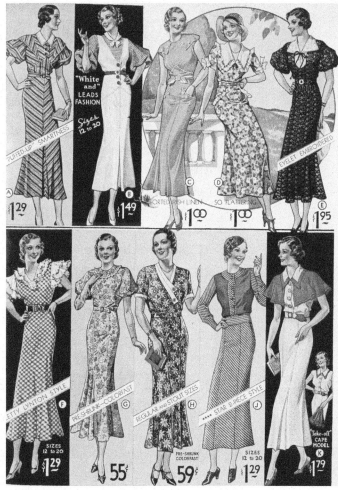

FIGURE 9.1 *Sears Roebuck Catalog from the 1930s.*
Source: © The Art Archive/Alamy

Planning the Advertisement

Buyers for major retailers spend a great deal of time planning ROP and direct mail advertising. Planning starts with accurate record keeping of last year's advertising and promotional events. The buyer should keep a copy of all advertisements, including the dates run and the actual sales results. If the style or merchandise was promoted at a discount, the buyer will record the sales generated for all dates of the promotion, not just the date on which the ad ran.

The buyer is responsible for presenting the featured merchandise and the copy to the advertising team. These advertising meetings usually consist of the buyer, photographer, fashion stylist, creative director, and copy writer. **Copy** is the written portion of the advertisement.

After the advertising meeting takes place, the merchandise is shot by the photographer, the rough draft of the advertisement is written, and the layout is configured. The buyer then must sign off on a series of proofs, sometimes up to three times before the advertisement is actually printed. Any and all corrections must be made at this time. This sometimes includes re-shooting the merchandise if it did not translate well or a mistake was made. **Proofs** are examples of the advertisement as it will appear, including the photograph and the written commentary.

Once the catalog or newspaper advertisement goes to print, no changes can be made. That is why it is extremely important to meticulously check the details of all proofs, including promotional price points. If something is wrongly advertised in a promotion, the buyer is still responsible for supporting the ad.

Advertising Allowance

Advertising expenses should be negotiated at the start of each season, before the advertisements occur, just as the markdown allowance was. **Advertising allowance** is a monetary contribution made by the vendor or manufacturer, which is used to support the retailer's advertising expenses.

$$\textbf{Advertising Allowance} \times \textbf{Total Purchase \$} \times \textbf{\% Vendor Contribution}$$

Cooperative advertising is vendor partnership on advertising, which translates into the dollar amount given to the retailer, or the passing of the advertising allowance. Refer back to markdown allowance for an example of the form that is completed by a buyer to apply the monetary contribution to the books.

Buyers maintain detailed and organized records to ensure that they collect all promised Advertising Allowances and exceed last year's performance. This includes keeping copies of past advertisements by date, with sales results for the time period of the specific advertisement. Excel spreadsheets are created that include all vendor agreements and advertising allowances passed, by month. There is also a summary of all vendors, by season, for easy TY/LY comparisons. The buyer brings this record to market and negotiates to anniversary all previous year performance. This means that the buyer's goal is to meet (anniversary), or exceed, all negotiations that were made last year.

Advertising and Markdown Allowances

Vendors have a variety of ways to meet retailer expectations through contribution to advertising and markdowns. As we discussed earlier, most vendors would prefer to negotiate a percentage of purchases up front for advertising and markdown coverage. For example, an agreement may state that the vendor is willing to contribute 10% of purchases at retail in markdown allowance, and an additional 5% of purchases at retail in advertising allowance. This demonstrates how advertising and markdowns are often tied to one another. This is because most advertisements include a promotional event or promotional price point.

Example

A vendor has agreed to contribute 10% of purchases (at retail) in markdown allowance, and an additional 5% of purchases (at retail) in advertising allowance. If the total purchases for this vendor are $250,000 at retail, what is the vendor willing to offer in markdown and advertising allowances?

Markdown Allowance = _____

Advertising Allowance = _____

This is usually a smart agreement type for vendors because it allows vendors to state up front what they are willing to give, without further negotiation throughout the season.

By-Style Advertising Allowances

In another agreement, a vendor may offer five cents on every unit that is bought in a particular style. If the buyer purchases 150,000 units, then $7,500 may be used for advertising **or** markdown allowance.

$$150,000 \text{ units} \times .05 = \$7,500$$

In this case, the use of the $7,500 may be specified or left up to the buyer's discretion. If this type of agreement was made on every style within a vendor, it could easily become very confusing for the buyer. This is why it is so important to keep accurate and detailed records of all agreements, and to make it a priority at the start of the season to confirm all agreements.

This is the answer to the question above.

Markdown Allowance = $25,000 ($250,000 × 10%)

Advertising Allowance = $12,500 ($250,000 = 5%)

Advertising Contribution for New Product Lines

In other instances, vendors may agree to pay for entire advertisements during the launch of a new product or line. This is also something that, if not offered, can be easily negotiated by the buyer. Vendors are willing to contribute if it means an opportunity to expand their current assortment in stores, or to add a new line altogether. The buyer does not know what the vendor will or will not do unless he/she asks. In this retail environment, be assured that the competition is asking, thus you should too.

Cooperative Advertising Simulation

In the following exercise, you will have the opportunity to see how markdown allowance and cooperative advertising are related, planned, and applied to the holiday and seasonal calendar.

You will be given a **percentage of purchases** for advertising and markdown allowance. Using this information, you will plan promotional events for the entire calendar year.

THE RULES FOR THIS EXERCISE

1. For every promotional event that you plan, you **must** also have an advertisement to support it.
2. Advertisements are paid for out of the advertising allowance, while markdowns are covered by the markdown allowance.

3. You may only use money allocated for advertising allowance for actual advertising. You may not borrow money from markdown allowance to pay for an advertisement.

4. A calendar or planner should be readily available for this exercise.

THE GOALS FOR THIS EXERCISE

1. Use up as much of your money as possible in both markdown allowance and advertising allowance.

2. Have as many advertisements and sale events as possible throughout the year, without neglecting any particular season.

3. Each quarter must have advertising.

4. Use at least one of each type of advertisement.

5. Take advantage of peak selling periods, as outlined in the rate of sale differences.

ALLOWANCE INFORMATION

Retail Purchases = $536,000

Advertising Allowance = 5% of retail purchases

Markdown Allowance = 10% of retail purchases

What is your advertising budget in dollars? _____

What is your markdown budget in dollars? _____

> **Note:** *Several of the promotional events have the* **same information**. *That is part of the simulation.*

PROMOTIONAL EVENTS

1. **Monthly Customer Appreciation Sales**—A 3-day promotional event that always occurs the second week of the month on Friday, Saturday, and Sunday. You can have as many of these events as you would like throughout the year. This event will generate **$18,400 in sales** with **markdowns of $6,127.**

2. **Columbus Day Sale**—A 5-day promotional event, including Columbus Day (OCT). You may pick the rest of the dates for this event. This event will generate **$18,400 in sales**, and **$6,127 in markdowns**.

3. **Labor Day Sale**—A 5-day promotional event including Labor Day (SEPT). You may pick the rest of the dates for this event. This event will generate **$18,400 in sales** with **markdowns of $6,127.**

4. **Pre-Thanksgiving Sale**—A 5-day promotional event leading up to Thanksgiving. This event will not include Thanksgiving, when most retailers are closed. This event will generate **$27,600 in sales** with **$9,191 in markdowns.**

5. **After Thanksgiving Sale**—A 5-day promotional event that starts the day after Thanksgiving. This event will generate **$27,600 in sales** with **$9,191 in markdowns**.

6. **Christmas/Holiday Sale**—A 5-day promotional event that can fall anywhere in the third or fourth week of December. This event will generate **$36,800 in sales** with **markdowns of $12,254.**

7. **New Year's Sale**—A 5-day promotional event that can fall anywhere in the last week of December or the first week of January. This event will generate **$36,800 in sales** with **markdowns of $12,254.**

ADVERTISING OPTIONS

1. **ROP full-page** newspaper advertisement, at any time except Thanksgiving, Christmas, or New Year's = **$5,000**

2. **ROP full-page** newspaper advertisement for Thanksgiving, or Christmas, or New Year's = **$7,500**

3. **Direct mail box** for any monthly customer appreciation sale = **$2,500**

4. **Direct mail half of page** for Labor Day = **$3,500**

5. **Direct mail half of page** for Columbus Day = **$3,500**

6. **Direct mail half of page** for Pre-Thanksgiving = **$4,000**

7. **Direct mail half of page** for After Thanksgiving = **$4,000**

8. **Direct mail full page** for Christmas = **$5,500**

9. **Direct mail full page** for New Year's = **$5,500**

You now have all information needed to complete this exercise. Your instructor may divide you into groups at this time. If you do this exercise as a group, come up with a group strategy. Remember, the goal is to use as much of your markdown and advertising allowance as possible without going over, and to keep customers coming into your stores throughout the season. **For every sale event chosen, at least one advertisement must be used to support the sale**. Use the chart that follows to record your answers.

Here are definitions of the terms used in the chart.

> **EVENT** = name of promotional event and dates chosen
>
> **MDWN$** = markdown allowance in dollars based on the event chosen
>
> **TYPE OF AD** = ROP or direct mail
>
> **ADV$** = advertising allowance in dollars, based on the type of advertisement chosen
>
> **TOTALS** = need only MDWN$ and ADV$ totals at bottom of page

EVENT/DATES	MDWN$	TYPE OF AD	ADV$
AUG			
SEPT			
OCT			
NOV			
DEC			
JAN			
FEB			
MAR			
APR			
MAY			
JUN			
JUL			
TOTAL $			

Simulation Results

After sharing the different strategies used for this exercise, you should have a firm grasp of how advertising, markdowns, and promotional events are related to one another in the planning process. Of course, this exercise was scaled down to make it easier to understand, but this example illustrates the concepts and challenges that buyers frequently face.

It is important to understand that while these negotiations occur at many large retailers, they are also possible for smaller retailers. A small boutique in an urban location, with celebrity patrons, will also be a business that vendors want to support. Buyers do not know what their vendors are willing to contribute unless they ask the question.

In the next chapter you will have the opportunity to practice simulations that incorporate last year history and vendor negotiations. Please review the concepts that follow before starting the next chapter.

Define the following concepts:

% to Total

_____

Sell Thru

_____

Markup

_____

Store Modules (A, B, C...)

_____

Weeks of Supply

_____

Summary

In this chapter, the importance of cooperative advertising partnership was emphasized. Vendor contribution was described in light of recent industry consolidation and the current saturation of the market. Both large and small retailers have made it a priority to negotiate advertising expenses up front, as part the purchasing process.

Buyers must keep accurate records and plan advertising according to last year history. Buyers negotiate to meet (anniversary), or exceed, last year advertising and markdown contribution. Advertising allowance and markdown allowance are often negotiated in conjunction with one another. In the simulation, you were able to clearly see how both allowance types are often tied to promotional events. Advertising allowance is given as a percentage of total purchases or based on units purchased by style.

10 Buying Simulations

11 End-of-Season Negotiations

12 Monday Morning Reports (Sales)

13 Monday Morning Reports (Markdowns)

PRIORITIZING
and Negotiating

UNIT 3

Buyers review selling history to determine retail price
Source: © Peepo/iStockphoto

BUYING
SIMULATIONS

CHAPTER OBJECTIVES

- Apply merchandising formulae to the analysis of LY performance.
- Recommend the addition/deletion of store modules based on LY sales performance.
- Pinpoint opportunities, by product classification, related to LY sales and markup results.
- Plan future purchases, by style, based on LY percent to total.
- Rank styles according to performance within a department.
- Convert planned sales into units using the retail ticket price.
- Perform buyer/vendor negotiations based on vendor assortment plans.

10

In an effort to experience the life of a buyer in fuller detail, the following simulations have been created to apply the concepts learned in previous chapters, and to bring actual problems from the buying office to the classroom. The first step is to analyze last year history for a department of goods through application of learned formulae. A recap of performance is calculated at the end of each season. This ongoing history puts all the information summarized at the buyer's fingertips when writing business plans.

At the end of each season, assistant buyers will be asked to create spreadsheets for better analysis of last season performance. Although there are several reports to choose from in most buying offices, each buyer likes to see the information in a specific format. Creating these spreadsheets in a timely manner requires that formulas are known, and a working knowledge of Excel exists.

Formatting Preferences

Most buyers create templates for how they wish to see last year history. This is a preference. An assistant buyer's job requires adherence to his/her buyer's formatting requirements. In any buying situation, it is advantageous to keep a record of spreadsheet formats on file. You never know when an old spreadsheet format may become advantageous in the present situation.

As we have discussed, failure to record accurate history results in poor buying decisions. Buyers who fail to condense and record last year history, such as the ranking of top sellers within a department, spend a lot of time retrieving this information for senior management. It is common in the buying office for several people to want to see the same information, but in different ways. If one had to retrieve records and create an entirely new spreadsheet every time a new request for information was submitted, nothing would get accomplished.

Instead of being *reactive*, plan to be **proactive** and have last year records calculated, organized, and on hand should the need arise.

The First Simulation

In the first simulation, you will complete LY history calculations step-by-step. If there are any formulas that you have forgotten, go back in the book and take note of them. Think about how this information is presented and why it is presented in this manner.

In this exercise, the buyer prefers to calculate sell thru, but we know from previous chapters that some companies prefer weeks of supply. How would you change this information to incorporate weeks of supply if required to do so? Where does it make sense to shift columns around on this spreadsheet? What is the most important information provided and where should it appear?

The first simulation includes LY statistics for a Men's Shoe Department. These shoes are part of the buyer's basic shoe collection and she replenishes them over several seasons. Her stores are broken down into A, B, C, and D modules. She usually tests new additions to the assortment in A and B stores, before rolling them out to the rest of the stores in the chain. LY history must be calculated before she can consider planning next year's buy.*

---

*Please round to the nearest tenth of a percent on all computations.

FIGURE 10.1 *Men's leather shoes on display in a department store*
Source: © Kheng Guan Toh/Shutterstock

Steps for Completing Men's Shoe Department Simulation

1. Total each classification by adding the **Retail $ Sold** for all styles, within each classification. A box has been highlighted under each classification to make this clear. The classifications are Casual Shoes, Slippers, Driving Shoes, and Dress Shoes. The **Casual Shoe** classification has been done for you—**$7,450.3 in sales**.

2. Add all classification sales together to get the **Total Shoe Dept Sales LY**. Double-check your answer by adding the Retail $ Sold for every style. You should get the same answer.

3. Complete **Sell Thru %** for all styles. A good sell thru for these styles is **80%** or higher.

4. This department is planned at a **+5% increase next year**. Add 5% to the **Total Shoe Dept Sales LY**, and write your answer on page 176 that follows, under **Next Year's Buy**. You are going to purchase only 5% more than what you sold last year.

5. Find the % to Total for each classification of goods using the **Retail $ Sold by classification** on page 175. Place your answer under **% by Class**.

6. Find the % to Total department for each style using the **Retail $ Sold by style** on page 175 of the simulation. Place your answer on page 176, under % by Style. Remember to round to one place after the decimal point.

7. **Rank the styles** in order, from highest to lowest, based on each style's **% by Style** (or % to Total department). Place your answer on page 176 under **Ranking Styles**. The highest ranking, or the style with the highest % to Total, should start with the #1 ranking. The next highest style will receive the #2 ranking, etc.

   • If two styles have the **same % to Total**, look at the actual dollars sold. In this case, the style with the **highest dollars** sold gets the highest ranking.

- If two styles have the **same dollars sold and % to Total**, choose the style with the higher markup, and give that style the higher ranking.
- If everything is **the same for two styles**, give them both the same numerical ranking.

8. You should have calculated **Next Year's Buy** and written it on page 176 of the simulation. For this exercise, our first consideration is to buy what we sold last year, +5%. Next Year's Buy is a plan of what the buyer will purchase, in units or dollars, for the coming year.

9. Break **Next Year's Buy** down by style using the % by Style (or % to Total) for each style. Place your answer under **Next Year $ Buy**.

10. Convert **Next Year $ Buy** into units, by style. Take **Next Year $ Buy** and divide it by **each style's Retail**, found on page 175. You are essentially taking the dollar buy for each style, and figuring out how many units that equals. The only way you can do that is to divide by the actual Retail price of each style. Make sure to round the units to the nearest whole number.

Example

You can't buy 11,023.5 pairs of shoes. However, you can buy 11,024 pairs of shoes.

The door/store modules are as follows: A, B, C, D

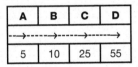

A	B	C	D
→	→	→	→
5	10	25	55

Place your answer under **Next Year Unit Buy** for each style.

11. Make a recommendation for the Store Modules for each style. Consider sell thru and sales performance. Your answer will go under **Next Year # of Doors** (doors = stores). The # of Doors each style was in last year is provided for you on page 175 of the simulation.

   Styles that are in A stores only, or the best performing stores, are in only 5 stores. Styles that are in 10 doors are in A and B stores. Styles that are in 25 doors are in A, B, and C stores. Styles that are in all doors (55) are in A, B, C, and D stores.

   Doors means the number of stores. A style that is in 10 doors is in 10 stores. In this example, the style is in 5 A stores and 5 B stores.

   If a style is in A stores and has adequate performance, you can roll it out to B and C stores, but you cannot roll it all the way out to D stores. This is too fast, too quick.

   Likewise, if a style is in all doors (A–D) and it has poor selling, you can roll it back to C or B stores, but not all the way back to A stores. This is too fast, and you would have to make up considerable volume somewhere else. Even with a poor sell thru, some styles do a tremendous amount of business and need to be gradually phased out and replaced with better options.

12. When you are finished, check your answers. Write a reflective paragraph summarizing the information provided in this simulation. Next, analyze the business considering factors such as: Sales, Sell Thru, % to Total, Vendor Assortment, Store Modules, Markup, Retail Price, Cost, and opportunities for newness. What classifications would you pursue in the future and why? What vendors would you develop further or try to narrow down? Where is there obvious opportunity? Where are there liabilities?

Next Year's Buy would not be the final answer, as you can see with the placement of your store module recommendations. This is, however, a starting point to develop by-style plans. We definitely want to buy what we did last year, assuming we are not discontinuing anything and we had favorable sales. Based on your finalized store modules by style, you would rework the by-style plans. You would also need to consider the larger Six-Month Merchandise Plan, and vendor placement within that plan.

Men's Shoe Department Simulation

VENDOR	STYLE #	DESCRIPTION	RETAIL	COST	MU %	DOORS	LY UNITS RECVD	LY UNITS SOLD	SELL THRU %	RETAIL $ SOLD
CASUAL										
A	10	DK BRWN BLUCHER	$145.00	$65.00	55.2%	55	14,000	11,440	81.7%	$1,658.8
A	20	BURG CASUAL PENNY	$135.00	$63.00	53.3%	55	20,000	17,160		$2,316.6
A	30	BLK CASUAL PENNY	$135.00	$63.00	53.3%	55	27,000	25,740		$3,474.9
							TOTAL CASUAL SHOE SALES			
SLIPPERS										
C	70	DK BRWN SHEARLNG SCUFF	$65.00	$26.00	60.0%	55	21,000	20,020		$1,301.3
C	80	BRWN PEBBL LEATHER SCUFF	$58.00	$22.00	62.1%	55	20,000	14,300		$829.4
							TOTAL SLIPPER SALES			
DRIVING SHOES										
D	90	DKGRY SUEDE DRIVER	$225.00	$92.00	59.1%	55	10,100	8,580		$1,930.5
E	100	BLK SUEDE DRIVER	$225.00	$92.00	59.1%	25	2,850	2,600		$585.0
							TOTAL DRIVING SHOE SALES			
DRESS SHOES										
F	200	BLK WING TIP	$290.00	$138.00	52.4%	55	15,000	8,580		$2,488.2
F	300	BRN CAPTOE	$280.00	$135.00	51.8%	55	30,000	25,740		$7,207.2
F	400	BLK CAPTOE	$280.00	$135.00	51.8%	55	34,000	28,600		$8,008.0
F	500	BLK SQUARE TOE	$310.00	$145.00	53.2%	55	22,000	20,020		$6,206.2
F	600	BRN SQUARE TOE	$310.00	$145.00	53.2%	55	15,000	8,580		$2,659.8
F	700	BLK BLUCHER	$290.00	$138.00	52.4%	25	15,000	10,400		$3,016.0
F	800	BRN BLUCHER	$290.00	$138.00	52.4%	25	15,000	13,000		$3,770.0
F	900	BLK PERF CAPTOE	$280.00	$135.00	51.8%	10	4,000	3,640		$1,019.2
F	1000	BURG FORML PENNY	$200.00	$98.00	51.0%	5	1,500	1,300		$260.0
F	1100	BRN FORML PENNY	$200.00	$98.00	51.0%	5	1,500	1,300		$260.0
F	1200	BLK FORML PENNY	$200.00	$98.00	51.0%	55	5,280	2,860		$572.0
							TOTAL DRESS SHOE SALES			
							TOTAL SHOE DEPT SALES LY			

Men's Shoe Department Simulation

NEXT YEAR'S BUY =

VENDOR	STYLE #	DESCRIPTION	% BY CLASS	% BY STYLE	RANKING STYLES	NEXT YEAR UNIT BUY	NEXT YEAR $ BUY	NEXT YEAR # OF DOORS
CASUAL								
A	10	DK BRWN BLUCHER						
A	20	BURG CASUAL PENNY						
A	30	BLK CASUAL PENNY						
SLIPPERS								
C	70	DK BRWN SHEARLNG SCUFF						
C	80	BRWN PEBBL LEATHER SCUFF						
DRIVING SHOES								
D	90	DKGRY SUEDE DRIVER						
E	100	BLK SUEDE DRIVER						
DRESS SHOES								
F	200	BLK WING TIP						
F	300	BRN CAPTOE						
F	400	BLK CAPTOE						
F	500	BLK SQUARE TOE						
F	600	BRN SQUARE TOE						
F	700	BLK BLUCHER						
F	800	BRN BLUCHER						
F	900	BLK PERF CAPTOE						
F	1000	BURG FORML PENNY						
F	1100	BRN FORML PENNY						
F	1200	BLK FORML PENNY						

Feedback on the First Simulation

In the Men's Shoe Department simulation you were asked to provide feedback and an analysis of the information. You should have noticed that the Slipper classification had the styles with the highest markup, and also had favorable sales. This would be an obvious growth category for the buyer.

Driving shoes was a small classification with equally great potential. It had a good sell thru and styles with higher than average markup. In the Casual shoe classification there was one style with an outstanding sell thru, the Black Casual Penny. The buyer would definitely go after this style next year and should ask vendor A if it comes in a shade of brown.

The Dress Shoe category is dominated by one vendor who does more than half of the entire department's sales. There are both good and poor selling styles within this classification. The buyer is also in a poor position to negotiate. When one vendor produces such a large percentage of business, with no other competitor within this classification, the vendor has little incentive to negotiate. This is apparent in the poor markup structure of these goods. The buyer should be searching the market for another vendor that can produce good-quality dress shoes, and test new styles with this additional vendor. This will keep vendor F on its toes and force it to compete in order to maintain this large assortment. The buyer should be asking vendor F to match the higher markup structure that is already in the department, or lose business to other vendors.

The Second Simulation

The second simulation gives you the opportunity to negotiate markup, vendor allowance, and markdown allowance. It requires that you build a vendor assortment plan that ties to your own floor plan, for a described target market. Upon completion of the first part of this simulation, your instructor will divide the class into vendor and buying teams. Each group will have the opportunity to be both the buyer and the vendor in these negotiations.

Directions for Simulation 2

1. Identify a target market for which you would like to buy. Describe the demographics, psychographics, and lifestyle of your customer briefly. Psychographics are the values and beliefs held by a particular target market.

2. Use ¼" square grid paper to draw a floor plan that equals 1,200 square feet, or 30' × 40'. Each square in ¼" grid paper equals one square foot. This is not a specialty store, but rather a pad in a department store of your preference. This is not a visual exercise, but rather a tool to plan your vendor and merchandise assortment. Do not include fitting rooms or anything other than fixtures and one cash wrap. The **cash wrap** is the counter space that holds the cash register.

3. After you have drawn the dimensions of your floor plan (selling pad), go shopping for fixtures. You can find many fixtures and their dimensions online, and simply by shopping the marketplace. Plot the fixtures on your floor plan, allowing for major walkways that are 3' in width. Aisles must be at least 3' wide to meet handicap accessibility requirements.

4. After you have decided on fixture types, make a list of the vendors you would like to include in your assortment. Allocate and plot vendors on the fixtures plotted on your floor plan. Keep in mind that your negotiating power is directly linked to the amount of space allocated to each vendor. The longer your vendor list, the less you are carrying of each vendor. This results in weak negotiating power. However, if you allocate **more than 50%** of your assortment to one vendor, you become too dependent on that vendor. At this point, the vendor knows that they have the upper hand in negotiation.

Example of a Vendor Worksheet

VENDOR	# of Fixtures	% to Total	MARKUP	MARKDOWN ALLOWANCE	ADVERTISING ALLOWANCE
7 For All Mankind	6	24.0%			
Rock & Republic	5	20.0%			
Citizens of Humanity	4	16.0%			
Joe's	3	12.0%			
Lucky	4	16.0%			
Antik	1	4.0%			
Private Label	2	8.0%			
TOTAL FIXTURES	25				

5. For this exercise you must have a private label assortment and allocate fixture space for it. Decide how much or how little space you would like it to occupy on your selling floor.

6. When you have completed your floor plan, create a spreadsheet similar to the example on page 178. You will list all vendors and the number of fixtures that each occupy on your selling floor. Make sure to have a **Fixture Total** at the bottom of the page. Next, find the **% to Total** for each vendor by dividing each vendor's fixture quantity by the Total Fixtures.

7. Now that you have created a vendor assortment plan, you are ready to begin negotiations. Your instructor will divide the class into groups of buyers and vendors. Each group will be briefed before negotiations begin.

Goals for Buying Teams

The goal of each buying team is to get the highest possible markup, markdown allowance, and advertising allowance possible. As you will soon find out, this is dependent upon each of your vendor's % to Total department. You will negotiate with each vendor separately and must have your worksheet with you. It is always smart to shop the market before making your final purchasing decision. When you are ready to make a final purchasing decision, you will be asked to sign the vendor's worksheet. You **cannot** change your mind after signing the vendor's worksheet.

Goals for Vendor Teams

The goal for each vendor team is to get the highest purchase amount and to give the buying teams the lowest end of the range on markup, markdown allowance, and advertising allowance. This means convincing the highest number of buying teams to agree to purchase with you, but also giving them the worst deals. Under no circumstances should the vendor grant the buyer a deal that is out of the range prescribed on the worksheet. To finalize a deal, you must obtain the buying team's signature on your worksheet. Vendors are either designer or private label. Your instructor will tell each team what they represent in the quick briefing before negotiations. There will be at least two of each represented for each negotiation session.

Other Information for Simulation

Remember that buyers have the opportunity to shop the vendor teams before signing with them. As vendors obtain confirmed orders with other buyers, they may be less likely to stick with the range they originally offered in the last negotiation. Vendors are not obliged to honor their original offers once the buying team has left their meeting to shop the market.

Vendor and Buyer Forms

The vendor forms must be completed by all vendor teams and signed by the buying team after it has agreed to the vendor deal. These will be turned in to your instructor when completed.

Buyers do not have any forms except for the spreadsheet they have completed. They must take notes of their agreements by hand, and then update the spreadsheet for homework. They are also responsible for signing the vendor form after they have made a final commitment.

While You Are Waiting to Negotiate

If you are waiting to see a vendor, listen to the arguments of other teams. Think about how you will present your argument. This can be a fun exercise if you are willing to have fun with it. Some students create mock discussions where they refer to shipping standards and late deliveries. If both parties will play along, the discussions can be very interesting.

Answer the following questions upon completion of the Second Simulation.

1. Who was the best negotiator in your class, and why?

_____

_____

_____

_____

2. How did he or she present his/her case?

_____

_____

_____

_____

3. How could you have been more assertive and formulated a better response?

_____

_____

_____

_____

_____

Summary

In this chapter you had the opportunity to refresh your basic merchandising math skills and calculate LY history. You did this in a number of ways, including looking at sales, sell thru, percent to total, and store breakdowns. You were then asked to analyze LY performance and come up with action plans. One of those actions was the initial breakdown of units by style for future purchases. You were able to view a recap of LY performance as a spreadsheet in Excel. You were then asked to create your own spreadsheet using this information. Buyer's particular formatting preferences for recording LY history were discussed.

You had the opportunity to participate in mock vendor and buyer negotiations. Here, you should have come to realize the importance of the vendor's square footage relative to the buyer's department when negotiating items such as markup, markdown allowance, and advertising allowance. In addition, you should have some new strategies for negotiation based on your own experience and listening to other students' negotiations.

END-OF-SEASON NEGOTIATIONS

CHAPTER OBJECTIVES

- Explain the details of buyer preparation for market week.
- Describe the sequence of events at a typical buyer/vendor appointment.
- Illustrate the financial topics of interest on a vendor market sheet.
- Calculate a department summary based on vendor market sheets.
- Determine the total dollars needed for the department to meet gross margin expectations.
- Rank vendors based on overall vendor performance and total department results.

End-of-season negotiations start with careful analysis of vendors and planning of the market trip. At the end of each season, most retailers send their buyers to market to review end-of-season results. The buyer quantifies each vendor's performance. This is usually a time when new lines for the upcoming season are previewed.

11

Placing Orders

Orders may be placed at these appointments, if buyers are well prepared. The advantage of getting your orders in first is that the orders are usually shipped in the order that they are received. If a vendor oversells inventory, the first orders in are not affected.

Being prepared to place orders during market week requires that:

- Business plans have been written and approved for the upcoming season.
- Vendor and assortment plans are completed.
- The vendor plan has been calculated and includes the number of styles, units, dollars, and an estimate of deliveries based on the Six-Month Merchandise Plan.
- The vendor plan may also include the total number of styles the buyer will purchase from each vendor, ranked by importance. The planned units for the #1 style will go to the style that shows best in market, followed by the #2 style, and so on.

Planning the Market Trip

Depending on a buyer's area of trade, different market weeks take place across the United States and around the world. The market weeks you attend depend on the merchandise categories for which you are buying. Major market centers, such as New York City, become quickly booked, so hotel accommodations and airline reservations should be made far in advance. Most buyers plan their hotel accommodations based on proximity to their market appointments. This makes going from one appointment to the next more efficient. If you are traveling to New York City, it is advantageous to bring a map and transportation information for the subway and bus system. Convention centers in large cities are also a place where small businesses attend trade shows. Attendance at these trade shows requires evidence that you are, in fact, a business owner, and registration must be booked in advance.

Vendor Appointments

Vendors fill appointments quickly, so all appointments must be made in a timely manner. Buyers for large retailers receive phone calls, sometimes several months before market week, from vendors requesting appointment times. Any new vendors that the buyer is interested in previewing must be included in this very tight schedule. In addition, vendors use this opportunity to promote goodwill by inviting buyers to dinner, fashion shows, and other events. This is a good time to socialize, but the goal is to keep it professional. A lavish dinner invitation one night may be followed by a tense negotiation the following day. A high degree of professionalism is required and necessary at all times.

Resident Buying Offices

Many retailers also work with Resident Buying Offices. One of the most famous Resident Buying Offices is the Doneger Group or Doneger Associates. They have offices in New York City and in Los Angeles.

Resident Buying Offices, often referred to as market specialists, work with retailers to develop new assortments, provide trend forecasting information, and act as a liaison to large manufacturers. They provide up-to-date information about what is happening in the marketplace, and are usually located in the middle of the wholesale market.

If a retailer works with a Resident Buying Office, the buyer must also schedule this meeting into their busy market week plans.

FIGURE 11.1 *At corporate buying meetings, buyers may be advised on how many units they should purchase*
Source: © Monkey Business/Fotolia

Corporate Buying Offices

Other industry leaders have in-house buying offices, or **Corporate Buying Offices**, that place orders across several divisions. The buyer must attend a series of corporate meetings, sometimes spanning several days. In these meetings, buyers meet with the corporate representative for their department and usually other buyers from many different divisions.

In corporate buying meetings, buyers may:

- Plan future product assortments.
- Place units for private label assortments.
- Place units for company-wide vendor assortments.
- Discuss overall LY performance.
- Decide on the addition or subtraction of a vendor to the Corporate Matrix.
- Defend their unit placement if it is too high or low, compared to other corporate divisions.
- Plan and discuss their negotiations with vendors for the rest of the week.

A **Corporate Matrix** is a list of preferred vendors with which a company wishes to do business. It is sometimes difficult for a buyer to order from a vendor that is not on a corporate matrix, if this concept applies.

Other Market Appointment Strategies

Smaller retailers must consider the competition to book important vendor appointments, and should start booking appointments very early in the season. Smaller retailers are often bumped by vendors that are eager to set an appointment with a larger retailer.

Some of the largest retailers, who have substantial buying power, request that vendors come to them. Some of them, in fact, refuse to visit the vendor in their showroom. This is a strategy used by powerful retailers, who realize the advantage of negotiating from home base. Their strategy is one of intimidation. They will often include several members of senior management in the negotiation, while only a few vendors are represented at the negotiation table. This strategy also reduces traveling expenses.

Adherence to the Market Week Plan

Once the market week schedule has been set, adherence to the plan is essential. Market appointments very often go over the allocated time, so overbooking is not favorable. Buyers should call vendors if they are running late. Showing up late to an appointment, without calling to warn the vendor, is not a good way to start off negotiations.

If the buyer is attending a market appointment at the end of the year, negotiations are extremely important. They will usually start off this market appointment with a recap of the year's business and a review of the buyer's market sheets. **Market sheets** are worksheets for each vendor that include a summary of results compared to the buyer's total department results.

Vendor Market Sheets

Assistant buyers help prepare the market sheets at the end of each season. Usually, a combination of retail reports is used to prepare these statements. Most retail reports show figures at the retail value, so specific reports will be needed to find cost figures. Actual statistics for this year are compared to LY and the departmental plan. Buyers use the total departmental results to negotiate with vendors that fall below the mean, in specific categories.

Vendors realize that the opportunity to grow their business depends on how their results compare to the departmental average. Those vendors that repeatedly fall short of the department plan, and are unwilling to meet gross margin expectations, risk losing future business. Buyers should be careful about threatening to drop a vendor from their assortment, and hold this card in reserve for serious matters. This is usually an unspoken concern.

First, buyers review the statistics with vendors and then they will compare each vendor to the department. Next, they discuss future business opportunities, including possibilities for newness and new product categories. If a vendor is pushing the buyer to add or test a new line of merchandise, the buyer should bring to the discussion any unproductive or old merchandise that is holding up his/her open-to-buy. In many instances, a trade of merchandise may be negotiated.

Example:

The vendor may ask the retailer to test $45,000 worth of new merchandise, in exchange for the return of $45,000 worth of old merchandise. Even if the vendor is only willing to return $35,000, this is a fairly good deal for the buyer, who may have been sitting on unproductive styles for an entire season. Some merchandise will not sell, no matter how much the ticket retail is reduced.

In many instances, vendors would rather return unproductive merchandise than reduce it to more than 50% off. At a certain point, merchandise that is drastically reduced affects the image of the brand. If vendors are

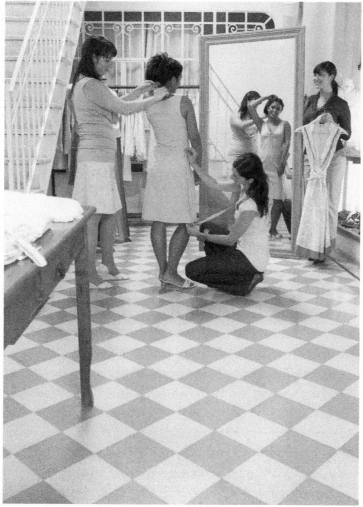

FIGURE 11.2
Source: Maria Teijeiro/Digital Vision/Thinkstock

unwilling to accept return merchandise, it may be possible to negotiate a markdown allowance. As discussed in previous chapters, it is important for the retailer to take timely markdowns on merchandise and to ask for coverage of those markdowns in the months that they accrue.

Negotiate Throughout the Season

If a buyer waits until the very end of the season to negotiate the entire season's markdown allowance, his/her chances of receiving it are slim. Consider the number of other buyers the vendor is negotiating with at the end of each season. They too are financially responsible for adhering to a plan.

In the retail industry, presentation and approach are everything. A good buyer will work on building a strong relationship with their resources over time. This does not mean becoming their best friends. It does mean being perceived as organized, efficient, reliable, and a tough negotiator. Socializing is part of the job requirement, and is a significant part of market week, but business is the purpose of the visit. The buyer must maintain a professional relationship at all times, so when it becomes time to negotiate, he/she does not hesitate to do what is best for the strength of the business.

Negotiation Tips

The first negotiation tip is, of course, to come well prepared. This means great premarket preparation, and includes bringing several copies of vendor market sheets. You never know exactly how many people will be present at each meeting and everyone present must be able to follow the statistics on the market sheets.

Next, establish and build rapport with the people present in the meeting. There is a moment when you first enter the meeting when you must make small talk. This usually includes a quick discussion about how your trip is going or something that you know about the vendor. The buyer is usually offered a beverage and/or food. This is not the time to order a complicated coffee drink; make it simple. If it is lunchtime, expect to eat something, because the vendors are also hungry and have very little time during market week. If you are well acquainted with the vendor representative, this is the time to ask him/her something casual. Remember to not get personal; it is not important that he/she know about your personal life. What is important is how you conduct business.

Always maintain good eye contact and smile, when it seems subtle. This naturally places people at ease. Throughout the discussion, keep your eyes up and look at everyone in the meeting, no matter what is said. Make sure to extend your hand and shake hands with those people you have not met. Do not wait for anyone to introduce you; instead, introduce yourself. It is just one way to show that you are not timid or intimidated. If you are already well acquainted with everyone in the room, you may not need to shake hands.

When you get into the discussion of the market sheets, know your statistics. Wake up early that morning to review the market sheets, or read them in the taxi, but come with that vendor's statistics in your memory. When discussions get a little more heated, some buyers become flustered. At this point, if you have your facts memorized, you will do well. You will be more respected in the market if you are prepared in this way.

All people like to be heard. It is as important for the buyer to listen as it is to speak. A good negotiator realizes that part of winning an argument is listening for the lack of validity in the other person's argument. You can also gain the trust of your vendor by admitting to mistakes and listening to feedback. After you are finished listening, act decisively. You should know how you are going to handle the possibilities of different outcomes before you get to that market appointment. When you are there, do not waver—make decisions.

Gross Margin Requirements

After briefly reviewing the statistics and discussing newness and return possibilities, the buyer discusses the vendor's gross margin results. Remember that the vendor has had this information for the entire season, so this should come as no surprise. The buyer should have been negotiating markdown coverage on a monthly basis, as well. Sales, markdowns, shortage, markup, and turnover are all reviewed in detail. In a large retailer, several buyers may purchase from each vendor, with freight having been predetermined through the corporate office. In this situation, it is not a negotiable factor. However, smaller retailers can negotiate freight and terms each season.

The market sheets on the following pages are examples of the vendor market sheets that will be calculated and brought to each vendor appointment. Several copies of each vendor market sheet should be made. It is common at end-of-season negotiations for several important executives to be present at each appointment. Buyers may be accompanied by their divisional merchandise manager, their planner, and an assistant buyer. In some cases, a general merchandise manager will also attend. Vendor representatives may be accompanied by the senior vice president of sales, a member of the design team, or any other executives who would like to take part in the discussion. Coming prepared and bringing extra copies of market sheets lets the vendor know you are ready to do business.

In the following pages, there are four vendor market sheets that equal an entire department. Only four vendors have been included, in order to make this exercise more easily understood. The goal for this exercise is to examine all of the components, on each sheet, that contribute to gross margin. Compare TY to LY and the department (DEPT) results. The plan for gross margin is given on each page, but the department results for categories such as turnover and markup are more important at this point in time.

When a vendor can clearly see that they fall below the department's actual results, this can feel threatening. They are usually willing to take action because they know the buyer will, if they do not. Purchases and shipping percentages have not been added to these negotiations, in an attempt to focus more clearly on key components and gross margin. Some parts of each vendor market sheet have been left open to be completed by you. Fill in the DEPT MU% on each sheet after you have completed the totals below. This will allow you to complete the analysis.

Complete the department totals below by adding up all four vendor market sheets. The first one has been done for you.

Complete these department totals:

Department Net Sales TY $544, 950

Department Net Sales LY _____

Department Sales % change _____

Department Purchases at Retail _____

Department Purchases at Cost _____

Departmental Markup % _____

After filling in the information on each vendor market sheet, analyze each vendor's results and complete the charts at the end of this chapter. Make sure to look at the amount, at cost, that the vendor needs to meet gross margin expectations. This is the most important part of negotiations for the buyer at the end of each season.

Vendor 1

	Cost	Retail		MU%
Gross Sales		105,000		
Returns		1,650	1.6%	
Net Sales		103,350		
				MU%
Stock Cost	$ 45,000	105,000		57.1%
Freight	$ 7,500		7.1%	
Markdowns	$ 3,500		3.3%	
Shortage	$ 1,390		1.3%	
Employee Discount	$ 1,735		1.7%	
Cost of Goods	$ 59,125			
Cost dollars needed to meet GM PLAN	$ 275			% of Sales
		58,850		
GM		44,500		43.1%
Departmental GM PLAN			43.1	

RECAP OF THIS YEAR'S PERFORMANCE

	SALES TY	SALES LY	% CHANGE	DEPT %
	103,350	98,000	5.5%	
	TURN TY	TURN LY	DEPT TURN	
	2.00	2.00		
	MU% TY	MU% LY	DEPT MU%	
	57.1%	57%		
	GM TY	GM LY	DEPT GM	
	42.8%	43%	43.1%	

Vendor 2

	Cost		Retail		MU%
Gross Sales			98,000		
Returns			4,100	4.2%	
Net Sales			93,900		
Stock Cost	45,000		98,000		54.1%
Freight	2,250	2.3%			
Markdowns	8,550	8.7%			
Shortage	1,600	1.6%			
Employee Discount	1,650	1.7%			
Cost of Goods	59,050				
Cost dollars needed to meet GM PLAN	5,575				% of Sales
			53,475		
	GM		40,425		43.1%

Departmental GM PLAN   43.1

RECAP OF THIS YEAR'S PERFORMANCE

SALES TY	SALES LY	% CHANGE	DEPT %
93,900	88,500	6.1%	

TURN TY	TURN LY	DEPT TURN
2.14	1.98	

MU% TY	MU% LY	DEPT MU%
54.1%	53.8%	

GM TY	GM LY	DEPT GM
40.8%	42.8%	43.1%

Vendor 3

	Cost		Retail	
Gross Sales			210,000	
Returns		3.5%	7,300	
Net Sales			202,700	
				MU%
Stock Cost	95,000		210,000	54.8%
Freight	4,800	2.3%		
Markdowns	10,000	4.8%		
Shortage	4,250	2.0%		
Employee Discount	3,500	1.7%		
Cost of Goods	117,550			
Cost dollars needed to meet *GM PLAN*	2,120			**% of Sales**
			115,430	43.1%
GM	87,270			
Departmental GM PLAN			43.1	

RECAP OF THIS YEAR'S PERFORMANCE

	SALES TY	**SALES LY**	**% CHANGE**	**DEPT %**
	202,700	200,000	1.4%	
	TURN TY	TURN LY	DEPT TURN	
	1.66	1.70		
	MU% TY	MU% LY	DEPT MU%	
	54.8%			
	GM TY	GM LY	DEPT GM	
	42.0%		43.1%	

Vendor 4

	Cost		Retail	
Gross Sales			150,000	
Returns			5,000	3.3%
Net Sales			145,000	
				MU%
Stock Cost	65,000		150,000	56.7%
Freight	3,500	2.3%		
Markdowns	12,000	8.0%		
Shortage	2,850	1.9%		
Employee Discount	2,500	1.7%		
Cost of Goods	85,850			
Cost dollars needed to meet GM PLAN	3,280			% of Sales
GM			82,570	
		GM	62,430	43.1%
Departmental GM PLAN			43.1	

RECAP OF THIS YEAR'S PERFORMANCE

	SALES TY	SALES LY	% CHANGE	DEPT %
	145,000	135,000	7.4%	
	TURN TY	TURN LY	DEPT TURN	
	1.98	1.88		
	MU% TY	MU% LY	DEPT MU%	
	56.7%			
	GM TY	GM LY	DEPT GM	
	40.8%		43.1%	

Make a statement about each of the following components using the information provided in each vendor's market sheets. Support your statement with statistics.

Vendor 1

Sales _____

_____

_____

Turnover _____

Markup _____

Shortage _____

Markdown % _____

Gross Margin _____

Vendor 2

Sales _____

_____

_____

Turnover _____

Markup _____

Shortage _____

Markdown % _____

Gross Margin _____

Vendor 3

Sales _____

_____

_____

Turnover _____

Markup _____

Shortage _____

Markdown % _____

Gross Margin _____

Vendor 4

Sales _____

_____

_____

Turnover _____

Markup _____

Shortage _____

Markdown % _____

Gross Margin _____

Be prepared to discuss your answers. Think about which vendor had the best and worst performance, compared to the department's performance.

In the following chapters, you will have the opportunity to review the procedures that a buyer encounters on a daily basis. These chapters focus on Monday, because this is the day that statistical results become available from the previous week. Several reports are analyzed, and re-projections of the open-to-buy are completed. Priorities are set for the week ahead.

Take a moment to review basic formulas from the preceding chapters. You will need to know sell thru, weeks of supply, % to Total, and stock to sales.

Summary

In this chapter, you were able to see the amount of planning and preparation that goes into end-of-season negotiations. All vendor appointments and travel arrangements have to be made far in advance, with an itinerary that is often overwhelming. Buyers must make appropriate effort to prepare and present accurate vendor market sheets. One of the most important tips for negotiating is adequate preparation and memorization of each vendor's results for the season. Buyers who come to market prepared to write orders usually get the best shipping results when next season arrives.

Corporate Buying Office meetings were described as an additional market week task, where units are placed and LY performance is discussed. Resident Buying Offices may also be a part of the market week visit, where buyers can gain valuable insight into what is happening in the market, as well as develop new assortments going forward.

The market sheet analysis enabled you to see exactly how vendor gross margins are calculated. You were able to analyze four different vendors within a department, and then compare each of their results to the department totals. You should have thought about what you would say to each of the vendors during an end-of-season negotiation, based on the statistics provided.

MONDAY

MORNING REPORTS

(SALES)

CHAPTER OBJECTIVES

- Visualize the tasks performed on a Monday morning in most buying offices.
- Explain how the reports printed on Monday affect the buyer's action plan for the week.
- Describe the Weekly Style Summary and its use in determining the Best Seller Report.
- Define the most important objective of the Vendor-by-Class Report.
- Determine the importance of the By-Location Sales Report and explain how it is used.

12

The next two chapters were designed to demonstrate a typical day in the life of a buyer. The information is presented from the perspective of a multi-chain retailer. However, the process of analyzing the business for a large or single-store retailer is the same. In fact, if you understand the mindset of a buyer for a large retailer, adapting to a single store retailer will be much easier and you will be more analytically prepared.

Monday Mornings

We start with Monday morning because it is the most important day in the life of a buyer. This is because most retailers print their last week results over the weekend and the results are collated for the buyer early Monday morning. A few exceptional retailers gain an advantage on the competition by printing and evaluating reports on Saturday, although this is not the norm.

Retailers that analyze the previous week's performance on Monday morning must arrive very early to get a head start. The buyer may arrive as early as 7 a.m. to start reviewing the many reports. The information and analysis that is done on Monday sets the agenda and tone for the rest of the workweek. The information found on this day helps the buyer schedule the week's events and allocate time to crucial business matters.

The reports that are provided in this chapter all include various ways of looking at sales. Remember, in the planning process the most important and first factor planned is sales, followed by stock. These reports also have stock information available so an accurate comparison of sales based on stock or inventory levels can be determined.

Sell Thru Review

Take a moment now to recall what you remember about sell thru and how it is used by the buyer.

Write down your definition of sell thru, using your own words.

_____

_____

_____

Now give the mathematical formula for determining sell thru.

_____

Received should have been part of the mathematical formula for sell thru.
Which two components make up the total received, if received is not available to calculate the sell thru?

_____

If you cannot remember the components of sell thru, refer back to Chapter 3.

The buyer first collects all of the reports printed over the weekend from the divisional merchandise manager's secretary or the reporting room. In some instances, the reports may already be on the buyer's desk when he/she arrives. At this time, the analysis and planning for the week begins. Depending on the buyer's sales volume, there may be several departments to analyze. Each department will have a separate set of reports to analyze.

Weekly Style Summary

The first and most valuable report analyzed is the Weekly Style Summary. This includes all sales information for each style in the buyer's department, and includes information regarding stock levels and on order amounts.

The **Weekly Style Summary**, or the **By-Style Report**, includes sales and inventory levels, by style, for the previous week, the month, and usually the season thus far. It also includes the style number, description, and the cost, retail, and markup of each style, as it is currently being promoted within the department.

Many buyers look through the Weekly Style Summary armed with a variety of highlighters. The main things that they are looking for are great sales, poor sales, and low inventory levels. For example, a buyer might highlight all the best sellers with a yellow highlighter. Poor sellers or styles that are slowing in sales and in need of a markdown might be highlighted in pink, and styles that need an immediate or urgent reorder might be highlighted in blue. The report can be quite large, so this method may be helpful when the buyer is trying to grasp the big picture at a glance.

Buying for a Small Chain or Single Store

A buyer for a single store or small chain of stores might consider creating a report similar to the Weekly Style Summary, in order to better analyze the business and create a Best Seller Report. Best Seller Reports can be used to educate the selling associates in the retail store on products that should be well stocked at all times and further emphasized. The ability to create the Weekly Style Summary and Best Seller Reports depends on the availability of information to the buyer.

How is the Weekly Style Summary Used?

The buyer utilizes the Weekly Style Summary to determine:

- **Selling by Style**—Which styles had the highest sell thru?
- **Selling by Vendor**—Which vendors have excellent selling? Which vendors are selling poorly?
- **New Deliveries**—Which styles had great sell thru the first week on the floor?
- **Old Deliveries**—Which past fashion styles have slowed in sales and may need a markdown?
- **POS Sale Events**—How did a 25% off sale on a specific delivery increase sales of those styles, relative to sales in an ordinary, non-sale week?
- **On Hand**—Are there any fashion styles that could use a reorder based on great selling and low on hands? Are there any styles that have favorable markup and good selling that could be reordered from the vendor?
- **Basic Goods**—Are there basics that have good sales and low on hands? Should the allocator or planner be updated on these successful styles and asked to raise the style's model stocks? (Raising the model stocks means increasing the minimum number of units that are required to be on hand in a store. This is an adjustment made in the computer ordering system.)
- **No Selling**—Are there any styles that have been delivered to the stores that show no selling? Are they on the floor? Are their UPC codes correctly attached?
- **On Order**—Does the On Order column correctly reflect what is on order for each style? How many weeks of supply are available, based on last week's rate of sale? How much should be available?

Many things can be determined by the Weekly Style Summary. This report acts as a starting point and reference for determining how the styles are performing in the department. After you have reviewed the Weekly Style Summary example in this chapter, review the previous bullet points and then draw conclusions about the information presented in the report. Before reviewing the Weekly Style Summary, review the following definitions in order to accurately read and analyze the report.

Definition Review

Please fill in the appropriate *definition* or *formula* for each of the following:

Class = _____

Vendor # = _____

Cost = _____

Retail = _____

MU % = _____

LW Sales = _____

MTD Sales = _____

OH Units = _____

OO Units = _____

The Weekly Style Summary

The Weekly Style Summary that follows is an excerpt from an intimate apparel department. This is an example of one page of the report. For a large store, this report may be over 200 pages long. That is why it is so important to learn to read the report efficiently and pinpoint key information. The items we are looking at throughout this exercise are pajamas in a variety of silhouettes, including pajama sets, pajama pants, and coordinating tops. The selling is indicative of any major retail chain with stores throughout the United States.

The information provided on the Weekly Style Summary will be used to determine the first report the buyer must complete. This report is called the Best Seller Report.

Best Seller Report

The Best Seller Report is created by the buyer and includes top selling styles for each department, determined by sales volume and sell thru. This report is often used to highlight emerging trends and includes high sell thrus on new styles, or styles that are driving a category for the season. Senior management uses this tool to educate retail store associates and to determine which departments need additional funding.

Usually, the divisional merchandise manager is asked to report on his/her division's "best sellers" at a meeting on Monday. In order to be sufficiently prepared, he/she asks his/her buyers to collate a list of the best sellers from each department, by a specified time (usually mid-morning).

This list may be referred to as the Best Seller Report. It may be hand written on a standardized form, or available for access through the retailer's internal networking system (**intranet**).

Complete the Best Seller Report on the following page, using the Weekly Style Summary provided.

Directions for Completing the Best Seller Report

You must choose and record the top five best sellers. In order to determine the best sellers, you must look at sales and sell thru, by style, for last week (LW) and the month (MTD). Both sales and sell thru are important, but for this exercise sell thru indicates an emerging trend. Likewise, the sales for last week are very important, but MTD sales are even more important, as they show the prolonged success of a style. Not every buyer will choose the same best sellers, although this exercise can be very objective.

Why Would a Buyer Not Report a Best Seller?

Be aware that buyers will not always report a best seller, especially if they have not ordered enough stock to support sales. If they skim over a best selling style in order to avoid drawing attention to the fact that they did not project high enough inventory for the style, senior management may still detect the error. Each

FIGURE 12.1

Source: © Suprijono Suharjoto/Fotolia

buyer has a different strategy for dealing with this situation. In other cases, the buyer may know the vendor has inventory on the best seller and want to reorder it, but not have the budget to do so. In this case, it is important for the buyer to add this style to the best seller report to draw attention to the fact that he/she needs more funding.

Do not look ahead in this exercise. Use the Weekly Style Summary on the next page to create your own Best Seller Report on the following page.

Upon completion of the Best Seller Report, you may check your top five best sellers against the answers in The Answered Best Seller Report.

WEEKLY STYLE SUMMARY

Total Vendor: 001

Class	Vendor	Style #	Description	Cost	Retail	MU%	LW Sales			MTD Sales			OH	OO
							Units	$	ST%	Units	$	ST%	Units	Units
20	1	5001	pnk dot pj bottom	$16.25	$34.00	52.2%	1125	$38.3	25.1%	4250	$144.5	55.9%	3350	1300
20	1	5002	blu dot pj bottom	$16.25	$34.00	52.2%	1020	$34.7	29.7%	3050	$103.7	55.9%	2410	1550
20	1	5003	pnk dot lg slv top	$10.50	$25.50	58.8%	550	$14.0	47.8%	1200	$30.6	66.7%	600	1250
20	1	5004	blu dot lg slv top	$10.50	$25.50	58.8%	475	$12.1	22.9%	800	$20.4	33.3%	1600	0
20	1	5005	blu check bottom	$16.00	$34.00	52.9%	829	$28.2	25.6%	3306	$112.4	57.8%	2415	4403
20	1	5006	pnk check bottom	$16.00	$34.00	52.9%	902	$30.7	20.8%	2700	$91.8	44.1%	3425	0
40	1	5007	pnk solid sslv top	$9.50	$20.00	52.5%	1001	$20.0	29.8%	5200	$104.0	68.8%	2354	500
40	1	5008	blu solid sslv top	$9.50	$20.00	52.5%	824	$16.5	14.1%	2450	$49.0	32.9%	5002	0
40	1	5009	wht logo sslv top	$9.50	$20.00	52.5%	1200	$24.0	49.2%	4825	$96.5	79.6%	1240	150

| Subtotal Vendor: 001 | | | | | | | 7926 | $218.4 | 26.1% | 27781 | $752.9 | 55.4% | 22396 | 9153 |

Handwritten annotations:

not only sell-thru but also sales

low (near style 5003 OO)
low (near style 5008 OH)

2 logo Cami
2 sslv tops logo $0 - basics
pj set - sslv

Colors
white/pink

Total Vendor: 002

Class	Vendor	Style #	Description	Cost	Retail	MU%	LW Sales			MTD Sales			OH	OO
							Units	$	ST%	Units	$	ST%	Units	Units
40	2	5020	gry solid bottm	$ 8.00	$ 20.00	60.0%	985	$ 19.7	33.5%	3954	$ 79.1	66.9%	1954	1020
40	2	5021	wht solid bottom	$ 8.00	$ 20.00	60.0%	550	$ 11.0	26.3%	1942	$ 38.8	55.7%	1542	0
40	2	5022	pnk solid bottom	$ 8.00	$ 20.00	60.0%	758	$ 15.2	36.4%	2900	$ 58.0	68.7%	1324	550
20	2	5023	yellw solid bottom	$ 8.00	$ 20.00	60.0%	456	$ 9.1	26.9%	865	$ 17.3	41.2%	1237	0
40	2	5024	pnk logo cami	$ 5.75	$ 17.50	67.1%	1250	$ 21.9	34.1%	5643	$ 98.8	70.1%	2412	1002
40	2	5025	wht logo cami	$ 5.75	$ 17.50	67.1%	1340	$ 23.5	49.2%	5542	$ 97.0	80.0%	1385	1250
Subtotal Vendor: 002							5339	$100.3	35.1%	20846	$ 389.0	67.9%	9854	3822

Total Vendor: 003

Class	Vendor	Style #	Description	Cost	Retail	MU%	LW Sales			MTD Sales			OH	OO
							Units	$	ST%	Units	$	ST%	Units	Units
20	3	5080	gry shrt sleeve pj set	$ 19.25	$ 45.00	57.2%	1030	$ 46.4	46.2%	2560	$ 115.2	68.1%	1200	1050
40	3	5081	wht shrt sleeve pj set	$ 19.25	$ 45.00	57.2%	1754	$ 78.9	32.3%	5620	$ 252.9	60.4%	3678	1350
40	3	5082	pnk shrt sleeve pj set	$ 19.25	$ 45.00	57.2%	2100	$ 94.5	44.7%	6100	$ 274.5	70.1%	2600	3500
40	3	5083	blu shrt sleeve pj set	$ 19.25	$ 45.00	57.2%	1850	$ 83.3	36.6%	4250	$ 191.3	57.0%	3210	2500
20	3	5084	yellw shrt sleeve pj set	$ 19.25	$ 45.00	57.2%	756	$ 34.0	50.2%	1645	$ 74.0	68.7%	750	360
Subtotal Vendor: 003							7490	$337.1	39.6%	20175	$ 907.9	63.8%	11438	8760

BEST SELLER REPORT

Division: _____

Buyer: _____

Date: _____

Style #	Vendor	Unit Cost	Unit Retail	Promotional Retail	Description of Merchandise	MTD Sales		LW Sales		OH	OO
						Units	$	Units	$	Units	Units

Explanation of Headings:

Style # = the mark style number used by the retailer

Vendor = Vendor name

Promotional Retail = If the style was on sale, what was the promoted retail?

MTD Sales = Month-to-date sales

LW Sales = Last week's sales

OH = units on hand (in stores)

OO = units on order, but not yet received

THE ANSWERED BEST SELLER REPORT

Division: Intimate Apparel

Buyer: Sleepwear

Date: _____

Style #	Vendor	Unit Cost	Unit Retail	Promotional Retail	Description of Merchandise	MTD Sales		LW Sales		OH Units	OO Units
						Units	$	Units	$		
5025	2	5.75	17.50	17.50	wht logo cami	5542	97.0	1340	23.5	1385	1250
5009	1	9.50	20.00	20.00	wht logo sslv top	4825	96.5	1200	24.0	1240	150
5024	2	5.75	17.50	17.50	pnk logo cami	5643	98.8	1250	21.9	2412	1002
5082	3	19.25	45.00	45.00	pnk shrt sleeve pj set	6100	274.5	2100	94.5	2600	3500
5007	1	9.50	20.00	20.00	pnk solid sslv top	5200	104.0	1001	20.0	2354	500

Explanation of Headings:

Style # = the mark style number used by the retailer

Vendor = Vendor name

Promotional Retail = If the style was on sale, what was the promoted retail?

MTD Sales = Month-to-date sales

LW Sales = Last week's sales

OH = units on hand (in stores)

OO = units on order, but not yet received

Vendor-by-Class Report

The **Vendor-by-Class Report** includes sales and stock dollars by vendor, classification, and subclass. It also shows stock-to-sales percent comparisons within each classification and subclass. This is an easy way to determine if stock levels are at adequate levels, based on rate of sale by classification and subclass. Once a buyer has used the Weekly Style Summary to analyze the business at the style level, he/she is ready to implement change at the classification level.

UPC (color/size) → Style → Class → Vendor → Department → Division

For a review of stock-to-sales comparisons, refer to Chapter 4.

What is the ideal ratio of stock-to-sales that you should aim to achieve?

_____

Example:

If we do 25% of sales in pajama bottoms, we should have _____ of the stock in pajama bottoms.

What Do Classification Sales Tell Us?

- Major areas of opportunity
- Where we are overstocked
- Where we are understocked
- Which vendors are in a balanced stock-to-sales ratio
- Where, by classification, we need to reorder
- Where, by classification, we have too much on order

Buyers in some retailers may compare their classification statistics to the statistics of other retail divisions within the company.

Example:

A comparison of The Limited and Express at the class level could compare denim stock-to-sales at these two retailers. The Limited buyer may see how strong sales are in denim for the Express buyer, and then decide to put more emphasis on that category of goods.

Buying for a Small Chain or Single Store

A buyer for a single store or small chain of stores can also create this type of report. The advantage of creating this report is the ability to determine quickly which classifications should be developed and which classifications should be minimized in future purchases.

Classifications

For the purpose of this report we have used the classifications, or classes, to break down our business into basic replenished goods, fashion goods, and novelty or holiday goods.

> **Note:** For the duration of this text, "allocator" is used to describe the person responsible for basic replenished goods and by-store breakdowns of purchase orders.

The classification Basic Goods is managed by the allocator and automatically reordered weekly, based on an advanced computer ordering system. They typically consist of classic styles that remain in vogue for long periods of time. Buyers do make adjustments and recommendations to the computer ordering system, which are then implemented by the allocator.

The classification Fashion Goods indicates the styles the buyer has bought in moderation, with the plan that they will sell out within the season or quarter. The buyer may decide to reorder these styles if they have great sell thrus and have a high markup structure.

The classification Novelty/Holiday Goods indicates styles that are driven by holidays and seasonality. They may include pajama bottoms with reindeer, Santa Claus, Valentine hearts, shamrocks, and so on. These items are bought conservatively, with the objective to sell thru very quickly. The buyer does not want to get stuck with these items after the holiday or event has passed.

Another example of Novelty Goods includes childlike cartoon figures seen on recent sleepwear, aimed at the young adult. Sanrio's collection of Hello Kitty on everything from bubble gum to television sets could also be classified as novelty.

Numerical equivalencies are used to describe each classification on the report for reporting purposes. Classifications are initially set up by the buyer based on how he/she wants to review the statistics for his/her department. Review the major classifications for this department below.

Major Classifications:

Class 20 = Fashion goods

Class 40 = Basic replenished goods

Class 60 = Novelty and holiday goods

Subclasses

Classifications can be further broken down into subclasses. A subclass is used to more accurately describe the merchandise type. This gives the buyer yet another way to analyze the business and compile specifically tailored reports.

Numerical equivalencies for each subclass on the report are provided below. In this case, the buyer has chosen to use the subclass to describe the exact silhouette.

Minor Subclass:

Subclass 100 = pajama bottoms

Subclass 200 = pajama tops

Subclass 300 = pajama sets (matching top and bottom, sold as 1 piece)

Subclass 400 = night shirts

Subclass 500 = short robes (knee length)

Subclass 600 = long robes (calf to ankle length)

Reading the Vendor-by-Class Report

One page of the Vendor-by-Class Report has been provided on the following page. Like the Weekly Style Summary, this report can be quite long. It is important to learn how to scan it quickly for pertinent information. This example includes six different vendors, and all class and subclass information, for stock and sales. Read the report carefully for stock-to-sales analysis, for order opportunities or liabilities, and for general areas of opportunity.

Each sales and stock section is separated by subclass. Vendor 1 and Vendor 2 have two sections each because they produce both pajama tops and pajama bottoms. Vendors 3 through 6 only have one section each, because they only produce one type of merchandise.

Example:

Vendor 3 produces only pajama sets. Subclass 300 is used to describe a pajama set. Class 20 refers to fashion pajama sets, while Class 40 refers to basic pajama sets. A subtotal has also been provided under each vendor section in order to show total vendor sales and stock levels.

In basic pajama sets, Vendor 3 is doing 76.1% of the sales on 82.9% of the stock. Thus, less inventory is needed in this category.

In fashion pajama sets, Vendor 3 is doing 23.9% of the sales on only 17.1% of the stock. Thus, *more inventory* is needed in this category.

THE VENDOR BY CLASS REPORT

Vendor: 001

Vendor: 003

Class	Sub-class	Description	Sales $	%	Stock $	%	OO $
20	300	fashion pj sets	80.4	23.9%	87.8	17.1%	63.4
40	300	basic pj sets	256.7	76.1%	426.9	82.9%	330.8
Subtotal: Vendor 003			337.1	100	514.7	100	394.2

Vendor: 004

Class	Sub-class	Description	Sales $	%	Stock $	%	OO $
20	400	fashion night shirts	91.1	34.3%	125.0	40.2%	180.2
40	400	basic night shirts	174.5	65.7%	186.3	59.8%	444.1
Subtotal: Vendor 004			265.6	100	311.3	100	624.3

Vendor: 005

Class	Sub-class	Description	Sales $	%	Stock $	%	OO $
20	500	fashion robes short	143.6	47.7%	221.6	43.2%	0
40	500	basic robes short	122.7	40.8%	285.4	55.6%	152.6
60	500	novelty robes short	34.6	11.5%	6.5	1.3%	0
Subtotal: Vendor 005			300.9	100	513.5	100	152.6

Vendor: 006

Class	Sub-class	Description	Sales $	%	Stock $	%	OO $
20	600	fashion robes long	25.1	21.5%	6.4	3.2%	0
40	600	basic robes long	88.9	76.3%	191	96.8%	50.7
60	600	novelty robes long	2.5	2.1%	0	0.0%	0
Subtotal: Vendor 006			116.5	100	197.4	100	50.7

Vendor: 001

Class	Sub-class	Description	Sales $	%	Stock $	%	OO $
20	100	fashion pj bottom	131.9	100%	394.4	100%	246.6
40	100	basic pj bottom	0	0%	0	0%	0
Subtotal: Vendor 001			131.9	100	394.4	100	246.6

Class	Sub-class	Description	Sales $	%	Stock $	%	OO $
20	200	fashion top	26.1	30.1%	56.1	24.6%	31.9
40	200	basic pj top	60.5	69.9%	171.9	75.4%	13.0
Subtotal: Vendor 001			86.6	100	228	100	44.9

Vendor: 002

Class	Sub-class	Description	Sales $	%	Stock $	%	OO $
20	100	fashion pj bottom	9.1	16.5%	24.7	20.4%	0
40	100	basic pj bottom	45.9	83.5%	96.4	79.6%	31.4
Subtotal: Vendor 002			55.0	100	121.1	100	31.4

Vendor: 002

Class	Sub-class	Description	Sales $	%	Stock $	%	OO $
20	200	fashion pj top	0	0%	0	0%	0
40	200	basic pj top	45.4	100%	66.4	100%	39.4
Subtotal: Vendor 002			45.4	100	66.4	100	39.4

Questions Based on the Vendor-by-Class Report

Use the Vendor-by-Class Report to answer the following questions. If you need to recall stock-to-sales analysis, refer back to Chapter 4.

1. Which vendor(s) did not have a basic pajama bottom classification?

   _____

2. Which subclass had the highest sales? What were the sales?

   _____

3. Which subclass had the lowest sales? What were the sales?

   _____

4. Which vendor had the highest sales? In which class were the majority of the sales?

   _____

5. Which vendor had the lowest sales? In which class were the majority of the sales?

   _____

6. Are fashion or basic styles of night shirts the most popular?

   _____

7. By how many dollars did basic robes outsell fashion robes?

   _____

8. Overall, are basic or fashion pajama bottoms the most popular?

   _____

9. In which categories are there balanced stock-to-sales ratios? Why?

   _____

10. In which areas (class & subclass), is more stock needed to support sales?

    _____

    _____

    _____

11. Where might it be acceptable to have a large sales percent on a very low stock percent? In this instance, a holiday might be very close to ending.

    _____

12. What categories (subclass) are responsible for 47.6% of the total business in this report? Almost half of the sales are generated in these subclasses.

    _____

13. For each of the following, make a recommendation for the categories RTV/Mdwn or Order, and the appropriate dollar amount.

Example:

In the first question, you must use Vendor 1 because it is the only vendor that has a comparison in this category. Vendor 2 only has basic pajama tops. You will create a stock-to-sales chart, like the one on the following page, to get the answer. The total stock available for this vendor is $228.0. Assuming that this vendor was bought to the original stock plan, we can apply the % Sales to this number to get the ideal stock value. Class 20, Subclass 200 is shown in the example below.

Total Stock $228.0 × 30.1% = $68.6 Ideal Stock

Ideal Stock $68.6 − Actual Stock $56.1 = $12.5 Order

Class	Subclass	% Sales	Stock	Ideal Stock	TV or Order
20	200	30.1%	$56.1	$68.6	$12.5 Order
20	400	69.9%	$171.9	$159.4	−$12.5 RTV

This is the example for Class 20, Subclass 400.

Total Stock $228.0 × 69.9% = $159.4 Ideal Stock

Ideal Stock $159.4 − Actual Stock $171.9 = $12.5 RTV

Fill in the chart below using the stock-to-sales method demonstrated above. If you need a review of stock-to-sales, see Chapter 4.

Class	Subclass	RTV/Mdwn	Order
20	200		$12.5
40	200	−$12.5	
20	100		
40	100		
20	300	40	300
20	400		
40	400		
20	500		
40	400		
60	500		
20	600		
40	600		
60	600		

14. What are the major areas of opportunity, based on the chart created in question 13?

_____

_____

15. What are the areas of liability, or areas where we are overstocked, based on current selling? Refer to the chart created in question 13.

_____

_____

_____

Pinpointing Opportunities and Liabilities

Once you have pinpointed areas of opportunity, you can use the Weekly Style Summary to determine the styles that were responsible for the classification sales. You can then decide which styles should be reordered. You may also determine which styles in that classification are poor performers, and then negotiate an early markdown on these styles with the vendor. The vendor, in some cases, may allow a return to vendor (RTV) if the color or fit is poor, or significantly differs from the market sample or description. As a buyer, you must always be aware of actual style versus the style you originally saw, or that was described to you during market week. Often, your vendor representative has not been alerted to a problem with a style's color or fit. You may be the first to discover this problem, with the help of a store associate. This is why it is extremely important to develop strong relationships with key selling associates and managers, who are in the actual stores.

Vendor-by-Class Reports are an excellent way to determine bigger areas of opportunity, both within a department and at the vendor level. Next, you can use the Weekly Style Summary to narrow down on opportunities even further.

After you have seen the big picture at the style, vendor, and classification level, you can look at selling by location to understand which regions and stores prefer particular styles.

By-Location Sales Report

The **By-Location Sales Report** includes sales, stock, and on order, by style, for all store locations. The sales are often shown for the week, month, and season. A total summary of sales, stock, and on order are shown at the bottom of the report. Sales and stock percent to total is also available for comparison on this report. This enables the buyer to determine if the right amount of stock is on hand in each store, based on the current rate of sale.

The By-Location Sales Report can be used to:

- Determine the reorders by style and location.
- Check the on order by style and location.
- Make sure that top A and B stores are adequately stocked, by style.
- Plan future fashion orders by classification subtotals, at the store level.
- Determine which stores have zero sales on new styles. This may indicate that new styles have not yet been placed on the selling floor.
- Determine the Weeks of Supply by store, based on current selling.
- Write basic booster orders by store, for big POS sale events, or strong holiday selling periods. These may be in addition to automatic replenishment orders submitted by the allocator.

Like the other reports, the By-Location Sales Report is quite long, so a one-page example has been shown on the following page. This report also includes a summary page by class and vendor, although it is not shown in this example. The summary page is useful for determining how a particular store sold a fashion style when planning future fashion purchases. Some store locations typically sell fashion goods better than others.

It would be advantageous for a buyer of a small chain to create this type of report, if it is not already produced by the retailer. This is a helpful tool in planning future purchases and also in the weekly analysis of sales and inventory by store location.

Review the By-Location Sales Report that follows. What information is provided in this report that is not on any of the previous reports mentioned?

_____

_____

_____

Take a moment to review the basic abbreviations used in the By-Location Sales Report.

Key for Headings

WTD = week-to-date	MTD = month-to-date	OO = on order
OH = on hand	Sales % and Stock % (are % to Total calculations)	

BY-LOCATION REPORT

Vendor #	Style #	Description
1	5005	blu check bottom

Sales

Stock

Store #	WTD Sales $	WTD Sales %	MTD Sales $	MTD Sales %	STD Sales $	STD Sales %		OH Stock $	Stock %	OO
1	0.8	2.8%	3.0	2.7%	40.6	2.8%		2.5	3.0%	4.8
2	0.7	2.5%	3.1	2.8%	36.6	2.5%		2.1	2.6%	2.2
3	0.2	0.7%	0.6	0.5%	1.6	0.1%		0.3	0.4%	0.1
4	0.1	0.4%	0.7	0.6%	5.1	0.3%		0.5	0.6%	0.2
5	0.6	2.1%	2.0	1.8%	31	2.1%		1.7	2.1%	3.0
6	0.4	1.4%	1.7	1.5%	20.8	1.4%		1.4	1.7%	2.1
7	0.9	3.2%	3.7	3.3%	46.5	3.2%		3.0	3.7%	5.1
8	0.5	1.8%	2.1	1.9%	25.7	1.8%		1.5	1.8%	0.2
9	0.8	2.8%	3.4	3.0%	41	2.8%		2.4	2.9%	4.1
10	0.7	2.5%	3.0	2.7%	36.1	2.5%		2.0	2.4%	4.5
11	1.0	3.5%	3.8	3.4%	52.5	3.6%		2.7	3.3%	6.5
12	0.1	0.4%	0.4	0.4%	5.6	0.4%		0.1	0.1%	0.3
13	1.3	4.6%	5.1	4.5%	70.1	4.8%		4.2	5.1%	7.9
14	0.4	1.4%	1.4	1.2%	20.4	1.4%		1.0	1.2%	2.1
15	0.6	2.1%	2.0	1.8%	31.9	2.2%		1.5	1.8%	3.2
16	0.3	1.1%	1.5	1.3%	15.8	1.1%		1.1	1.3%	1.0
17	0.4	1.4%	1.7	1.5%	20.1	1.4%		1.2	1.5%	2.9
18	0.2	0.7%	0.6	0.5%	10.1	0.7%		0.4	0.5%	2.4
19	0.9	3.2%	3.3	2.9%	46	3.2%		2.7	3.3%	5.1
20	0.8	2.8%	3.0	2.7%	41.9	2.9%		2.1	2.6%	4.9
21	0.7	2.5%	3.0	2.7%	37.2	2.6%		2.4	2.9%	4.2
22	0.7	2.5%	2.7	2.4%	36.1	2.5%		2.1	2.6%	3.7
23	1.0	3.5%	3.9	3.5%	52.8	3.6%		3.1	3.8%	5.8
24	1.2	4.3%	4.7	4.2%	62.8	4.3%		4.0	4.9%	7.1
25	0.5	1.8%	2.1	1.9%	25.4	1.7%		1.6	1.9%	3.1
26	0.4	1.4%	1.5	1.3%	20.4	1.4%		1.1	1.3%	2.5
27	0.7	2.5%	2.9	2.6%	36.4	2.5%		2.2	2.7%	4.6
28	0.6	2.1%	2.2	2.0%	31.2	2.1%		1.7	2.1%	3.1
29	0.3	1.1%	1.0	0.9%	15.1	1.0%		0.4	0.5%	1.0
30	0.8	2.8%	3.0	2.7%	41.9	2.9%		2.1	2.6%	2.0
31	0.8	2.8%	3.4	3.0%	41	2.8%		2.7	3.3%	2.4
32	1.0	3.5%	4.1	3.6%	51.8	3.6%		3.4	4.1%	3.0
33	0.3	1.1%	1.5	1.3%	15.8	1.1%		1.0	1.2%	2.5
34	0.3	1.1%	1.3	1.2%	15.7	1.1%		0.9	1.1%	1.9
35	1.4	5.0%	5.8	5.2%	71.5	4.9%		4.0	4.9%	8.5
36	1.1	3.9%	4.5	4.0%	57.9	4.0%		3.0	3.7%	2.8
37	0.6	2.1%	2.1	1.9%	31.6	2.2%		1.5	1.8%	3.7
38	0.7	2.5%	2.9	2.6%	36	2.5%		1.9	2.3%	4.0
39	0.9	3.2%	3.7	3.3%	46.5	3.2%		2.4	2.9%	5.9
40	0.4	1.4%	1.4	1.2%	20.9	1.4%		0.5	0.6%	3.6
41	0.3	1.1%	1.0	0.9%	15.1	1.0%		0.6	0.7%	1.4
42	0.5	1.8%	2.1	1.9%	26.4	1.8%		1.7	2.1%	3.8
43	0.3	1.1%	1.4	1.2%	15.9	1.1%		0.8	1.0%	1.1
44	1.0	3.5%	4.1	3.6%	52.5	3.6%		2.6	3.2%	5.4

Total										
Style	28.2	100%	112.4	100%	1457.3	100%		82.1	100%	149.7

Questions Based on the By-Location Sales Report

In the box below are basic facts that accompany the **By-Location Sales** Report.

> - "A" stores are those with STD sales % of 4% or higher.
> - "B" stores are those with STD sales % of 3% or higher.
> - There are a total of 44 stores for this report.
> - The report shows the categories Sales and On Hands for only one style, style #5005.

Using the **By Location Sales** Report, determine the answers to the following problems.

1. According to STD sales information, which are the A-volume stores?

   _____

2. According to STD sales information, which are the B-volume stores?

   _____

3. Of the A and B stores, which are understocked, according to the stock-to-sales ratio?

   _____

4. Of the A and B stores, which stores are overstocked, according to the stock-to-sales ratio?

   _____

5. Are the STD sales percents for the A and B stores consistent with the WTD sales percents?

   _____

6. Find the weeks of supply for the A stores, based on the WTD sales $, OH stock $, and the OO $. (Based on your On Hand and On Order categories, how many weeks of supply do you have for each store?)

   _____

   _____

7. Based on current on hand stock $, write an order to get the A and B stores to an adequate stock level based on MTD sales %. You must subtract what they have on hand, minus ideal stock, to determine the order.

   _____

8. Using the MTD sales % and comparing it to the stock %, where would you recommend a markdown or return to vendor, for the A and B stores only?

   _____

9. Comparing WTD sales % to STD sales % in the A and B stores, which stores have selling last week that has slowed, based on sales trend for the season?

   _____

10. In all stores, which stores have picked up in sales trend versus the season average?

    _____

These are just a few examples of how the buyer uses this report.

As mentioned previously, at the end of each vendor's individual style pages there is a subtotals page for the total vendor. This page would look identical but, instead of style selling, would include total vendor on hands and sales by location. This is very useful information for planning future orders.

In addition, there are classification and vendor subtotal pages. For example, all of the style selling for fashion pajama bottoms from Vendor 1 would be grouped together on a subtotals page at the end of the section. This information could be used to plan next year's buy for fashion pajama bottoms at the vendor level, assuming that sales next year would be similar to this year's.

The four reports you have reviewed in this chapter are the core reports used to determine selling and stock opportunities and liabilities. This usually takes most of Monday to complete and analyze sufficiently. Several things can be learned from the previous week of selling, and should be used to prioritize actions for the coming week.

A quick and efficient way to prioritize is to base actions on dollar volume. Execution of plans can follow a logical approach, such as by estimated dollar return on investment.

- What are my hot sellers?
- From which vendors are my biggest sales coming?
- What are my key product classifications?
- Which styles and classifications have high margins?

Buyers will contact these vendors first, and adjust replenishment and fashion orders accordingly.

- Where can I clean up unproductive stock?
- Which vendors are due to take fashion markdowns?

A buyer then contacts these vendors to negotiate markdowns or returns to vendor, if applicable.

A buyer typically spends the first half of the day reviewing the reports that deal with sales and inventory. Vendors who are effective usually request a copy of their selling results from the buyer on Monday. The second half of the day includes a careful analysis of markdowns. In the next chapter you will have the opportunity to plan, track, and analyze markdowns.

Summary

In this chapter, you were able to view four different reports and see how they are used. Monday morning was emphasized as a day when the buyer analyzes last week's performance and creates an action plan for the week ahead. The buyer starts with analysis at the style level, using the Weekly Style Summary. A Best Seller Report, or recap of best-selling styles and emerging trends, is created using the Weekly Style Summary. This recap is used by senior management to communicate to the stores the key areas of business and to determine where future funding should be allocated.

The Vendor-by-Class Report is then used to determine, by classification and vendor, where sales and inventory levels are out of balance. At a glance, the buyer can determine where funds should be shifted to best serve the current trends and provide the best customer satisfaction.

Finally, the By-Location Sales Report is used to analyze sales, stock, and on order by store location. Stock-to-sales analysis is used to determine, by store location, where inventory is out of balance based on the current rate of sale. It is also easy to determine, through this report, which stores have not placed new deliveries on the selling floor. At the end of each season, the buyer uses this report to determine how future orders for fashion goods should be placed.

Buyers begin inputting orders upon their return from market week

Source: © Peter Atkins/Fotolia

MONDAY MORNING REPORTS (MARKDOWNS)

CHAPTER OBJECTIVES

- Describe the importance of taking timely markdowns and accounting for them in the month that they occur.
- Review the reasons for taking both POS and permanent markdowns.
- Explain why the creation and vendor negotiation of a POS sale event calendar is essential to the buyer's success.
- Determine the amount of a POS and permanent markdown based on current inventory levels and sales.
- Summarize the components of the Markdown Report and how it is used by the buyer.
- Establish the usefulness of the Markdown Update and how vendor allowance increases the buyer's overall profitability.

13

After reviewing sales and the variety of reports that determine the appropriate steps a buyer must take in order to maximize opportunities, you now have the chance to further investigate markdowns and their relevance to the buyer's business. As we have seen in previous chapters, the degree to which a buyer has mastered record keeping and strategically planned his/her business helps determine the overall health of the business. While sales determine the overall strategy and plan of action the buyer must immediately take, markdowns determine the overall profitability of the business, for which vendor contribution is essential.

How Are Markdown Reports Used by the Buyer?

The following reports are designed to guide you through a buyer's thinking process, while providing you with a basic report template for analysis. These reports, like all sales reports previously described, are simply examples of the types of reports many buying offices use. These reports may be altered, based on the type of business being analyzed and the retailer's preferences. Many new computer programs have been designed that suggest to buyers the types and the timing of markdowns, based on factors such as sell thru and comparison of style information. However, computer applications must be interpreted and are never fail proof. A buyer must use sound business judgment, coupled with instinct and an understanding of customers, to ensure success and profitability.

POS and Permanent Markdown Review

Markdowns are a reduction in an item's retail ticket price, either temporarily or permanently, due to slow selling or the need to drive sales for a period of time.

In some cases, buyers may take markdowns to make room for new merchandise, although this is not always the most strategic approach. Markdowns should be taken due to the obvious need to drive sales, and the slowing of an item's popularity, which is determined by sales and sell thru. The two types of markdowns frequently taken are permanent markdowns and point-of-sale markdowns. A permanent markdown is often referred to as a perm, while a point-of-sale markdown may be referred to as a POS.

A point-of-sale markdown is a temporary reduction in the selling price of an item, for a specified amount of time. Markdowns are only accrued if the item sells, because this is not a permanent reduction in the retail ticket price.

A popular example would be a 25% off sale on new bathing suits, over Memorial Day weekend. After the Memorial Day weekend is over, these bathing suits will scan at the register at the original ticket price.

A permanent markdown is a permanent reduction in the ticket retail of an item. The actual retail value of the item is permanently reduced the moment that the perm is processed. These are usually taken on fashion items when their sales have slowed and their shelf life has come to an end.

Unlike POS markdowns, the dollar markdown on a perm is taken up front; no items need to sell for the markdown to accrue. For example, at the end of July, bathing suits have become broken in size and are at the end of their fashion life cycle for the season. A buyer at this time might decide to redline these items, and permanently reduce the retail ticket price. If the original ticket price for bathing suits was $60.00, the buyer might take them to $30.00 to sell thru the remaining pieces and make room for fall merchandise.

The term *red tag* simply refers to crossing out the old ticket price of $60.00 and writing the new retail ticket price of $30.00 over it, with a red pen. Many retailers still do this today, but the color of the writing may differ. As the sales associate is retagging the items, ownership in the item is concurrently changed to the new ticket retail of $30.00.

For the buyer, this means a reduction in his/her total inventory, based on the number of units owned at the time of the perm. If the number of units owned by the buyer at the time of the perm is large, this will create a substantial increase in the buyer's open-to-buy.

Why, then, would a buyer not just take perms in order to increase his/her open-to-buy, if he/she was overbought one month?

Markdowns Erode the Positive Effects of Markup

This is where markup must be considered. Remember that markup is simply the difference between the cost and retail of an item. When a buyer takes a perm, the reduction in the ticket retail compared to the cost creates a much smaller markup structure. For example, if a buyer takes a perm of 50% on an item that originally had a 50% markup, he/she will make no money on the item at the reduced price. Assume the cost of a bathing suit was $15.00, and the original ticket retail price was $30.00. The item was then reduced 50%, to a new red tag ticket retail of $15.00. The buyer is no longer making any money on this item.

Planning for Markdowns

Both types of markdowns require careful planning and analysis by the buyer. In many buying offices, a time frame for reducing fashion groups or items may be three months, or less, if the item or group has insufficient sales. A good question to ask, as a new buyer, would be what the average time frame is for taking fashion markdowns for a specific department. In many departments, specific vendors have promotional events, or POS sales, at the same time every year. A new buyer might ask for the vendor list of POS sale events planned for the current season. If a calendar of these events has not yet been created, it would be advantageous for the new buyer to create such a document.

Keeping a History of POS Sale Events

A POS sale event calendar may include:

- The vendor's name
- The product on sale
- The timeframe for the POS markdown
- The actual POS markdown %, or promotion
- The dates of the promotion last year (LY), if applicable
- The anticipated units and/or dollars sold from each event
- Advertising medium, if it is advertised
- A copy of the advertisement, if applicable

An example of one vendor sale event is provided on the following page. For a large department, several vendors will have different promotions throughout the season. If accurate record keeping is maintained, a history of the markdowns that were needed to obtain last year's sales result is evident. This is extremely important to the planning process of the buyer. If this information is not properly kept, a buyer must sort through tedious Markdown Reports and hypothesize about what exactly happened last year.

An Example of a Vendor Sale Event

TY	LY
Calvin Klein Intimate Sale	Calvin Klein Intimate Sale
POS 25% off	POS 25% off
May 5–8	May 5–10
Direct mail (box)	Direct mail (half a page)
Estimated units sold 1250	Units sold 2500
Estimated dollars sold $62,500	Dollars sold $125,000
Estimated markdown $15,625	Markdown $31,250

A copy of the TY and LY advertisement might be attached here or catalogued in a separate binder, with advertising information for future reference.

This is important because sales and traffic generated from past advertisements must be duplicated TY in order to project the same sales and markdowns as LY. Remember, we use LY history as a basis, or starting point, for this year's projections.

How to Determine the Markdown of a Sale Event

In the previous example, the vendor has decided to run the same 25% POS sale event, but the length of the event has changed. Last year the event ran for six days, while this year the event will only run for three days. The average retail price of the Calvin Klein inventory is $50.00 per unit, both TY and LY.

If 2,500 units were sold last year at an average retail of $50.00, the total sales were $125,000.

2,500 Units Sold × $50.00 Ticket Retail = $125,000 Sales

A straight 25% POS would generate a markdown of $125,000 × 25%, which equals $31,250.

$125,000 Sales × 25% POS Markdown = $31,250 Markdowns

This year the event is only three days, so the buyer has estimated average daily sales of 417 units per day, based on LY.

$$\frac{\text{LY Units Sold 2,500}}{\text{6 Days}} = \text{416.6 units per day, or 417 units per day}$$

Unit sales of 417 per day times a three-day event equals approximately 1,250 units sold TY.

If 1,250 units sold at an average retail price of $50.00, it would equal $62,500 sold.

1,250 Units Sold × $50.00 Ticket Retail = $62,500 Sales

At a 25% POS markdown, the markdown will equal $15,625, or $62,500 times 25%.

$62,500 Sales × 25% POS Markdown = $15,625 Markdowns

Calculating a 25% POS Markdown at .333

Now consider that a 10% off coupon has been included for the event in a direct mail advertisement for which Calvin Klein is *not exempt*.

Buyers often calculate a 25% off markdown at .333 instead of .25, to allow for any other coupons or promotions that may be advertised during this event. If this were the case, the projected markdown would increase to $20,813, or

$62,500 Sales × 333 Markdown = $20,813 Markdowns

Advertising Changes

As we have discussed, it is very important for the buyer to anniversary last year's vendor agreements and advertising to ensure the same or better sales results. Anniversary means that the buyer must offer or obtain what was generated last year. Of course, beating last year is preferred.

In this example, something else has changed as well. The advertising space allocated for the Calvin Klein Intimate 25% POS event has been reduced from a half a page in the direct mailer, to one box. This may also negatively impact the sales for this event. This is something that can only be projected based on previous experience. Another consideration for this sale may be whether or not the vendor agreed last year to help pay for the advertisement. If the vendor had contributed to advertising, this should be noted here, or in a separate advertising report. Again, an emphasis on accurate record keeping is essential to the success of the buyer's business.

To understand the calculation of both permanent and POS markdowns, the following problems have been created. Take a moment to review this chapter, particularly the calculation of the **CK POS Sale Event**, before starting to work through these problems.

POS and Permanent Markdown Problems

1. A buyer has 1,500 bathing suits at a $45.00 retail ticket price. The buyer has planned to permanently reduce these bathing suits to $29.99. What will the markdown be?

   _____

   By how much will the buyer's inventory be reduced, once the markdown has been taken?

   _____

2. A buyer has an average inventory of $300,000 in holiday sweaters. The retail ticket price of a holiday sweater is $75.00. The buyer has planned a POS sale event of 50% off for the week before Christmas. If she projects selling 3,500 units, what will be the sales volume generated from this event, and the value of the markdown?

   _____

   How many units will be left after the sale event?

   _____

3. A buyer has several unproductive denim styles left after a Back-to-School event. He plans on taking these denim styles permanently to $19.99 from $45.00. If the original ticket retail of these styles was $45.00 and the cost was $15.00, what was the original markup on these items?

   _____

What will the new markup be on these styles after the permanent markdown?

_____

4. The dress buyer has several junior prom dresses that did not sell, and it is now July. What type of markdown should this buyer use, a permanent or POS markdown?

_____

5. The coat buyer has 3,400 units of leather coats left after the January end-of-season sale. They have already been permanently reduced from $185.00 to $99.99. If the buyer wants to take another permanent reduction of 50%, what will the new redlined retail and total markdowns equal?

_____

_____

6. This year's 50% POS beach towel sale event will run from July 1st through July 6th and include 4,500 towels regularly priced at $15.00 each. Last year's event ran from July 1st through July 4th and generated $80,000 worth of sales. What are your projections for this year's sales and total markdowns, based on last year's performance?

_____

_____

7. On November 1st, all Halloween candy that was not sold at full price will be permanently reduced by 50%, with an additional 25% POS sale. If the candy buyer owns 20,000 units of a particular candy, at an average ticket retail of $4.50 per unit, what is the total value of the candy before the reduction?

_____

What is the total value of the permanent markdown?

_____

What is the POS markdown if the buyer sells 15,000 units?

_____

Now that you have completed some sample problems for computing both permanent and point-of-sale markdowns, you will have the opportunity to review the Markdown Report.

The Markdown Report

The Markdown Report includes both types of markdowns, by day and by vendor. This report allows the buyer to obtain precise information regarding the markdowns accrued within a department, and it is an important negotiation tool. In many cases, a buyer can tell a vendor specifically what types of markdowns the vendor is responsible for with a by-day breakdown. In addition, the buyer can show the vendor which classification of goods is responsible for each markdown.

For example, if a permanent markdown was taken in novelty holiday sweaters, the exact markdown accrued is documented in the Markdown Report. This serves as appropriate evidence and supporting documentation that the buyer did in fact take the markdown, while allowing the vendor to see the markdown value.

The following information demonstrates, at a glance, what information may be obtained from the Markdown Report.

What Information Is Available on the Markdown Report?

- Both permanent and POS markdowns by day, week, vendor, and classification
- Total permanent markdowns for the week, by vendor and classification
- Total POS markdowns for the week, by vendor and classification
- Total markdowns for the month may be obtained by adding all vendor totals for the number of weeks within a month

The Markdown Report on pages 226–27 is an example of a much larger report. Only three vendors are shown to enable you to more clearly understand the information derived from this report. The vendors considered are numbered 10, 11, and 12. Review each vendor's permanent and POS markdowns by day and by week, and then compare their results.

Which vendors had the most POS markdowns versus permanent markdowns?

_____

The classifications are identical to those in Chapter 12, where we examined the Vendor-by-Class Report.

> Classification 20 = Fashion goods
> Classification 40 = Basic goods
> Classification 60 = Novelty/holiday goods

Review the vendor classification results carefully, and then try to answer the following questions.

- What classifications of goods had the highest markdowns within each vendor?
- Was there a distinguishable trend?
- If these were the only vendors in a buyer's department, how would the buyer determine the total markdowns for the week?
- What totals or subtotals are important for determining this number?

Remember that everything flows back to the buyer's open-to-buy, and as markdowns accrue that are not planned for, the dollars available to spend on new inventory are negatively affected. What types of markdowns are more easily controlled? What types of markdowns would you not expect to be over the original planned figure? Review the following report, and then answer the questions on the following pages. Circle or highlight important subtotals as you review the report.

Markdown Report

VND # 10

		S	M	T	W	TH	F	S	Total POS	Total Perms	Total Mdwns
Class: 20	POS	1.0	0.1	0.1	0.2	0.2	0.5	1.0	3.1		3.1
	PERM	0.0	0.0	4.3	0.0	0.0	0.0	0.0		4.3	4.3
	Subtotal	1.0	0.1	4.4	0.2	0.2	0.5	1.0			7.4
Class: 40	POS	1.3	0.1	0.2	0.1	0.2	1.0	2.0	4.9		4.9
	PERM	0.0	0.0	1.0	0.0	0.0	0.0	0.0		1.0	1.0
	Subtotal	1.3	0.1	1.2	0.1	0.2	1.0	2.0			5.9
Class: 60	POS	1.7	0.2	0.1	0.1	0.2	1.4	2.4	6.1		
	PERM	0.0	0.0	2.3	0.0	0.0	0.0	0.0		2.3	
	Subtotal	1.7	0.2	2.4	0.1	0.2	1.4	2.4			8.4
Total Vendor # 10		4.0	0.4	8.0	0.4	0.6	2.9	5.4	14.1	7.6	21.7

VND # 11

		S	M	T	W	TH	F	S	Total POS	Total Perms	Total Mdwns
Class: 20	POS	0.1	0.0	0.0	0.0	0.1	0.2	0.5	0.9		0.9
	PERM	0.0	0.0	3.6	0.0	0.0	0.0	0.0		3.6	3.6
	Subtotal	0.1	0.0	3.6	0.0	0.1	0.2	0.5			4.5
Class: 40	POS	0.3	0.0	0.0	0.0	0.0	0.6	1.2	2.1		2.1
	PERM	0.0	0.0	1.3	0.0	0.0	0.0	0.0		1.3	
	Subtotal	0.3	0.0	1.3	0.0	0.0	0.6	1.2			3.4
Class: 60	POS	0.9	0.0	0.0	0.0	0.0	1.0	1.5	3.4		3.4
	PERM	0.0	0.0	1.7	0.0	0.0	0.0	0.0		1.7	
	Subtotal	0.9	0.0	1.7	0.0	0.0	1.0	1.5			5.1
Total Vendor # 11		1.3	0.0	6.6	0.0	0.1	1.8	3.2	6.4	6.6	13.0

VND # 12

Class: 20										
POS	0.0	0.0	0.1	0.0	0.1	0.3	0.7	1.2		
PERM	0.0	0.0	4.8	0.0	0.0	0.0	0.0		4.8	
Subtotal	0.0	0.0	4.9	0.0	0.1	0.3	0.7			6.0
Class: 40										
POS	0.2	0.0	0.0	0.1	0.1	0.8	1.7	2.9		
PERM	0.0	0.0	2.0	0.0	0.0	0.0	0.0		2.0	
Subtotal	0.2	0.0	2.0	0.1	0.1	0.8	1.7			4.9
Class: 60										
POS	0.5	0.1	0.0	0.0	0.0	1.4	2.1	4.1		
PERM	0.0	0.0	1.1	0.0	0.0	0.0	0.0		1.1	
Subtotal	0.5	0.1	1.1	0.0	0.0	1.4	2.1			5.2
Total Vendor # 12	0.7	0.1	8.0	0.1	0.2	2.5	4.5	8.2	7.9	16.1

Markdown Report Questions

Answer the following questions regarding the Markdown Report provided on the previous pages.

8. Which vendor had the *highest* total markdowns for the week, and what were their markdowns?

   _____

9. Which vendor had the *lowest* markdowns for the week, and what were their markdowns?

   _____

10. Which classification of goods had the highest markdowns across all vendors?

    _____

    Why might this be?

    _____

11. Within Vendor 11, which classification of goods had the highest markdowns, and what were they?

    _____

    Was this consistent with the overall vendor classification trend?

    _____

12. If these were all the vendors within the department, what would the total markdowns for the week be?

    _____

    What is the easiest way to determine this answer?

    _____

    What would the total POS markdowns be for this department?

    _____

    What would the total permanent markdowns be for this department?

    _____

13. Overall, which day of the week had the highest total markdowns?

    _____

    Do you think this is consistent with sales trends?

    _____

14. Permanent markdowns are often processed on the same day every week by retailers. This is due to a deadline for entering the markdowns into the computer system, and it allows for the printing of the price change at the store level.

    On what day of the week are permanent markdowns taken for this particular retailer?

    _____

15. For Vendor 12, on what day of the week are the most markdowns taken?

    _____

    Within which classification of goods are the most markdowns taken?

    _____

16. All vendors have permanent markdowns taken in classification 40. Why might permanent markdowns be taken in this particular classification?

    _____

The Markdown Update

In previous chapters, you learned the importance of markdowns as they pertain to sales. Many retailers do not already have this information coordinated in a report that allows for an adequate comparison of both figures, so they must create their own. The following report may be referred to as the Markdown Update. It is an example of how buyers may put together the individual pieces of information derived from various reports. The Markdown Update highlights markdowns and sales by day and week, while allowing for a comparison of TY, LY, and Plan.

Importance of Markdown Percent to This Report

The Markdown Update also provides a line that derives the markdown percent or markdown rate. As mentioned previously, it is the markdown percent, not the actual markdown dollars, that is most important to a buyer.

$$\frac{Markdown\ \$}{Sales\ \$} = Markdown\ Percent\ or\ Markdown\ Rate$$

As a department's sales increase, markdowns may also increase, as long as the markdown percent remains favorable or within the planned markdown percent. Additionally, if a buyer's actual markdown percent is higher than plan, gross margin may start to diminish. This is why vendor contribution and partnership in regard to markdowns is vital.

$$Gross\ Margin = Net\ Sales - Cost\ of\ Goods\ Sold$$

Vendor Allowances (VAs)

In this report you will see a total called "VAs". This is a vendor allowance or a markdown allowance. This is the difference between the actual markdowns accrued and the markdown plan, which includes the markdown percent. The total of the VAs is the amount needed from vendors for the buyer to make their planned markdown percent. As you will see, this is a number that is always fluctuating, based on sales. This is why a Markdown Update is essential to the buyer's business. Continually comparing the results of sales and markdowns to the plan allows buyers to partner with vendors throughout the season. If buyers wait until the end of the season to ask vendors for markdown contributions, the amount of the contributions may be overwhelming and the chance of receiving them low. The end of the season also comes at a time when vendors are being asked for markdown allowance from multiple buyers.

> **Note:** It is always advantageous to resolve markdown issues as they occur, on a month-by-month basis.

What Information Is Available on the Markdown Update?

- Actual TY results for sales and markdowns, by day
- Actual TY markdown percent, by day
- TY, LY, and planned sales, markdowns, and markdown percent for each week
- Total POS and permanent markdowns, by week
- The vendor allowance, or VA, needed to obtain the planned markdown percent for each week

Directions for Reading the Markdown Update

The Markdown Update that follows includes an example of one five-week month. It is usually updated on a weekly basis, and is compiled from other reports. For a single store buyer, creating something similar to the Markdown Update would be advantageous. It is updated weekly, with the assumption that vendors will be contacted *each week*, with their individual markdown results. Most vendors require a weekly update on sales figures; this is the perfect opportunity for a buyer to discuss markdowns, as well. Individual markdowns by vendor and classification can usually be obtained from the Markdown Report.

As you review the Markdown Update, pay particular attention to TY, LY, and Planned results, as compared to the VA for each week. Last year's sales and markdowns have been provided from last year's reports. The planned sales and markdowns are taken from the buyer's business plan for the season. The by-day markdowns are actual results this year, for the month. The subtotal refers to the total markdowns taken each week. It is restated next to the VA in order to clearly restate the markdown total, compared to the VA needed to reach the planned markdown percent.

> **Note:** *Markdowns in every week except Week #3 exceed last year. This is partly because sales were higher; thus, the markdowns are higher. However, in Week #1 the actual markdowns this year are drastically higher than last year. This is an example of how calendar shifts, and specifically holiday shifts from year to year, can dramatically affect the Markdown Update.*

Questions have been provided on pages 230–32 in order to guide you through the thought process of the buyer as he or she formulates this report. Try to analyze the report before answering the questions.

Questions to Consider in Your Analysis

- How is the VA, or vendor allowance, calculated?
- What are the planned markdowns each week, and the planned markdown percent?
- In what weeks have sales and markdowns exceeded last year results?
- Are more POS or permanent markdowns taken this month? Why?
- What are the total markdowns taken this month, and the total VA needed to meet the planned markdown percent?

Markdown Update Questions

Answer the following questions using the Markdown Update.

17. What were the total markdowns TY, in week 1 of this month?

_____

Were these markdowns above or below Plan?

_____

Were these markdowns above or below LY?

_____

18. Are the markdowns, as a percentage of sales or the markdown rate, in line with the planned markdown rate for week 1?

_____

19. Did the actual sales meet the planned sales goal in week 1?

_____

20. Did the actual sales exceed LY sales in week 1?

Markdown Update

Week		For the Week			By Day Markdowns							Total POS	Total Perms	Sub-Total	VAs
		TY	PLAN	LY	S	M	T	W	TH	F	S				
Week 1	Date														
	Sales	550	576	530	88	49.5	44	66	77	99	126.5	135	30	165	136
	Mdwn	165	29	55	20	5	30	6	20	35	49				
	% to Sales	30.0%	5.0%	10.4%	22.7%	10.1%	68.2%	9.1%	26.0%	35.4%	38.7%				
Week 2	Date														
	Sales	630	628	577	100.8	56.7	50.4	75.6	88.2	113.4	144.9	94	1	95	63.5
	Mdwn	95	31.5	52	15	8	1	12	14	20	25				
	% to Sales	15.1%	5.0%	9.0%	14.9%	14.1%	2.0%	15.9%	15.9%	17.6%	17.3%				
Week 3	Date														
	Sales	665	660	605	106.4	59.9	53.2	79.8	93.1	119.7	152.9	40	0	40	7
	Mdwn	40	33	60	4	2	0	1	2	13	18				
	% to Sales	6.0%	5.0%	9.9%	3.8%	3.3%	0.0%	1.3%	2.1%	10.9%	11.8%				
Week 4	Date														
	Sales	635	640	586	99.5	57.9	50.8	77.2	86.9	115.9	146.8	78	2	80	48
	Mdwn	80	32	59	10	4.5	2	11	13	18	21.5				
	% to Sales	12.6%	5.0%	10.1%	10.1%	7.8%	3.9%	14.2%	15.0%	15.5%	14.6%				
Week 5	Date														
	Sales	575	560	514.1	92	51.8	46	69	80.5	103.5	132.2	52	0	52	24
	Mdwn	52	28	51	11	4.5	0	6	8.5	9	13				
	% to Sales	9.0%	5.0%	9.9%	12.0%	8.7%	0.0%	8.7%	10.6%	8.7%	9.8%				

21. What is the value of the VA needed to meet the planned markdown percent of 5% in week 1?

_____

22. In week 2, which days of the week was the markdown percent at, or below, the week's total planned markdown percent?

_____

23. In which week was the actual markdown rate TY closest to making the planned markdown rate?

_____

24. In week 3, what do the actual markdowns need to be in order to meet the planned markdown rate, based on the actual sales TY?

_____

25. In which weeks are the actual sales TY higher than the planned sales?

_____

26. If the five weeks provided in the Markdown Update were for the entire month, what would this month's actual sales, markdowns, and markdown rate be?

_____

What would the VA need to be to make the monthly planned markdown rate of 5%?

_____

27. In week 4, what do the actual markdowns need to be to meet the planned markdown rate of 5%, based on actual sales TY?

_____

28. Overall, were more POS or permanent markdowns taken for this month, and what was that total?

_____

29. In which week were the most VAs needed to meet the planned markdown rate?

_____

30. Was the planned markdown rate for each week and the month less than or more than, the markdown rate LY?

_____

31. What are the total VAs needed for the month in order to meet the planned markdown rate of 5%?

_____

32. What were the total markdowns taken this month?

_____

33. In which week was the fewest VAs needed, and why might this be?

_____

_____

Although the Markdown Update contains a lot of information and may take some time to analyze thoroughly, it contains information vital to the health of the buyer's business. Both Markdown Reports were designed to demonstrate what information is most useful to the buyer. In addition, they allow you to see how a report may be created as a tool for making the buyer's job more productive, while providing excellent record keeping for future business planning.

Summary

In this chapter, accurate record keeping and analysis of reports was further emphasized, with a focus on markdowns. You were able to review when POS and permanent markdowns are used, and how to calculate the total markdown when inventory and sales are applied. An example of a POS event calendar demonstrated the importance of TY and LY history of advertisements and sale events.

The Markdown Report provided information on POS and permanent markdowns by vendor, classification, and day. This report is used to determine total markdowns by day and also to support negotiations with vendors. Throughout this chapter, an emphasis was placed on negotiating vendor allowances (VAs) as they accrue (monthly). Buyers who wait until the end of a season to negotiate VAs usually end up with lower gross margins than buyers who negotiate with their vendors monthly. The Markdown Update was an example of a report that is usually created by the buyer to keep track of vendor allowance needs and actual markdown results, as compared to plan. Reaching the desired markdown percent each month is the essential goal of the markdown tracking and planning process.

glossary

% by Class – Units or dollars sold in a particular classification of goods, divided by the department or division's total units or dollars sold.

4th quarter – November, December, and January, looked at as a collective whole.

account executive (vendor) – The individual responsible for selling a manufacturer's line to retailers and negotiating the terms of the sale.

advertising allowance – A monetary contribution made by the vendor or resource to support the retailer's advertising expenses.

advertising allowance – Total Purchase $ × % Vendor Contribution

advertising allowance – Total Units Purchased × $ Contribution

ASN (Advanced Shipping Notice) – A computerized notification of when a basic order will be shipped, with a projected receive date and carton count.

assortment plan – The buyer's mix of appropriate vendors, colors, sizes, and classifications of goods that are needed to achieve planned sales for a season.

automatic replenishment – Basic goods that are reordered through a computerized ordering system.

Average Stock (Average Inventory) – The typical amount of stock that is held in inventory for a specific period of time, usually a season or a year.

Average Stock Formula –

$$\frac{\text{(All BOM Stocks + the last month's EOM Stock)}}{\text{the number of stocks}}$$

basic goods – Classic styles that are reordered on a continual basis through an automatic replenishment system.

Basic Stock Method – A method for planning monthly BOM stocks relative to monthly sales that requires a known turnover and a season sales plan.

best sellers – Styles with a higher than average sell thru and favorable sales volume.

Best-Seller Report – A retail statement compiled by the buyer that includes best-selling styles within a department. It usually includes sales, on hand, and sell thru for the week, month, and season; a summary of top-selling styles and emerging trends within a department, determined by sales volume in dollars and sell thru.

BOM stock (beginning-of-month stock) – The stock value on hand, in dollars, at the start of each month.

bottom-up plan – A method of planning that starts at the SKU level and then works into a total department and company plan.

By-Location Sales Report – A summary of sales, stock, and on order, by style, for all store locations.

cancel date – The last date that a vendor or manufacturer can ship a purchase order before it becomes null and void.

cash discount – A reduction (usually a percentage) applied to purchases for paying an invoice early.

cash wrap – The counter space that holds the cash register.

chargeback – A fee charged to the vendor by the retailer for violation of a shipping standard.

closing inventory – The amount of stock on hand when the profit and loss statement is configured.

comparative sales (Comp %) – Only include sales for stores that have been open an entire year this year, and last year. Also called same-store sales.

cooperative advertising (Ad Co-op) – Vendor contribution or partnership on expenses related to advertising.

copy – The written portion of the advertisement.

Corporate Buying Office – An in-house buying office that places orders across several divisions.

Corporate Matrix – A list of preferred vendors with which a company wishes to do business.

cost of goods sold (COG) – Expenses associated with the actual sale of the merchandise that includes the actual stock cost (purchases), freight, cash discount, and workroom expenses.

COG % of Net Sales – $\dfrac{\text{Cost of Goods Sold \$}}{\text{Net Sales \$}}$

daily flash – A report or online database of retail sales, often comparing sales this year to sales last year. May also include a comparison of actual sales to planned sales.

dating – The amount of time a retailer has to pay for the goods they receive from the vendor.

direct expenses – Costs that directly impact the department of interest.

direct mail – Company-generated advertisements that are mailed to the customer's home.

DUNS number – A universal identification code that is used for billing and payment.

employee discount – The dollar amount of the reduction in an employee-generated retail sale for which a percentage off is applied. It is measured as a percentage of sales.

EOM stock (end-of-month stock) – The stock value on hand, in dollars, at the end of each month.

exclusives – Brands that have the attachment of a celebrity or designer and are only offered at one retailer.

fashion goods – Styles bought for a season that are in line with current trends; styles that are bought in moderation, with the plan that they will sell out within the season or quarter.

fashion order – An order that includes items intended to sell through without being replenished.

flagship store – A store that is located in a large city and does an abnormally higher percentage of business for the company than any other store in the chain.

freight – The total cost of shipping the merchandise to the store.

freight on board (FOB) – When an order is in the process of transit or shipment.

full price – Styles that are currently at the original ticket retail.

gross cost of goods sold – Total Goods at Cost − Closing Inventory

gross margin (GM) – A measure of profitability of an item or classification of goods, after the cost of selling the goods is subtracted: the first measure of profitability; derived by subtracting the cost of goods sold from net sales.

gross margin driven – A focus on profit that aims to generate the highest possible markup on each item.

gross margin formula – Net Sales − Cost of Goods Sold

GM % of Net Sales – $= \dfrac{\text{Gross Margin \$}}{\text{Net Sales \$}}$

gross sales – The total sales achieved before any customer returns or adjustments are accounted for; total company sales before any returns and merchandise credits are calculated.

holiday/seasonal goods – Styles bought for a particular holiday or season with the intention to sell out of them completely, in a limited amount of time.

ideal stock – The optimal stock level indicated by the current rate of sale.

indirect expenses – Costs that are related to the operation of the entire company.

initial markup – The original cost and retail of the merchandise before any reductions have occurred,

intranet – A retailer's internal computer networking system.

inventory – A physical hand count of the merchandise in a store.

jobber – A company that buys old or discontinued merchandise from retailers for a deep discount and sells the merchandise to off-price retailers.

keystone – A 50% markup, or doubling the cost, to obtain the retail price of an item.

liability (stock) – The stock percentage is higher than the sales percentage, indicating a need to reduce the current level of inventory in order to match current sales trends.

LY – Last year.

maintained markup – The final cost and retail at a point in time that reflects any permanent markdowns that have been taken.

markdown – A reduction in the ticket retail price of an item, either permanently or temporarily.

markdown allowance – The vendor agrees to pay for a reduction in the retail price of a product or style; money paid to the retailer by the vendor to cover the cost of a promotional event.

markdown percent (markdown rate) – The value of markdown dollars when compared to sales by day, week, season, or year.

markdown percent formula – $\dfrac{\text{Total MD\$}}{\text{Total Sales\$}}$

markdown percent Excel formula – Total MD$/Total Sales $

Markdown Report – A summary of POS and permanent markdowns by vendor, classification, and day.

Markdown Update – A comparison of actual markdowns and sales versus plan and last year, with a projected vendor allowance to meet the planned markdown percent.

market sheets – Worksheets calculated for each vendor that include a summary of results compared to the buyer's total department results.

market week – Buyers visit vendors in a major market center, where vendors showcase their goods for upcoming seasons and buyers negotiate the terms of the purchase.

mark style – The retailer's style number.

markup – The difference between the cost to the consumer, or ticket retail, and the price paid by the retailer for an item or style; the difference between the cost and retail of an item, for which there is a desired range, based on retail store format and product type.

Markup Formulas

> **When you have retail and cost**
>
> $$\text{markup formula} = \frac{(\text{Retail} - \text{Cost})}{\text{Retail}}$$
>
> markup Excel formula = (Retail − Cost)/Retail
>
> **When you have cost and markup**
>
> The formula is Retail = Cost/(1 − MU%)
>
> **When you have retail and markup**
>
> The formula is Cost = Retail × (1 − MU%)

merchandise overage – The difference between physical and book inventory, when the physical inventory is higher than the book inventory, or system on hands.

merchandise plan – The budget a buyer has planned for the season, or year, that includes sales, stock, and markdowns.

modules – Store groupings or breakdowns, based on sales history.

monthly sales percent (% Sales by Month) – The month's sales compared to total season sales that results in a percentage.

monthly sales percent formula – Monthly Sales ÷ Season Sales

MTD – Month-to-date.

net cost of goods sold – Gross Cost of Goods Sold − Cash Discount

net loss – A negative balance after all company revenue and expenses are considered for a period of time.

net profit – A positive dollar amount that is left after all company revenue and expenses are considered for a period of time.

Net Profit/Loss % of Sales – $\dfrac{\text{Net Profit/Loss \$}}{\text{Net Sales \$}}$

net sales – The sales achieved after all customer returns and adjustments are deducted; the sales that are left after returns and adjustments are calculated.

Net Sales Formula – Gross Sales − Returns and Adjustments

next year's buy – A plan of what the buyer will purchase, in units or dollars, for the coming year.

novelty/holiday goods – Styles that are driven by holidays and seasonality.

obsolete – Merchandise that shows no selling and has not been marked down for over 13 months.

OH – On hand (stock).

on hand (OH) – The number of units or dollar amount of the goods available in stores.

OO – On order (stock).

opening inventory – The stock the retailer started with, for the period of time the profit and loss statement reflects.

open-to-buy (OTB) – The amount of dollars available to purchase new inventory, based on current business trends.

opportunity (stock) – The sales percentage is higher than the stock percentage, indicating a need for additional orders based on current sales trends.

percent change (% Change) – Derived by subtracting LY sales from TY sales, and then dividing by LY sales. This is also referred to as percent increase or decrease.

percent change formula – $\dfrac{(TY - LY)}{LY}$

percent change Excel formula – (TY − LY)/LY

perceived value – The worth of an item or style based on the consumer's opinion of the style's quality and image; the customer's quantifiable opinion of a style's worth.

percent to total (% to Total) – Taking a portion of a business and dividing it by the total business, to determine what percentage it represents to the total. Typically calculated using units or dollars in retail buying.

percent to total formula – $\dfrac{\text{Category of Business}}{\text{Total Business}}$

percent to total Excel formula – (Category of business/Total business)

permanent markdown (perm) – A physical reduction in the ticket retail price and ownership of a style; when the actual owned retail price of an item is reduced, and the cost of the reduction accumulates based on current ownership of that item.

plan – The buyer or company plan for achieving seasonal and yearly business goals.

point of sale markdown (POS) – A temporary reduction in the retail price of an item that does not permanently change the retail value of the item in the retailer's computer system.

POS Sale Event Calendar – A record kept by the buyer of all POS sale events, by vendor, that includes the type of advertisement, the length of the sale, and the actual promotion.

pre-pack – Grouping styles, colors or sizes together under one style number with a minimum quantity purchase, in order to streamline the shipping and tracking of many styles for both vendor and buyer. An example is a predetermined size distribution.

private label – In-house brands.

proactive – A forward thinking approach to business.

profit and loss (P&L) statement – A financial summary of a business that reflects its overall health, for a specific period of time.

proofs – Examples of the advertisement as it will appear in print; includes the photograph and the written commentary.

purchase formula – (EOM Stock + Deductions) – BOM Stock

Purchase Journal (PJ) – A report that lists all purchase orders and summarizes purchase order information by department.

purchase order – A paper or computer document that contains all information regarding the purchase of a style, or many styles, with specific shipping guidelines.

purchases – The amount of inventory the buyer can bring into the store each month.

quarters – Three-month buying cycles.

ROP (run off press) – An advertisement that is placed on the pages of a newspaper.

red tag – Styles that have had a permanent price reduction and have the new ticket retail written over, or next to, the original retail price of the style.

replenishment analyst – The person responsible for inputting, tracking, allocating, and reordering all basic merchandise.

Resident Buying Office – Market specialist; a company that works with retailers to develop new assortments, provide trend forecasting information, and act as a liaison to large manufacturers.

retail buyer – The individual responsible for negotiating the purchase of wholesale goods, for resale to the ultimate consumer.

retail buying – The purchase of a large quantity of wholesale goods, for resale to the ultimate consumer.

Retail $ Sold – The amount of dollars sold at the ticket price.

Return % of Gross Sales – $\dfrac{\text{Returns/Adjustments \$}}{\text{Gross Sales \$}}$

return to vendor (RTV) – The vendor or designer agrees to take back a damaged or unsuccessful style or group of merchandise; merchandise is sent back to the vendor without a penalty to the retailer.

rolling forecast – The update and re-projection of the merchandise plan based on actual results.

sell thru – The total units or dollars sold for a style, divided by the total units received.

sell thru formula – $\dfrac{\text{Units Sold}}{\text{Units Received}}$ or $\dfrac{\text{Dollars Sold}}{\text{Dollars Received}}$

sell thru Excel formula – Units Sold/Units Received

sell thru % – Units sold divided by units received or dollars sold divided by dollars received.

shortage – The difference between a retailer's physical inventory and book inventory, when the physical count is lower than the book inventory, or stock on hand.

silhouette – The shape or outline of an item or style.

ship date – The first date that a vendor or manufacturer can ship a purchase order.

Six-Month Merchandise Plan – The buyer's plan and ongoing record of inventory, sales, and markdowns.

Six-Month Seasons – Fall/winter (August through January), and spring/summer (February through July).

stock-to-sales analysis – A comparison of on-hand inventory to current rate of sale that results in a recommendation for increasing or decreasing current inventory levels, in order to meet sales demand.

stock-to-sales ratio – A method for planning BOM stocks relative to sales, and a calculation that indicates the amount of BOM stock needed to support sales within a month.

stock-to-sales ratio formula – BOM stock divided by the same month's sales.

store planner – The individual responsible for the allocation of space within the retail sales floor, based on sales and gross margin goals. This person usually resides in a retailer's corporate offices.

supplemental order (booster order) – An additional order needed to meet current sales demand.

target market – The individual or group of people that a retailer aims to reach.

total cost of goods sold – Net Cost of Goods Sold – Alterations

Top-down Plan – A method of planning that starts with the total company plan and then breaks it down to the SKU level.

total deductions – Everything that reduces the value of inventory on the merchandise plan. This may include sales, markdowns, return to vendor, shortage, and employee discount.

total expenses – Direct Expenses + Indirect Expenses

total goods at cost – Opening Inventory + Purchases + Freight

total on hand – The quantity of a style, in units or dollars, that is currently available in stores.

total on-hand formula – Total Received – Total Sold

total received – The quantity of a style, in units or dollars, physically taken in by the stores throughout the season, or during another specified period of time.

total received formula – Total Sold + Total On Hand

total sold – The quantity of a style, in units or dollars, that has been purchased by the consumer.

total sold formula – Total Received – Total On Hand

total stock – BOM stock + Purchases on the merchandise plan.

transfer – The movement of merchandise from one store to another, usually based on the ability to sell the merchandise and provide adequate floor space.

trunk show – A private screening of a vendor's seasonal collection that is often held at upscale stores.

turnover – The number of times you buy and sell through an average amount of stock, for a season or year.

turnover formula – $\dfrac{\textbf{Season Sales}}{\textbf{Average Stock}}$

turnover Excel formula – Season Sales / Average Stock

TY – This year.

UCC catalog – A universal computer catalog that contains vendor UPC codes by season.

UPC code – A unit product identification code (number) placed under the bar code of each style that includes the vendor style number and DUNS number.

ultimate consumer – The individual or group that will use or consume the product.

vendor/markdown allowance – Money paid to the retailer by the vendor or manufacturer to cover the cost of a markdown or sale event.

Vendor-by-Class Report – A summary of sales, stock dollars, and percent to total, by vendor, classification, and subclass.

Vendor Merchandise Plan – A breakdown of the Six-Month Merchandise Plan by vendor.

visual merchandiser – The individual responsible for the presentation of goods on the sales floor.

volume – Another word used to describe the amount sold in dollars or units.

volume driven – A sales-driven focus on selling as many of each item as possible.

WTD – Week-to-date.

Weekly Style Summary (By-Style Report) – A summary of sales and inventory levels, by style, for the previous week, the month, and usually the season.

weeks of supply – The number of weeks of inventory left in a particular style, based on that style's current rate of sale.

weeks of supply formula – $\dfrac{\textbf{(On Hand Stock + On Order Stock)}}{\textbf{WTD Sales}}$

weeks of supply Excel formula – (OH + OO) / WTD Sales

workroom and alteration fees – an expense that includes any adjustments to merchandise in order to make it floor-ready

YTD – Year-to-date.

Index

account executives, 28
Ad Co-op (cooperative advertising), 160–165
adjustments, 146–147
advanced shipping notice (ASN), 98
advertising
cooperative, 160–165
new product lines and, 163
planning, 162
sale events, 223
advertising allowance, 162–163
alteration and workroom fees, 148
anniversary, 223
ASN (advanced shipping notice), 98
assistant buyers, 98, 186
assortment plan, 26, 29–31
authorization code, 89
automatic replenishment, 97–98, 99
availability, 26
average stock, 125–126

basic goods, 83, 97–98
Basic Stock Method, 119–120
beginning-of-month (BOM) stock, 117, 120–121
Best Seller Reports, 37, 199, 200–201, 204–205
best sellers, 37
Black Friday, 151
BOM (beginning-of-month) stock, 117, 120–121
booster orders, 62
bottom line, 151
bottom-up planning method, 116
boutiques, 5
brands. *see* private label brands
build orders, 62–63
buyers. *see* assistant buyers; retail buyers
buying cycles, 11
buying offices, 184–185
buying simulations, 172–179
By-Location Sales reports, 212–216
By-Style Report, 198–200

calculations. *see* formulas
calendars, 90, 221
cancel date, 98
cash discount, 148
cash wrap, 177
category killers, 5
chargebacks, 101
classes, 207
classification of goods, 28, 31–32
sales analysis by, 206–212
stock-to-sales analysis by, 61
closing inventory, 148
Collect on Delivery (COD), 101
colors, stock analysis by, exercise, 25–27

comparative sales, 11–13
competition, 26
computerized logarithms, 122
consumers, ultimate, 4
controllable expenses, 150–151
cooperative advertising (Ad Co-op), 160
copy, 162
corporate buying offices, 185
corporate matrix, 185
cost, extended, and retail, 106
cost and markup, 74
cost of goods sold (COG), 147–149

daily flash, 10
Data Universal Numbering System (DUNS), 96, 97
date of invoice (DOI), 100
dating, 100–101
department stores, 4, 13, 76
descriptions, style, 97
designers, 14
direct expenses, 150
direct mail, 161
discount stores, 5, 14–16, 76
discounts, 36, 148
employee, 141
shipping, 101
DUNS (Data Universal Numbering System), 96, 97

employee discounts, 141
end-of-month (EOM) stock, 117, 120–121
exclusives, 76–77
expenses, 150–151
extended cost and retail, 110

fashion goods, 83
fashion orders, 99–100
flagship stores, 51
forecasting, 14
forecasts, 138–140
forms
purchase order, 102–109
UPC add/change, 97
vendor add/change, 97
formulas
average stock, 125
cost based on markup, 79
50% markup, 77
GM% of Net Sales, 149
gross cost of goods sold, 148
gross margin (GM), 146
markdown percent, 84
markdowns, 81, 82

markup, 74
monthly sales percent, 118
net cost of goods sold, 148
Net Profit/Loss % of Sales, 151
percent change, 10
percent to total, 24
permanent markdowns, 81, 85
point-of-sale (POS) markdowns, 82, 84
purchases, 127
retail price markup, 78
Return % of Gross Sales, 146
sale event markdowns, 222, 223
sell thru, 36
stock-to-sales, 121–122
total deductions, 134
total expenses, 237
total goods at cost, 147
total on hand, 237
total received, 37
total sold, 238
total stock, 134
turnover, 51, 119
weeks of supply, 43
4th quarter, importance of, 11
freight, 147, 188
freight on board (FOB), 101
full price, 36, 37

gross cost of goods sold, 148
gross margin driven, 76
gross margin (GM), 26, 188–189
in Profit and Loss statements, 149
sell thru and, 36
gross sales, 10, 146

holiday goods, 83, 207

ideal stock, 53–54
income statement, 145
incremental sales, 161
indirect expenses, 150
initial markup, 148
intranet, 97
inventory, 141–142. *see also* stock
average, 125–126
closing, 148
determination of, 44
merchandise plans and, 115
opening, 147
invoices, 100

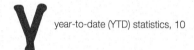

Calculating Build Orders

Sales

Store #	WTD Sales $	WTD Sales %	MTD Sales $	MTD Sales %
1	1.8	5.9%	5.2	4.6%
2	1.5	4.9%	6.1	5.3%
3	1.1	3.6%	4.5	3.9%
4	0.7	2.3%	2.4	2.1%
5	1.6	5.2%	5.4	4.7%
6	1.3	4.2%	4.3	3.8%
7	0.8	2.6%	2.7	2.4%
8	1.4	4.6%	4.9	4.3%
9	0.9	2.9%	3.6	3.2%
10	1.6	5.2%	5.4	4.7%
11	2.0	6.5%	8.5	7.4%
12	1.0	3.3%	3.7	3.2%
13	2.3	7.5%	9.7	8.5%
14	2.5	8.1%	10.1	8.8%
15	1.6	5.2%	6.0	5.3%
16	1.2	3.9%	4.1	3.6%
17	1.4	4.6%	5.2	4.6%
18	1.1	3.6%	3.9	3.4%
19	2.1	6.8%	7.4	6.5%
20	2.8	9.1%	11.1	9.7%
Total Style	30.7	100%	114.2	100%

Stock

OH Stock $	Stock %	OO Stock $
4.5	6.2%	2.8
4.1	5.7%	0.0
2.3	3.2%	0.5
1.5	2.1%	1.2
2.7	3.7%	3.0
3.4	4.7%	2.1
3.0	4.1%	0.1
3.5	4.8%	0.0
1.8	2.5%	2.1
2.4	3.3%	3.5
4.7	6.5%	1.5
1.1	1.5%	1.3
6.2	8.6%	0.9
6.4	8.8%	5.1
5.2	7.2%	0.0
2.1	2.9%	1.0
4.2	5.8%	1.1
2.4	3.3%	2.4
4.2	5.8%	5.1
6.7	9.3%	1.9
72.4	100%	35.6

Based on the concept of weeks of supply covered in Chapter 1, determine a build order by store for this basic collection.

For this exercise, we need four weeks of supply. Use the month-to-date (MTD) selling to determine the projected sales for the next four weeks. In most cases, you would look at both WTD and MTD selling.

Consider stock on hand (OH) and on order (OO).

Example: Store #1 has MTD sales of $5.2, stock OH of $4.5, and stock OO of $2.8.

Add the **OH Stock 4.5** + **OO Stock 2.8** = **7.3**.
Total stock available will be 7.3, once the OO arrives.

If projected sales for the four week period are the same as this month (MTD) at 5.2, do we have enough stock?

Total stock 7.3 − **5.2 MTD sales** = **2.1**.

Yes, and we have 2.1 extra! **Store #1 does not need a build order.**

Store #	Build Order in $s
1	$–
2	$2.0
3	
4	
5	
6	
7	
8	
9	
10	
11	
12	
13	
14	
15	
16	
17	
18	
19	
20	
Total Style	

End of Season Selling for Fashion PJ Sets

Store #	Season Units Sold	Sales % to Total	Total Recvd	Total OH	Sell Thru %
1	158	3.6%	240	82	65.8%
2	110	2.5%	120	10	91.7%
3	107	2.4%	120	13	89.2%
4	221	5.0%	240	19	92.1%
5	254	5.8%	360	106	70.6%
6	395	9.0%	480	85	82.3%
7	104	2.4%	120	16	86.7%
8	102	2.3%	120	18	85.0%
9	301	6.8%	360	59	83.6%
10	225	5.1%	240	15	93.8%
11	341	7.7%	480	139	71.0%
12	79	1.8%	120	41	65.8%
13	206	4.7%	240	34	85.8%
14	194	4.4%	240	46	80.8%
15	456	10.3%	480	24	95.0%
16	403	9.1%	480	77	84.0%
17	77	1.7%	120	43	64.2%
18	85	1.9%	120	35	70.8%
19	388	8.8%	480	92	80.8%
20	206	4.7%	240	34	85.8%
Totals	4,412	100%	5,400	988	81.7%

Next Year Buy: 7,800 units

The Buyer has decided to purchase 7,800 units next year based on this year's total sell thru by style. She was pleased with the 82% sell thru, because the style arrived late and did not receive the benefit of the full selling period. Break down the order by location and consider the following:

1. Sell Thru by store

2. Stock OH

3. % sales by store

Which of these concepts is most helpful?

Congratulations, you have completed Chapter 4! The Merchandising Math packet at the end of this chapter is meant to be a comprehensive review of Unit One, before we start pricing concepts. Try these exercises without referring to your notes and formulas. By now you should have a firm grasp of these ideas and when to use them.

Planned Future Buy

Store #	Next Year Unit Buy	Sales % to Total
1		
2		
3		
4		
5		
6		
7		
8		
9		
10		
11		
12		
13		
14		
15		
16		
17		
18		
19		
20		
Total		100%

Name _____

Merchandising Math Packet Review

A. % Increase or Decrease

What is the formula?

(Known as % CHANGE in Retailing)

1/ **Chico's FAS**

Dec '05 STD Sales	Dec '04 STD Sales	% Change
$1,314.0	$999.0	_____

2/ **The Limited**

Dec '05 Sales	Dec '04 Sales	% Change
$8,961.0	$8,700.0	_____

3/ **Saks Inc.**

Dec '05 Sales	Dec '04 Sales	% Change
$5,562.0	$6,000.0	_____

4/ **Wilson's Leather**

Dec '05 Sales	Dec '04 Sales	% Change
$371.1	$411.0	_____

5/ **Federated Department Stores**

Dec '05 Sales	Dec '04 Sales	% Change
$21,000.0	$15,000.0	_____

6/ **Target Corporation**

Dec '05 Sales	Dec '04 Sales	% Change
$47,700.0	$42,600.0	_____

7/ How can you double check your answers on these problems?

B.   **Percent to Total**
     What is the formula?

The denim buyer needs help determining % to Total for the following Denim sizes. After you have completed the chart below, answer the corresponding questions.

Size	Sales	% to Total
8/ 25	$55.4	_____
9/ 26	$76.3	_____
10/ 27	$61.9	_____
11/ 28	$80.4	_____
12/ 29	$69.1	_____
13/ 30	$50.0	_____
14/ 31	$39.6	_____
15/ 32	$41.0	_____
16/ Total $		

17/ What size would you invest the most in?

18/ What size would you invest the least in?

19/ What three sizes are worth 47.7% of this business?

20/ If you had to get rid of one size what would it be based on % to Total?

21/ Is it a sound business decision to get rid of the size mentioned in question #20? Why or why not?

22/ You have **$600.0** to invest in these sizes next year. How will you invest those dollars?

Size	LY Sales	Planned $ Buy
25	$55.4	_____
26	$76.3	_____
27	$61.9	_____
28	$80.4	_____
29	$69.1	_____
30	$50.0	_____
31	$39.6	_____
32	$41.0	_____

The fine jewelry buyer needs help determining the % to Total for the following styles in her ring collection. Please determine the % to Total for each style and then answer the questions below.

	Style #	Description	Sales	% to Total
23/	6100	Platinum diamond band	$ 158.4	_____
24/	6101	White gold diamond band	$ 149.2	_____
25/	6102	Silver diamond band	$ 78.3	_____
26/	6103	Platinum ruby and diamond band	$ 149.5	_____
27/	6104	White gold ruby and diamond band	$ 141.1	_____
28/	6105	Silver ruby and diamond band	$ 117.4	_____
29/	6106	Platinum sapphire and diamond band	$ 172.0	_____
30/	6107	White gold sapphire and diamond band	$ 128.6	_____
31/	6108	Silver sapphire and diamond band	$ 104.4	_____
		Total $	_____	

32/ What five styles are responsible for approximately 64% of this business?

_____

33/ What two styles are worth 27.5% of this business?

_____

34/ What color setting above do you think this buyer could live without? Platinum, white gold, or silver?

_____

35/ Based on the type of stone used, what is the top seller? Ruby and diamond, sapphire and diamond, or diamond only?

_____

36/ Based on current trends in settings and stones, what might the buyer add to this assortment to make it more appealing?

_____

_____

_____

B. **Percent to Total applied to a purchase**

The men's Divisional Merchandise Manager needs help determining the % to Total, by department, within his division.

Men's departments	LY Sales	% to Total
37/ Sport coats	$98.9	_____
38/ Suits	$489.0	_____
39/ Pants	$300.4	_____
40/ Shoes	$256.1	_____
41/ Shirts	$312.6	_____
42/ Golf	$64.3	_____
43/ Coats	$111.2	_____
44/ Big & Tall	$148.9	_____
Total Dept	_____	

The men's denim buyer needs help determining her % by vendor for last year.

		LY Sales	% to Total
45/	AG Jeans	$128.4	_____
46/	Ben Sherman	$100.2	_____
47/	Chip & Pepper	$210.4	_____
48/	Diesel	$112.9	_____
49/	G-Star	$198.6	_____
50/	Lacoste	$142.1	_____
51/	Lucky	$169.3	_____
52/	Quicksilver	$86.4	_____
	Total Dept	_____	

The men's denim buyer has $1,500 to spend on purchases for next season. Break down the order in dollars by vendor, based on last year's % to Total.

		LY Sales	Next Year Buy
53/	AG Jeans	$128.4	_____
54/	Ben Sherman	$100.2	_____
55/	Chip & Pepper	$210.4	_____
56/	Diesel	$112.9	_____
57/	G-Star	$198.6	_____
58/	Lacoste	$142.1	_____
59/	Lucky	$169.3	_____
60/	Quicksilver	$86.4	_____

C.   Sell Thru

What is the formula?

The children's buyer nees help determining the Sell Thru's for last season in her novelty slipper collection. Some slippers included a sound chip, as noted in the description.

	Style	Description	Units Sold	Units Recvd	% Sell Thru
61/	100	Frogs	8,542	10,800	
62/	101	Ducks that quack!	9,750	10,800	
63/	102	Pigs	7,420	10,800	
64/	103	Dogs that bark!	10,013	10,800	
65/	104	Monkeys	8,890	10,800	
66/	105	Cats that meow!	9,856	10,800	

67/   If these were Sell Thru's for the season, were they acceptable? Why or why not?

68/   What could you add more of to the assortment next year, based on this information?

The women's hosiery buyer needs help determining Sell Thru's for third quarter of the fall season, in her sock department. Start by calculating Units Received.

	Class	Description	Units Sold	Units OH	Units Recvd	ST%
69/	2	Basic socks	10,010	14,562		
70/	4	Athletic socks	6,112		6,112	
71/	6	Fashion socks	8,450	5,510		
72/	8	Knee highs		6,100	6,100	

73/   Are these good Sell Thru's for third quarter, considering there are 3 months left in the season?

74/ Why might basic socks have a below average Sell Thru but such a large amount received? Did the buyer forget to review LY history?

_____

D. Stock to Sales

What is the formula?

The buyer for the Men's Casual Shirt Department would like to know if his stock levels are consistent with his sales volume by department.

	Sales $	% to Total Sales	Stock $	% to Total Stock	Ideal Stock $	RTV/Markdown or Order $
75/ Long-sleeve sport	64.5		120.1			
76/ Short-sleeve sport	180.4		164.8			
77/ Polo	160.5		135.2			
78/ Tropical	45.3		65.8			
79/ Stripe	55.4		75.8			
80/ Basic solid	204.6		236.5			
81/ T-shirt	356.8		300.1			

82/ Which classification has the most stock?

83/ Basic Solid Shirts are doing _____ % of the sales on _____ % of the stock.

84/ Which classification is the biggest liability?

85/ What is the total department order, based on this analysis?

86/ If you had to eliminate a classification from this assortment, what would it be?

STORE NAME IN FANCY FONT

PO# _____

Dept # _____

Vendor # _____

Date Entered: _____

Ship Date: _____

Cancel Date: _____

Shipping Terms: _____

QTY	Style #	DESCRIPTION	SIZE	COLOR	Unit COST	Unit RETAIL	Store #	Store #	Store #	Store #	Total UNITS	Total COST	Total RETAIL

Total Order COST _____

Total Order RETAIL _____

Order Markup % _____

Planned Dept. Markup % _____

STORE NAME IN FANCY FONT

PO# _____

Dept # _____

Vendor # _____

Shipping Terms: _____

Date Entered: _____

Ship Date: _____

Cancel Date: _____

QTY	Style #	DESCRIPTION	SIZE	COLOR	Unit COST	Unit RETAIL	Store #	Store #	Store #	Store #	Total UNITS	Total COST	Total RETAIL

Total Order COST _____

Total Order RETAIL _____

Order Markup % _____

Planned Dept. Markup % _____

STORE NAME IN FANCY FONT

PO# _____

Dept # _____

Vendor # _____

Date Entered: _____

Ship Date: _____

Cancel Date: _____

Shipping Terms: _____

QTY	Style #	DESCRIPTION	SIZE	COLOR	Unit COST	Unit RETAIL	Store #	Store #	Store #	Store #	Total UNITS	Total COST	Total RETAIL

Total Order COST _____

Total Order RETAIL _____

Order Markup % _____

Planned Dept. Markup % _____

Merchandise Plan

	AUG	SEPT	OCT	NOV	DEC	JAN	FALL SEASON
BOM Stock	277,703	293,303	297,203	298,303	322,703	313,103	
+ Purchases							
= Total Stock							
Markdowns	10,345	8,246	7,980	13,452	23,453	35,000	98,476
+ Sales	120,000	135,600	139,500	140,600	165,000	155,400	856,100
= Total Deductions							
EOM Stock	293,303	297,203	298,303	322,703	313,103	300,385	

	AUG						FALL SEASON
% Sales by Month	14.0%						100.0%
Markdown Rate	8.6%						
Stock-to-Sales	2.3%						
Average Stock							
Turnover							

Formula Review:

% Sales by Month = Monthly Sales ÷ Season Sales

Markdown Rate = Monthly Markdowns ÷ Monthly Sales

Stock-to-Sales Ratio = BOM Stock ÷ Monthly Sales

Average Stock = All BOMs + Jan EOM ÷ 7

Turnover = Season Sales ÷ Average Stock

Total Stock = BOM Stock + Purchases

Total Deductions = Sales + Markdowns

Purchases = (EOM Stock + Total Deductions) − BOM Stock

Merchandise Plan for Junior Department

	AUG	SEPT	OCT	NOV	DEC	JAN	FALL SEASON
BOM Stock							
+ Purchases							
= Total Stock							
Markdowns							
Sales							
Total Deductions							
EOM Stock							

% Sales by Month							
Markdown Rate							
Stock-to-Sales							
Average Stock							
Turnover							

	FEB	MARCH	APRIL	MAY	JUNE	JULY	SPRING SEASON
BOM Stock							
+ Purchases							
= Total Stock							
Markdowns							
Sales							
Total Deductions							
EOM Stock							

% Sales by Month							
Markdown Rate							
Stock-to-Sales							

Average Stock		
Turnover		

Six-Month Merchandise Plan for Fragrance (Spring)

	FEB	MAR	APR	MAY	JUN	JULY	SPRING SEASON
BOM Stock							
Basic Purchases	119,000	125,300	119,720	83,480	63,440	120,125	631,065
Fashion Purchases	48,500	70,100	66,480	150,220	115,160	39,975	490,435
Total Purchases							
Total Stock							
RTV's							
Markdowns							
Sales							
Total Deductions							
EOM Stock							

% Sales by Month			
Markdown Rate			
Stock-to-Sales			

Average Stock		
Turnover		

Six-Month Merchandise Plan for Fragrance (Fall)

	AUG	SEPT	OCT	NOV	DEC	JAN	FALL SEASON
BOM Stock							
Basic Purchases	98,100	83,000	72,500	68,400	78,000	141,200	541,200
Fashion Purchases	98,800	145,000	235,000	296,700	236,300	215,400	1,227,200
Total Purchases							
Total Stock							
RTV's							
Markdowns							
Sales							
Total Deductions							
EOM Stock							

% Sales by Month		
Markdown Rate		
Stock-to-Sales		

Average Stock	
Turnover	

Rolling Open-to-Buy Forecast

	SEPT	OCT
BOM Stock	345,000	375,000
ACTUAL BOM Stock	384,000	365,000
Basic Purchases	83,000	72,500
ACTUAL Basic Purchases	81,000	
Fashion Purchases	145,000	235,000
ACTUAL Fashion Purchases	95,000	
Total Purchases	228,000	307,500
ACTUAL Purchases	176,000	
Total Stock	573,000	682,500
ACTUAL Total Stock	560,000	
RTV's	–	–
ACTUAL RTV's	1,500	
Markdowns	8,000	7,500
ACTUAL Markdowns	9,500	
Sales	190,000	225,000
ACTUAL Sales	184,000	
Total Deductions	198,000	232,500
ACTUAL Total Deductions	195,000	
EOM	375,000	450,000
ACTUAL EOM	365,000	

In the following example, September "Actual" figures are actually what occurred for the month of September. We are using September's statistics to project the entire month of October. First, calculate the PERCENT CHANGE for September.

Sept Sales Plan $190,000 − Sept Actual Sales $184,000 = $6,000

$6,000/190,000 Sales Plan = **−3.2%**

When you compare the original sales plan to what actually occurred, you will determine the department's sales trend. This trend will either be over, or under, the original sales plan. Apply this percent to next month's (OCT) projection. Fill in your October projection under the "Actual" boxes. This is very similar to how you would reproject your Open-to-Buy in a corporate forecasting system. Some buyers will need to reproject the *entire season*, every two to four weeks.

Cooperative Advertising Simulation

EVENT = name of promotional event and dates chosen

MDWN$ = markdown allowance in dollars based on the event chosen

TYPE OF AD = ROP or direct mail

ADV$ = advertising allowance in dollars, based on the type of advertisement chosen

TOTALS = need only MDWN$ and ADV$ totals at bottom of page

EVENT/DATES	MDWN$	TYPE OF AD	ADV$
AUG			
SEPT			
OCT			
NOV			
DEC			
JAN			
FEB			
MAR			
APR			
MAY			
JUN			
JUL			
TOTAL $			

Men's Shoe Department Simulation

VENDOR	STYLE #	DESCRIPTION	RETAIL	COST	MU %	DOORS	LY UNITS RECVD	LY UNITS SOLD	SELL THRU %	RETAIL $ SOLD
CASUAL										
A	10	DK BRWN BLUCHER	$145.00	$65.00	55.2%	55	14,000	11,440	81.7%	$1,658.8
A	20	BURG CASUAL PENNY	$135.00	$63.00	53.3%	55	20,000	17,160		$2,316.6
A	30	BLK CASUAL PENNY	$135.00	$63.00	53.3%	55	27,000	25,740		$3,474.9
								TOTAL CASUAL SHOE SALES		
SLIPPERS										
C	70	DK BRWN SHEARLNG SCUFF	$65.00	$26.00	60.0%	55	21,000	20,020		$1,301.3
C	80	BRWN PEBBL LEATHER SCUFF	$58.00	$22.00	62.1%	55	20,000	14,300		$829.4
								TOTAL SLIPPER SALES		
DRIVING SHOES										
D	90	DKGRY SUEDE DRIVER	$225.00	$92.00	59.1%	55	10,100	8,580		$1,930.5
E	100	BLK SUEDE DRIVER	$225.00	$92.00	59.1%	25	2,850	2,600		$585.0
								TOTAL DRIVING SHOE SALES		
DRESS SHOES										
F	200	BLK WING TIP	$290.00	$138.00	52.4%	55	15,000	8,580		$2,488.2
F	300	BRN CAPTOE	$280.00	$135.00	51.8%	55	30,000	25,740		$7,207.2
F	400	BLK CAPTOE	$280.00	$135.00	51.8%	55	34,000	28,600		$8,008.0
F	500	BLK SQUARE TOE	$310.00	$145.00	53.2%	55	22,000	20,020		$6,206.2
F	600	BRN SQUARE TOE	$310.00	$145.00	53.2%	55	15,000	8,580		$2,659.8
F	700	BLK BLUCHER	$290.00	$138.00	52.4%	25	15,000	10,400		$3,016.0
F	800	BRN BLUCHER	$290.00	$138.00	52.4%	25	15,000	13,000		$3,770.0
F	900	BLK PERF CAPTOE	$280.00	$135.00	51.8%	10	4,000	3,640		$1,019.2
F	1000	BURG FORML PENNY	$200.00	$98.00	51.0%	5	1,500	1,300		$260.0
F	1100	BRN FORML PENNY	$200.00	$98.00	51.0%	5	1,500	1,300		$260.0
F	1200	BLK FORML PENNY	$200.00	$98.00	51.0%	55	5,280	2,860		$572.0
								TOTAL DRESS SHOE SALES		
								TOTAL SHOE DEPT SALES LY		

Men's Shoe Department Simulation

NEXT YEAR'S BUY =

VENDOR	STYLE #	DESCRIPTION	% BY CLASS	% BY STYLE	RANKING STYLES	NEXT YEAR UNIT BUY	NEXT YEAR $ BUY	NEXT YEAR # OF DOORS
CASUAL								
A	10	DK BRWN BLUCHER						
A	20	BURG CASUAL PENNY						
A	30	BLK CASUAL PENNY						
SLIPPERS								
C	70	DK BRWN SHEARLNG SCUFF						
C	80	BRWN PEBBL LEATHER SCUFF						
DRIVING SHOES								
D	90	DKGRY SUEDE DRIVER						
E	100	BLK SUEDE DRIVER						
DRESS SHOES								
F	200	BLK WING TIP						
F	300	BRN CAPTOE						
F	400	BLK CAPTOE						
F	500	BLK SQUARE TOE						
F	600	BRN SQUARE TOE						
F	700	BLK BLUCHER						
F	800	BRN BLUCHER						
F	900	BLK PERF CAPTOE						
F	1000	BURG FORML PENNY						
F	1100	BRN FORML PENNY						
F	1200	BLK FORML PENNY						

Vendor 1

	Cost		Retail		MU%
Gross Sales			105,000		
Returns			1,650	1.6%	
Net Sales			103,350		
					MU%
Stock Cost	$ 45,000		105,000		57.1%
Freight	$ 7,500	7.1%			
Markdowns	$ 3,500	3.3%			
Shortage	$ 1,390	1.3%			
Employee Discount	$ 1,735	1.7%			
Cost of Goods	$ 59,125			% of Sales	
Cost dollars needed to meet GM PLAN	$ 275				
		GM	58,850		
			44,500	43.1%	
Departmental GM PLAN			43.1		

RECAP OF THIS YEAR'S PERFORMANCE

	SALES TY	SALES LY	% CHANGE	DEPT %
	103,350	98,000	5.5%	

	TURN TY	TURN LY	DEPT TURN	
	2.00	2.00		

	MU% TY	MU% LY	DEPT MU%	
	57.1%	57%		

	GM TY	GM LY	DEPT GM	
	42.8%	43%	43.1%	

Vendor 2

	Cost	Retail		MU%
Gross Sales		98,000		
Returns		4,100	4.2%	
Net Sales		93,900		
				MU%
Stock Cost	45,000	98,000		54.1%
Freight	2,250	2.3%		
Markdowns	8,550	8.7%		
Shortage	1,600	1.6%		
Employee Discount	1,650	1.7%		
Cost of Goods	59,050			
Cost dollars needed to meet GM PLAN	5,575			% of Sales
		53,475		
GM		40,425		43.1%
Departmental GM PLAN	43.1			

RECAP OF THIS YEAR'S PERFORMANCE

	SALES TY	SALES LY	% CHANGE	DEPT %
	93,900	88,500	6.1%	
	TURN TY	TURN LY	DEPT TURN	
	2.14	1.98		
	MU% TY	MU% LY	DEPT MU%	
	54.1%	53.8%		
	GM TY	GM LY	DEPT GM	
	40.8%	42.8%	43.1%	

Vendor 3

	Cost		Retail	
Gross Sales			210,000	
Returns			7,300	3.5%
Net Sales			202,700	
				MU%
Stock Cost	95,000		210,000	54.8%
Freight	4,800	2.3%		
Markdowns	10,000	4.8%		
Shortage	4,250	2.0%		
Employee Discount	3,500	1.7%		
Cost of Goods	117,550			% of Sales
Cost dollars needed to meet GM PLAN	2,120		115,430	
		GM	87,270	43.1%
Departmental GM PLAN				43.1

RECAP OF THIS YEAR'S PERFORMANCE

	SALES TY	SALES LY	% CHANGE	DEPT %
	202,700	200,000	1.4%	
	TURN TY	TURN LY	DEPT TURN	
	1.66	1.70		
	MU% TY	MU% LY	DEPT MU%	
	54.8%			
	GM TY	GM LY	DEPT GM	
	42.0%		43.1%	

Vendor 4

	Cost		Retail	
Gross Sales			150,000	
Returns			5,000	3.3%
Net Sales			145,000	
				MU%
Stock Cost	65,000		150,000	56.7%
Freight	3,500	2.3%		
Markdowns	12,000	8.0%		
Shortage	2,850	1.9%		
Employee Discount	2,500	1.7%		
Cost of Goods	85,850			
Cost dollars needed to meet GM PLAN	**3,280**			**% of Sales**
			82,570	
		GM	62,430	43.1%
Departmental GM PLAN			43.1	

RECAP OF THIS YEAR'S PERFORMANCE

	SALES TY	SALES LY	% CHANGE	DEPT %
	145,000	135,000	7.4%	
	TURN TY	**TURN LY**	**DEPT TURN**	
	1.98	1.88		
	MU% TY	**MU% LY**	**DEPT MU%**	
	56.7%			
	GM TY	**GM LY**	**DEPT GM**	
	40.8%		43.1%	

BEST SELLER REPORT

Division: _____

Buyer: _____

Date: _____

Style #	Vendor	Unit Cost	Unit Retail	Promotional Retail	Description of Merchandise	MTD Sales		LW Sales		OH	OO
						Units	$	Units	$	Units	Units

Explanation of Headings:

Style # = the mark style number used by the retailer

Vendor = Vendor name

Promotional Retail = If the style was on sale, what was the promoted retail?

MTD Sales = Month-to-date sales

LW Sales = Last week's sales

OH = units on hand (in stores)

OO = units on order, but not yet received

THE VENDOR BY CLASS REPORT

Vendor: 001

Class	Sub-class	Description	Sales $	%	Stock $	%	OO $
20	100	fashion pj bottom	131.9	100%	394.4	100%	246.6
40	100	basic pj bottom	0	0%	0	0%	0
		Subtotal: Vendor 001	131.9	100	394.4	100	246.6

Vendor: 001

Class	Sub-class	Description	Sales $	%	Stock $	%	OO $
20	200	fashion pj top	26.1	30.1%	56.1	24.6%	31.9
40	200	basic pj top	60.5	69.9%	171.9	75.4%	13.0
		Subtotal: Vendor 001	86.6	100	228	100	44.9

Vendor: 002

Class	Sub-class	Description	Sales $	%	Stock $	%	OO $
20	100	fashion pj bottom	9.1	16.5%	24.7	20.4%	0
40	100	basic pj bottom	45.9	83.5%	96.4	79.6%	31.4
		Subtotal: Vendor 002	55.0	100	121.1	100	31.4

Vendor: 002

Class	Sub-class	Description	Sales $	%	Stock $	%	OO $
20	200	fashion pj top	0	0%	0	0%	0
40	200	basic pj top	45.4	100%	66.4	100%	39.4
		Subtotal: Vendor 002	45.4	100	66.4	100	39.4

Vendor: 003

Class	Sub-class	Description	Sales $	%	Stock $	%	OO $
20	300	fashion pj sets	80.4	23.9%	87.8	17.1%	63.4
40	300	basic pj sets	256.7	76.1%	426.9	82.9%	330.8
		Subtotal: Vendor 003	337.1	100	514.7	100	394.2

Vendor: 004

Class	Sub-class	Description	Sales $	%	Stock $	%	OO $
20	400	fashion night shirts	91.1	34.3%	125.0	40.2%	180.2
40	400	basic night shirts	174.5	65.7%	186.3	59.8%	444.1
		Subtotal: Vendor 004	265.6	100	311.3	100	624.3

Vendor: 005

Class	Sub-class	Description	Sales $	%	Stock $	%	OO $
20	500	fashion robes short	143.6	47.7%	221.6	43.2%	0
40	500	basic robes short	122.7	40.8%	285.4	55.6%	152.6
60	500	novelty robes short	34.6	11.5%	6.5	1.3%	0
		Subtotal: Vendor 005	300.9	100	513.5	100	152.6

Vendor: 006

Class	Sub-class	Description	Sales $	%	Stock $	%	OO $
20	600	fashion robes long	25.1	21.5%	6.4	3.2%	0
40	600	basic robes long	88.9	76.3%	191	96.8%	50.7
60	600	novelty robes long	2.5	2.1%	0	0.0%	0
		Subtotal: Vendor 006	116.5	100	197.4	100	50.7

BY-LOCATION REPORT

Vendor #	Style #	Description
1	5005	blu check bottom

Sales

Store #	WTD Sales $	WTD Sales %	MTD Sales $	MTD Sales %	STD Sales $	STD Sales %
1	0.8	2.8%	3.0	2.7%	40.6	2.8%
2	0.7	2.5%	3.1	2.8%	36.6	2.5%
3	0.2	0.7%	0.6	0.5%	1.6	0.1%
4	0.1	0.4%	0.7	0.6%	5.1	0.3%
5	0.6	2.1%	2.0	1.8%	31	2.1%
6	0.4	1.4%	1.7	1.5%	20.8	1.4%
7	0.9	3.2%	3.7	3.3%	46.5	3.2%
8	0.5	1.8%	2.1	1.9%	25.7	1.8%
9	0.8	2.8%	3.4	3.0%	41	2.8%
10	0.7	2.5%	3.0	2.7%	36.1	2.5%
11	1.0	3.5%	3.8	3.4%	52.5	3.6%
12	0.1	0.4%	0.4	0.4%	5.6	0.4%
13	1.3	4.6%	5.1	4.5%	70.1	4.8%
14	0.4	1.4%	1.4	1.2%	20.4	1.4%
15	0.6	2.1%	2.0	1.8%	31.9	2.2%
16	0.3	1.1%	1.5	1.3%	15.8	1.1%
17	0.4	1.4%	1.7	1.5%	20.1	1.4%
18	0.2	0.7%	0.6	0.5%	10.1	0.7%
19	0.9	3.2%	3.3	2.9%	46	3.2%
20	0.8	2.8%	3.0	2.7%	41.9	2.9%
21	0.7	2.5%	3.0	2.7%	37.2	2.6%
22	0.7	2.5%	2.7	2.4%	36.1	2.5%
23	1.0	3.5%	3.9	3.5%	52.8	3.6%
24	1.2	4.3%	4.7	4.2%	62.8	4.3%
25	0.5	1.8%	2.1	1.9%	25.4	1.7%
26	0.4	1.4%	1.5	1.3%	20.4	1.4%

Stock

OH Stock $	Stock %	OO
2.5	3.0%	4.8
2.1	2.6%	2.2
0.3	0.4%	0.1
0.5	0.6%	0.2
1.7	2.1%	3.0
1.4	1.7%	2.1
3.0	3.7%	5.1
1.5	1.8%	0.2
2.4	2.9%	4.1
2.0	2.4%	4.5
2.7	3.3%	6.5
0.1	0.1%	0.3
4.2	5.1%	7.9
1.0	1.2%	2.1
1.5	1.8%	3.2
1.1	1.3%	1.0
1.2	1.5%	2.9
0.4	0.5%	2.4
2.7	3.3%	5.1
2.1	2.6%	4.9
2.4	2.9%	4.2
2.1	2.6%	3.7
3.1	3.8%	5.8
4.0	4.9%	7.1
1.6	1.9%	3.1
1.1	1.3%	2.5

BY-LOCATION REPORT

27	0.7	2.5%	2.9	2.6%	36.4	2.5%	2.2	2.7%	4.6
28	0.6	2.1%	2.2	2.0%	31.2	2.1%	1.7	2.1%	3.1
29	0.3	1.1%	1.0	0.9%	15.1	1.0%	0.4	0.5%	1.0
30	0.8	2.8%	3.0	2.7%	41.9	2.9%	2.1	2.6%	2.0
31	0.8	2.8%	3.4	3.0%	41	2.8%	2.7	3.3%	2.4
32	1.0	3.5%	4.1	3.6%	51.8	3.6%	3.4	4.1%	3.0
33	0.3	1.1%	1.5	1.3%	15.8	1.1%	1.0	1.2%	2.5
34	0.3	1.1%	1.3	1.2%	15.7	1.1%	0.9	1.1%	1.9
35	1.4	5.0%	5.8	5.2%	71.5	4.9%	4.0	4.9%	8.5
36	1.1	3.9%	4.5	4.0%	57.9	4.0%	3.0	3.7%	2.8
37	0.6	2.1%	2.1	1.9%	31.6	2.2%	1.5	1.8%	3.7
38	0.7	2.5%	2.9	2.6%	36	2.5%	1.9	2.3%	4.0
39	0.9	3.2%	3.7	3.3%	46.5	3.2%	2.4	2.9%	5.9
40	0.4	1.4%	1.4	1.2%	20.9	1.4%	0.5	0.6%	3.6
41	0.3	1.1%	1.0	0.9%	15.1	1.0%	0.6	0.7%	1.4
42	0.5	1.8%	2.1	1.9%	26.4	1.8%	1.7	2.1%	3.8
43	0.3	1.1%	1.4	1.2%	15.9	1.1%	0.8	1.0%	1.1
44	1.0	3.5%	4.1	3.6%	52.5	3.6%	2.6	3.2%	5.4

Total Style									
	28.2	100%	112.4	100%	1457.3	100%	82.1	100%	149.7